Scribe Publications
FUTURE FILES

Richard Watson advises organisations on the future, focusing on innovation and scenario planning. He is the author and publisher of *What's Next*, a quarterly report on global trends, and is a columnist for a number of magazines including *Fast Company* (USA).

For NDVW & MAVW

FUTURE FILES

A HISTORY OF
THE NEXT
50 YEARS

RICHARD WATSON

SCRIBE
Melbourne

Scribe Publications Pty Ltd
PO Box 523
Carlton North, Victoria, Australia 3054
Email: info@scribepub.com.au

First published by Scribe 2007

Typeset in 11.5/16 pt Minion by the publisher
Cover designed by Design by Committee
Printed and bound in Australia by Griffin Press

National Library of Australia
Cataloguing-in-Publication data

Watson, Richard, 1961- .
 Future files.

 ISBN 9781921215414 (pbk.).

 1. Forecasting. 2. Social prediction. I. Title.

303.49

www.scribepublications.com.au

I was a peripheral visionary.
I could see the future, but only way off to the side.
–Steven Wright

Contents

Preface | 1

1   Society and Culture:
    why we'll take longer baths in the future | 3
2   Government and Politics: us and them | 27
3   Science and Technology: the rise of the machines | 55
4   Media and Entertainment: have it your way | 77
5   Money and Financial Services: everyone is a bank | 103
6   Automotive and Transport:
    the end of the road as we know it | 131
7   Food and Drink: faster *and* slower | 157
8   Retail and Shopping:
    what we'll buy when we've got it already | 183
9   Healthcare and Medicine: older and wiser | 207
10 Travel and Tourism: 'Sorry, this country is full.' | 231
11 Work and Business: the new right-brain economy | 251
12 Conclusions: where to next? | 269
    Sources | 277
    Acknowledgements | 279

Preface

I have seen the future, and it's very much like the present,
only longer.
–Woody Allen

This book contains various forecasts and scenarios, but its aim is not to predict the future. Anyone who says they can do this is either a liar or a fool. My intention is to liberate the imagination. Hopefully you will see familiar things in a new light and unfamiliar things with greater clarity. The objective — if a book can have such a thing — is to broaden perspectives and widen horizons; to make as many individuals and organisations as possible think twice about where they are going and to consider whether, once they get there, it will be worth staying. This is not easy. To do it one must first observe what is already happening and then make an educated guess as to where some of what is happening may lead. This may, in turn, cause us to do some things we would not otherwise have done or perhaps stop us from blindly accepting so-called inevitabilities. The future, after all, is not a forgone conclusion. It is something that we shape every day by our present decisions and actions.

The date of up to fifty years hence (let's call it the year 2050 for the sake of simplicity) has been chosen because it is sufficiently far away to avoid accusations of incompleteness or incorrectness (who, after all, can tell if I'm right?). Presumably by 2050 most readers will have forgotten about this book entirely or time will have healed any mental wounds created by misjudged ideas or incorrect dates. As someone once said, even if my past is chequered with failed forecasts, my future predictions and extrapolations will be spotless. Ironically, it is usually easier to make predictions about the distant future than next month or next year because it can take a long time for patterns to emerge or new ideas to replace old habits and conventions. For example, hydrogen-powered cars and digital wallets are coming, but nobody can yet say for sure when they will be adopted by mainstream society.

For that reason this book is partly a look backwards at new things that have already happened, which, up to a point, we can assume will continue to happen and thus shape our future. This is a dangerous game because the future is never a straight linear extrapolation from the present or the past. Totally unexpected ideas and events usually conspire to trip up future plans and predictions, but it's usually better than not thinking about the future at all.

The selection of innovations and trends in this book is entirely personal. It's based upon material I have collected from a number of sources over the years, many of which have been featured in my *What's Next* report published by nowandnext.com.

Chapter 1

Society and Culture: why we'll take longer baths in the future

If you want to know your past, look at your present conditions.
If you want to know your future, look into your present actions.
–Buddhist saying

Early in 2006, Joyce Vincent, a middle-aged woman, was discovered dead in her London flat. There was nothing remarkable about this, except for the fact that she'd been dead for more than two years and her television was still on. How could this happen? Where was everyone? The answer, of course, was that everyone was somewhere else. London, like most major cities, no longer has neighbourhoods; it has collections of individuals leading increasingly isolated, selfish, and narcissistic lives. Neighbours keep to themselves, and people don't ask questions or volunteer information. In an age when everyone is increasingly connected to everyone else through the internet, nobody really knows anyone any more.

We have lots of friends, but few of them dig deep to understand our hopes and fears. The general feeling is that you'll live longer if you keep yourself to yourself.

In Japan there is a social phenomenon called 'hikikomori'. The phrase roughly translates as 'withdrawal' and refers to boys who retreat into their bedrooms and rarely, if ever, come out. In one case a young man shut his bedroom door in his early twenties and played video games, watched TV, and slept for fourteen years. Food was supplied by his mother, who lived downstairs, virtually alone. The phenomenon is a particularly Japanese condition, although nobody can quite understand who or what is to blame. According to experts, there are somewhere between 100,000 and 1 million hikikomori in Japan, caused by everything from absent (always-working) fathers to over-protective mothers.

There are a number of simple explanations for problems like this, and most are wrong. Some people blame individualism; others point the finger at urbanisation, technology, education, or even government. The reality is that it's all of these, but ultimately we have nobody to blame but ourselves. We, and only we, have let this happen. And if it's like this now, what will it be like in another fifty years?

Perhaps this is a strange way to start what is essentially a business book, but I think it's important to understand the bigger picture first.

I'm sitting in a budget hotel room at Miami International Airport. It's 10.30 p.m. My room is basic, but I have free access to the internet — either from my own computer or via a giant TV in my room. There is a coffee machine, complete with non-dairy creamer, and a small bar of hypoallergenic soap in the bathroom. Outside, on the other side of the freeway, a large neon sign reads 'Girls'. Unfortunately, inside the hotel, humans are rather absent. Indeed, while I can check up on the news in London through my TV, I can't order a sandwich because the restaurant closed thirty minutes ago. There is no room service either, presumably due to a focus on 'essential services'. The hotel is pretty full, but I don't expect to come into contact with anyone else. If you placed the 'Do not disturb' sign outside my door (and my credit rating was good enough) I could probably drop dead inside my room with the TV on and nobody would notice. My email isn't working either because my email provider has thoughtfully 'recently completed an upgrade of all services to enhance security and reliability'. Believe it or not, I can't access my email because they have sent me a new password, but I can't access that because I don't have the password to open my email. Brilliant.

If you want a vision of the future, this is a good one. I could be anywhere. In another ten or twenty years I will be able to access every film ever made in any language through the TV. The room will be personalised, too, in the sense that the hotel chain will know where I come from and what I like — so Triple J will be playing on the radio as I enter my room, and decaf coffee and real milk will be in the fridge. The sandwich will still be an impossible request, unless I'm staying at one of the company's premium hotels, but I guess I'll be able to order one through the TV for twenty-four hour delivery. In twenty-five years time I will enter the hotel by placing my finger on a security panel by the entrance, and both the receptionist and the 'girls' will be holograms. I will gain access to my room with my world-phone or the chip inserted in my jaw and be able to customise the room myself to look and smell just like home — but I still won't be able to get a sandwich from the restaurant at 10.30 p.m., and my email still won't work.

Two big trends at the start of the twenty-first century are urbanisation and the increase in the number of people living alone. In 2006, 25 per cent of homes in the United Kingdom were single-person households. In Australia it was 17 per cent, while in the United States single-person households have grown by 30 per cent in thirty years, due to factors such as couples staying single for longer, easier divorces, and longer life-spans, especially for women. We have also seen a significant reduction in the number of children born and a massive increase in the number of old people. In short, there is a lack of births and deaths, which means that the global population will go into decline around 2050, putting an end to fears of global overcrowding. You can see this already in statistics — 22 per cent of women in the UK say that that don't expect to have children.

Home alone

The growth of urban singles is driving everything from a growth in late-night convenience retailing (for example, buying a single portion of chicken fillet at 1.00 a.m.) to how the tables and chairs are laid out in your local McDonald's. Reasons for this urban renaissance are various.

Twenty years ago it seemed as though everyone was moving out of the cities. In the US the term 'white flight' was coined to describe white, middle-class families fleeing inner-city crime and grime to start new lives in the suburbs. Nowadays the reverse is happening. Known as boomerang migration, singles and childless couples are flooding back into cities like New York, London, and Melbourne because that's where the action is and the commute isn't. Indeed, by the year 2050, if this trend continues, most inner cities will be made up almost entirely of rich singles, wealthy families, and gay couples with high disposable incomes and liberal political persuasions. Rural areas that still exist will be populated by rich hobby-farmers interspersed with down-shifters and digital nomads.

But it's not just the cities that are changing. In 1950, 80 per cent of US households comprised the traditional husband, wife, and one or more kids. Now it's under 50 per cent. The rest are singles and same-sex couples (increasingly with kids). There are also 'blended families' — mother, father, plus two or more children from different relationships or marriages and extended financial families — homes with more than one generation living under the same roof.

In other words, shifts in social attitudes (what is considered normal or acceptable), together with changes in demographics, housing stock, and even retailing are making it easier to live however you like. And for many people this means by themselves. Even if you don't live alone you will increasingly be able to do whatever you want unencumbered by family pressure or practical considerations. This is freedom without responsibility. For example, at a recent new home show in the US, a dream home was displayed that allowed each family member to enter the house via a different entrance. Individuals could watch TV or surf the internet in their own room, and choose separate kitchen facilities and bathrooms, so as not to interact with other family members. And to think that back in the 1980s people were worried about families not eating breakfast together. In the middle of the twenty-first century the problem will be how to get individual members of the family to even talk to each other.

In Australia in 2005, adults spent on average three hours watching TV every day — and twelve minutes talking to their partner. In the US over 25 per cent of two-year-olds have a TV in their bedroom, and children aged two to seventeen spend twenty hours a week watching TV versus thirty-eight minutes talking to their parents.

No wonder the fastest growing reason for women seeking a divorce in some countries is absent (always-at-work or always-working) partners. There is already a growing gulf between the sexes, and this will open up even further in the future as women become more economically self-sufficient. Even when both sexes are together physically, men are usually emotionally somewhere else. Women just want to talk, while men just want women to be quiet. In the future there will be a law passed in Europe that requires married men to be at home by 9.00 p.m. on Thursdays or else they will be fined 500 euros. There will also be tax breaks for people who choose not to live alone, and pet owners will be taxed if the owners live alone as an incentive for people to have children rather than child substitutes.

Of course, there is an irony here. We are increasingly leading separate lives, and in the future it will become much easier to physically isolate oneself from other people at home or at work — which, for some people, will be the same place.

At the same time we are becoming increasingly connected. One of the most popular websites in the UK is Friends Reunited. MySpace (now Rupert's Space) in the US has well over 100 million members and regularly receives more hits per month than Google. Both websites simply seek to put like-minded individuals and groups in touch with one another, but maybe something more profound is happening. To a large degree, the history of the next fifty years will be about the relationship between technology and people. Moreover, there is an inherent instability built into this relationship because technology changes fast and exponentially, while people change slowly and incrementally. What this means, in effect, is that the more technology gets embedded into our lives, the more we will run away from it. As a result, there will be a greater demand for human-to-human physical contact and direct experiences.

There will also be more interest in spiritualism and philosophy — unless, of course, humans and technology are merged together, in which case things will get very confusing indeed.

By the year 2025 artificial intelligence (AI) will have become a reality. In simple terms, this means that when you phone your bank and have a twenty-minute argument about credit-card charges you'll be speaking to a computer without realising it. More spookily, by the year 2050 there will be two highly intelligent species on Earth — traditional, genetically pure humans and technologically aided hybrid humans. The latter will be 'people' who have been genetically manipulated by the insertion of DNA segments to prevent certain diseases or to create certain emotions or personality traits. They will also be robotically and computer-enhanced to improve strength, sight, vision, or intelligence. Again, one will evolve very slowly, and the other will change as rapidly as technology and ethics permit.

Do we want this to happen? Perhaps the question is whether or not we can stop it.

Some people will say that this won't happen. We will understand the threat and pass laws to prevent such enhancements, much in the same way that human cloning is already outlawed. But if history can serve as a guide to the future, it shows us that mankind is curious. Someone, somewhere, legally or illegally, will be tempted to answer the question 'what if?'

In Los Angeles you can already visit a reproductive technologist and choose sperm or eggs based on IQ or appearance: 'blonde hair, blue eyes, and an aptitude for tennis, please'. If you can't make it to LA, you can always order sperm over the internet. And if we are already doing this, it's only a very small step before we add non-biological elements to our children. Given that companies such as Nike sponsor thirteen-year-old soccer stars it's probably also just a matter of time before a company signs up a promising foetus on a thirty-five-year sponsorship deal.

If such experiments simply involved the insertion of technological elements into a human brain or body, this would be almost no threat to the human species. But what if the enhancement involves nanotechnology or computers, and the machine elements really do start to think for themselves? What happens when we produce machines that are more intelligent than us? What happens if these machines develop some kind of self-awareness (consciousness) and become self-replicating? Once that gene is out of the bottle it will be very difficult indeed to put it back in.

OK computer

Our relationship with objects is going to change in the future. In the past, objects were neutral. They were not intelligent and did not possess a state of mind. If they had a personality, it was given to them by their designers and was entirely skin-deep. Otherwise we imbued personality into objects via our own imagination. This won't be the case in the future. Take children's dolls, for example. Historically these were inert, rather poor representations of the human form. They are already becoming more realistic and more intelligent. Owners of the 'Amazing Amanda' can already chat with their doll, and 'intelligence' is available in the form of facial recognition, speech recognition, and radio-frequency identification device (RFID) impregnated accessories. If you're a bit older (and presumably no wiser) you can even buy a physically realistic, life-sized 'love partner' for US$7,000 from a company called realdoll. com. But you 'aint seen nothing yet.

In a few years' time you will be able to personalise your doll's face (one of your own choice or, more likely, a famous face), communicate with your doll by telephone or email, have real conversations, and experience your entire life history through the eyes, ears (and nose) of your doll. The latter will be achieved by the doll and other linked devices preserving your emails, phone calls, and other images and information captured through its artificial eyes, ears, and nose. In other words, the doll will become a digital storage device with the capacity to document your entire life. The so-called 'life-caching' industry is already worth US$2.5 billion annually. This will in turn give rise to a debate about the ethics of information, because questions will arise as to who owns such information, whether or not it can be sold or traded, and what happens to the information once the 'owner' dies.

Dead, but increasingly not forgotten

In the past, when you died there was very little of you left. One hundred years ago you might have left some letters or drawings. Fifty years ago you may have left some fading photographs. Currently you can seek or accidentally attain digital immortality through video clips, sound files, digital photographs, and emails on your own website or sites belonging to others. There is even a website called mylastemail.com that promises to send out your last email once you've died and you can even check what date that might be at deathclock.com. But there are already problems. The tragic death of seventeen-year-old Anna Svidersky became problematic recently because she had a page on MySpace.

She is still there, unaware of her fate in the physical world. And because her MySpace page is protected by a password known only to her, the page — her digital afterlife — will stay there, potentially forever. Of course, there are counter-trends. Scrapbooking is phenomenally popular at the moment as a low-fi way of preserving memories and as a way of engaging in physical contact with other people across generations.

It might not be so low-tech either. Some people believe we are presently living in the digital dark ages because most of what we are currently preserving will be unreadable by future generations. I already have a stack of floppy discs from the early 1990s that I can't read, and it's entirely possible that the photographs of my children (4,753 at the last count) won't be readable or printable in twenty years' time.

You think I'm kidding? NASA can't read some of the records of its 1976 Viking Mars space landing, and the BBC can't read the digital copy of the Doomsday Book it produced in 1986 to celebrate the 900th anniversary of the original. Of course, the original paper copy remains perfectly readable.

In the not-too-distant future, everyday objects such as shoes, carpets, and toothbrushes will contain technology that will collect information about us. We will then be able to personalise objects, allowing them to change physical state (like colour) or respond to our daily mood. They will also be able to exchange data with other objects and send information to other people. For example, your toothbrush will be able to analyse your breath, and book an appointment with your doctor if it detects the smell of lung cancer. In other words, what were once just ordinary objects will be increasingly networked and intelligent. Manufacturers will use the information generated by these smart products to sell us other services or enhance our 'ownership experience' — although whether people will want such a relationship with their toothbrush remains to be seen.

In Japan you can already buy school blazers embedded with GPS tracking technology. This means that, as a parent, you can elect to receive an email or SMS alert when your child arrives safely at school each morning (or at least when the blazer does). This idea is no doubt linked to the rise in paranoid parenting and so-called 'stranger danger', but there will be other services linked to similar products in the future. For example, kitchen appliances will monitor their own performance, and order spare parts and service calls all by themselves — much in the same way that the McLaren F1 supercar already alerts the factory when something goes wrong, thanks to onboard monitoring and GPS tracking.

Equally, ordinary clothes will be able to monitor their condition, arrange for dry-cleaning pick-ups, or alert their owner to new design upgrades. But what are some of the likely attitudinal and behavioural implications of these developments?

At the East Sutton Park Young Offenders Institution and Open Prison in Kent (UK), offenders with low self-esteem are encouraged to do gardening. Even something as simple as raking up fallen leaves has been shown to have an instant effect, delivering instant satisfaction. As twenty-year-old Leah says, 'If I'm angry I dig.' Gardening will enjoy a huge surge of popularity in the years ahead because it will be an antidote to the future. It will deliver the solitude and peace and quiet that will be so lacking in people's lives. It will be a way of dealing with too much technology. Washing dishes by hand and baking your own bread will similarly become popular for much the same reasons. They will provide physical results, and people will feel that they've achieved something by themselves.

One of the consequences of ubiquitous technology is that some of us will unplug some or, in extreme cases, all of our lives. In theory, new technologies will make our lives easier. Things will move faster saving us time and money. Things will also be more reliable. Technology will make things that were previously difficult or impossible easier and more affordable. But history suggests that the opposite is much more likely to happen.

Do you remember the predictions of the paperless office and the leisure society? Between 1999 and 2002 global use of paper increased by 22 per cent and we now seem to have less spare time than ever. We are also sleeping less than we used to — down from nine hours per day in 1900 to 6.9 hours today, and everything from computers to home-loan decisions are getting faster. Indeed, the benefits of the computer age can be seen everywhere except in the productivity statistics, because we are inventing new ways of making ourselves busy.

Comfortably numb

This obsession with 'busyness' can be seen in the way that the work ethic has invaded childhood. Children must be kept busy at all times. As a result, children are becoming over-scheduled, and we are creating a generation that cannot think for itself, a generation of passive citizens and comfortably numb consumers with almost no imagination or self-reliance.

In Japan the word 'benriya' loosely translates as convenience-doers. These are people, usually older men, who fix leaking taps, change lightbulbs, remove cockroaches from sinks, and generally do things that require an ounce of commonsense. In other words, there is a section of Japanese society that is totally incapable of fending for itself.

Another obvious problem is that complex technologies fail. In the past, when things broke down they were relatively easy to fix.

If your car wouldn't start there were only three or four things that could be wrong, each one easily fixable. These days breakdowns are more complex, and chances are you won't be able to fix it yourself. Moreover, as things become smarter and more networked, these failures will become even more catastrophic. The term 'cascading failure' refers to the failure of one element of a network being able to bring the entire network to its knees. If you lose your house keys today it's a problem, but hardly the end of the world. In the future, though, you won't have house keys; you'll have smartcard or biometric entry, and if your card gets lost or the fingerprint reader breaks down it really will be a headache because it will be linked to all the other devices inside your house. So you won't be able to switch on the central heating or make a cup of coffee because the central-heating settings and the coffee machine will have been personalised and linked to individual smartcards for each member of the household or the biometric door entry system.

People will therefore seek out older products with less technology or hack into new products to remove the unnecessary features. In the long term, technology may solve this complexity problem itself, but don't bet on it. A more likely scenario is that companies will keep inventing useless gadgets like internet fridges — and some deluded souls will even buy them — but most of us will stick with what we know. Our lives are complicated enough already, and we won't buy into technological dreams like smart homes until it can be demonstrated that the new really is superior to the old. This means faster and cheaper, but it also means taking into account the bigger picture. 'Does this make my life easier?' as well as 'Does this make the world a better place?' After all, as a very old friend of mine, Douglas Slater, once reminded me: 'Old things become old because they are good. They are not bad simply because they are old.' Door keys, books, and bank notes have survived for centuries because they are extremely well designed for their purpose. Don't get me wrong here: keyless entry, e-books, and digital money are all coming, but most people will prefer to use the original tried and tested versions for a number of practical, historical, and emotional reasons.

Things cannot get faster or more complicated forever. Our minds (at least our current minds) won't be able to cope — there is only so much information we can take on board. For example, there's a trend called too much information (TMI) that has a distant cousin called too much choice (TMC). In a nutshell, mankind is producing too much stuff. The amount of new information we now produce is estimated to be around 2 billion exabytes annually. That's (very roughly) 2 billion billion bytes or about twenty billion copies of this book. The average large corporation similarly experiences a doubling of the amount of information it produces annually.

It is no longer information that is power; it is capturing and maintaining a person's attention. The problem is so bad that the world's largest bank (Citibank) is testing something called Auditory Display Software as a way of delivering vital information to traders via music because visually based information just isn't getting through.

A Japanese company has already invented a way to move a cursor across a screen just by thinking about it, so ultimately we may be able to send and receive messages telepathically. Will such innovations make our lives better? It depends. Some people will rush to embrace these developments, while others will seek temporary or permanent solitude in everything from alcohol and country pursuits to memory-erasing pills (probable slogan: 'Take one to forget what happened to you today.') There will even be a boom in people buying remote real estate and islands to get away from it all. However, most of us will live somewhere in the middle, or will mentally commute between both extremes.

Hence there will not be a single future because we will all experience the future in different ways; there will be multiple, often contradictory, futures. The future will arrive faster if you live in a metropolis such as London, Sydney, or New York than if you live in a remote town or village. Equally, the level of change you will experience will vary according to your age, your income, and your occupation, although there will be exceptions everywhere.

New theories of time and space

There will also be tensions generated by these differences. People living in metropolitan areas will tend to push for the rapid deployment of innovations, while older, more conservative rural and semi-rural populations will generally seek to limit them. It will also be a battle between the technology haves and the new Luddites (the technology have-nots and want-nots). The first tribe will tend to have money, but they will suffer from time famine and space anxiety because they won't have either of these. The second tribe, conversely, will tend to have time and space but little or no income, relatively speaking, because this will be tied up in real estate or spent on healthcare costs. So, for example, young people will enjoy very high salaries, but they will be unable to afford the overall standard of living enjoyed by their parents and grandparents because of long work hours, the high cost of real estate, and the lack of private space. What was 'free' to their forebears (fresh air, public parks, public beaches, libraries, roads, etc) will all cost money.

Overall, people will cope — just — with the avalanche of change, uncertainty, and anxiety, but many of them will seek refuge in the past. They will escape the present through various nostalgic pursuits, although their love of the new will sit alongside a fondness for the past.

They will mentally return to the eras they grew up in, which they will perceive (often incorrectly) as being safer, warmer, and more certain than the present or the future. They will covert old cars, old clothes, old music, and even old technology. Again, this is already happening. Just look at the popularity of old arcade video games (Pong), old car designs (the 'new' VW Beetle), old running shoes, and 'old' food (recipes). Indeed, as people and products become more perfect (humans through surgery and gene modification, products through quality control and innovation), we will seek out imperfect people and products.

Patina will be big in the future. Women with facial lines will be highly desirable, while new hydrogen-powered cars will be available with used-looking paintwork and worn leather seats as optional extras. Another example is pornography. The fastest-growing segment of the pornography industry worldwide is 'real' or 'amateur' pornography using real people rather than airbrushed or surgically enhanced 'models'. In other words porn like it used to be. Nostalgic pornography for the over-seventies crowd? That will be coming along shortly, too.

We will also, where possible, shut the outside world away completely by locking our front doors and turning our homes into either high-security compounds or — more likely — miniature holiday resorts. An interesting fact I came across recently is that the ratio of gated communities to trailer parks in the US is 1:1. People will withdraw into themselves because they will feel impotent in the face of change and believe their lives lack meaning. This will be a problem because if the majority of people withdraw and take refuge inside their homes and inside individual obsessions, governments (and companies) will have carte blanche to behave exactly as they like. To misquote Woody Allen, all that future dictators will need to be successful is for nobody else to show up. The opposite of good isn't evil — it's indifference.

Meet mini-me

For the technically minded, doorbells will disappear in favour of proximity indicators. We will constantly know where our friends and family are thanks to the descendents of services like Friendfinder, and we will be able to screen out the unknown and the unfamiliar.

This will undoubtedly increase our safety, but it will remove the element of surprise from our lives.

Amazon's recommendation software already removes chance encounters with totally unrelated books. Other types of software could do the same with people in the future. This is bad news for society and especially bad news for new ideas, which thrive on social interaction, cross-fertilisation, and serendipity. We will therefore meet more people like ourselves in the future and be protected from people and ideas that are strange or unfamiliar. This is hardly a recipe for global harmony and understanding.

We will also be taking longer baths in the future as an antidote to modern stress, anxiety, and change. However, we will be contradictory. Many of us will embrace natural-looking materials and bath scents rather than the real thing because we will have so little experience of the real thing. Research conducted by the US Taste Research Foundation recently found that people generally prefer artificial smells to the real thing, partly because they are nostalgic about fake smells from their childhood. In the future, fake will thus become more real than real. Any (fake) experience we want will also be available via smart drugs, nanomedicine, and screen-based products, making the real strange and unfamiliar to most people.

The fully wired smart home will thus exist for some, but many of us will reject it in favour of its opposite. David Bowie allegedly once said, 'I spend all day in a recording studio surrounded by technology. When I get home all I want to do is have a cup of tea and touch some wood.' Even those who fully embrace technology (generally the younger generations) will use it to escape from reality. This will mean further growth in fantasy-related industries, ranging from gaming to virtual sex — the latter becoming increasingly realistic and acceptable to a vast swathe of society. People will take virtual vacations and have serious relationships with real people who they never meet in person.

The real will also become virtually indistinguishable from the virtual. Again, some of this is already happening right now. It has been estimated that Everquest is the seventy-seventh largest economy on Earth despite the fact that it doesn't really exist. Gamers are even spending real currency to buy virtual currencies and virtual real estate. In another example of our escape from reality, the top five worldwide grossing movies in 2005 were all escapist fantasies: *Harry Potter and the Goblet of Fire, Star Wars Episode III, The Chronicles of Narnia, War of the Worlds*, and *King Kong*. Why? I'd suggest that if present realities are too much for people, one way to deal with it is to escape into a fantasy world. If we experience another Great Depression I'd fully expect the entertainment industry — movies, for example — to do rather well.

By 2050 Hollywood, the computer industry, neuroscience, and the pharmaceuticals industry will have all merged into one. This will enable people, legally and illegally, to spend days inhabiting what are quite literally (according to all five of our human senses) other worlds — like the films *Matrix* and *Logan's Run*, but for real.

What are the implications of this? First, we will become socially and emotionally inept. Relationships will be originated, consummated, and terminated digitally. A court in Malaysia recently upheld a divorce that a husband sent to his wife via SMS; while I don't think that this will catch on, relationships will undoubtedly become more superficial and fleeting. People will still get together physically, but it will be less common, and they will commit to each other through renewable ten-year contracts downloaded from the internet. Divorce will be even more common (it hit 60 per cent in the US in 2006), but when people do finally settle down they will tend to stay together for longer, more out of fear of loneliness than love in many cases. Virtual adultery will become a reasonable cause for a divorce, although everyone will be doing it.

Second, we will be exposed to more experiences earlier, so childhoods will be compressed, while the ability for adults to remain 'children' indefinitely will become easier. Indeed, childhood, adolescence, and adulthood will become less distinct in the future. Ten-year-olds will want the same birthday presents, and forty-year-olds and sixty-year-olds will dress identically to eighteen-year-olds. At least buying birthday presents will become easier.

Inventing new types of fear

What will people be running away from in the future? What will we be afraid of in the year 2050? The answer is reality. People will be disorientated and uncomfortable due to the level and speed of change, so they will seek refuge in other places (holidays, books, games, films, and so on). The entertainment industry will therefore become the biggest game in town. Add to this the natural human inclination to see what's next, and you have a society that will refuse to tackle current problems such as debt, education, healthcare, and transport, while simultaneously worrying about things that happened in the past or might happen in the future (such as asteroid strikes).

We will be afraid of not knowing. We will be afraid of things that are outside our control. We will be afraid of uncertainty. Most of all, perhaps we will be afraid of 'them' — people who come from somewhere else, and I don't mean the planet Mars. These fears will drive the accumulation of information. We will crave 'scientific' data on the statistical probability of everything while simultaneously seeking out the personal stories of people, products, and organisations as some kind of faux reassurance.

By the year 2020 people, products, and organisations will have reliability ratings. These will be ratings of honesty, integrity, and transparency created by and available to everyone. You will be able to rank everything from politicians to personal computers based on past claims, actions, and performance, much in the same way that buyers and sellers are currently rated on eBay. Reputations will therefore be actively managed and, in some cases, even traded or stolen.

However, as an interesting counterpoint, it will be almost impossible to maintain a perfect record because everything you say and do and everywhere you go will be monitored and recorded. Secrecy will be history, in the future. People, products, and corporations will therefore be assumed guilty until investigated. This will eventually give rise to the idea of ethical bankruptcy, which will be a clean slate for reputations.

If none of this appeals to you, we will also see the appearance of disappearance. In the future, people will pay professionals to help them disappear. This will be difficult due to the level of electronic surveillance but not entirely impossible, especially for younger people already familiar with the concept of using multiple identities on the internet or for older people who have never existed online. For the rest of us, saddled with credit cards, GPS-embedded mobile phones, and biometric identity cards, it will be just another fantasy.

Many of the institutions and other anchor points in many people's lives, especially in developed western societies, have already vanished or had their reputations eroded to the point where people no longer implicitly trust them. The family, the church, government, business, science, and even the local bank manager have lost or are losing their ability to unite or be trusted. This cynicism and antipathy will continue in the future. People will focus even more on themselves, and a culture of self-reliance — the do-it-yourself society — will emerge. People will live in isolation bubbles and won't trust doctors, hospitals, or pharmaceutical companies, so self-diagnosis and self-medication will become commonplace. In 2050 smart software packages will be available to identify what's wrong with you, and websites like Genes Reunited will offer genetic histories enabling people to anticipate hereditary diseases and defects. You will also be able to hire or purchase robotic surgeons to perform operations in your own home or office.

At this point, you are probably thinking that most of what you have just read is wishful thinking; more science fiction than science fact. My response to this is simple. Make a list of what exists now and what you are able to do now that didn't exist or couldn't be done fifty years ago. Now add a multiplier to take into account the fact that technology tends to advance exponentially, and you may start to see that the future really is 'out there'.

Having said this, many of the things around today will still be around tomorrow. The basics won't change much. Our basic hopes and fears will be the same. We will still want to be acknowledged. We will still want our time on Earth to have made a difference. We will still want to achieve something, and we will still crave respect. We will also still want to know whether our collective existence is anything more than a cosmic accident.

Like Joyce Vincent, alone in her London apartment, we will still want to love and be loved.

Plus ça change, plus c'est la même chose.

14 November 2030

Dear Renée

This will knock you out. I'm sending you something I've just found called 'Leaves'.™ It's a new product from Past Toyz in Shanghai featuring a giant biodegradable plastic bag containing real farm-grown leaves that have been hygienically dried and treated with an anti-bacterial agent for 'safe outdoor fun'.™ Can you believe it? Why didn't we think of that? I think you empty the bag in your backyard and play with the leaves. Either that or you can drive that hygiene and order-fixated neighbour of yours crazy by placing a single leaf on his plastic lawn every night for the next two years. I suppose the company did some research with trend-setters and early adopters which said that people in urban areas aren't getting as close to nature as they like. Back in my day leaves grew on trees but the colours weren't manipulated and the bugs were kept in check by other bugs, not chemicals. Anyway, it certainly made me laugh. You can always send it back if the joke is lost on you.

What's next — aerosol dirt?

All the best

Sing

Five trends that will transform society

Globalisation   Globalisation used to mean Americanisation, but these days it means exposure to people, products, and ideas from everywhere. Globalisation impacts on the sourcing of products and services, and on market-expansion opportunities. It also means connectedness and mobility. Everything from countries and computers to gadgets and global banking will be hyper-linked together. In the future, this trend will accelerate even faster, thanks to devices such as GPS, RFIDs, sensor motes, and smart dust (all essentially tiny wireless transmitters and/or receivers of some kind). Hence privacy will all but disappear, but transparency and risk may increase.

Localisation   Localisation (or re-localisation) is a perfect example of a trend creating a counter-trend. Localisation will occur because people don't like globalisation or homogenisation. The European Union will therefore splinter and ultimately collapse. This new tribalism will drive city states, locally tailored products, economic protectionism, and the sale of flags.

Polarisation   The future is an either/or kind of place with most things polarising in some form or another. First there will be multiple futures, some of them speeding up and others slowing down. Some people with embrace technology, while others will reject it. Industrial markets will split between luxury and low-cost options, with access to services like health and education, transport, and security similarly polarising, depending on your ability to pay. The middle class will eventually disappear in most developed countries, with people either moving upwards into a new global managerial elite or downwards into a new enslaved working (or not working) class.

Anxiety   If 'they' don't get you, a global pandemic probably will. At least that's how many people will feel in the future. Trust in institutions will all but evaporate, and the speed of change will leave people longing for the past. This insecurity is to some extent generational, but whether you are eighteen or eighty there will be a growing feeling of powerlessness and a continual state of anxiety that will fuel everything from an interest in nostalgia and escapism to a growth in narcissism, localisation, and tribalism.

Meaning   One of the most fascinating questions about the future is whether religion will be a victim or a beneficiary of change. Some people predict that faith will decline because the spread of information will undermine the mindset necessary to support belief. Physics will produce a unified theory of everything and this will destroy old-fashioned superstitions such as religion. In other words, science will become our new religion. I'm not so sure. If science, technology, and complexity become key ingredients of the future, this will drive change and uncertainty. And the more this happens, the more people will seek out safety, comfort, and guidance from religion. This could just lead to an increase in individual spirituality, but I suspect that globalisation, mixed with a general feeling of powerlessness and anxiety, will drive group actions and beliefs. Hence we will witness an increase in tribalism, nationalism, and xenophobia, which at the extreme will fuel Islamic fanaticism and muscular Christianity.

Chapter 2

Government and Politics: us and them

The empires of the future are the empires of the mind.
–Winston Churchill

Former British prime minister Harold Macmillan once observed that his biggest problem was 'events'. Predicting anything is a recipe for failure and frustration, but politics is almost impossible due to such events. Indeed, the only thing you can say with any degree of certainty about politics is that, if you take a long enough timeframe, almost anything is possible. Predictions about the end of history now seem as ridiculous as Thomas Jefferson saying that 'History, by apprising (people) of the past, will enable them to judge the future: it will avail them of experience of other times and nations.' If this were true, why did UN officials decide to cover up a copy of Picasso's *Guernica*, which hung outside the entrance to the UN Security Council, on the very day that Colin Powell addressed the UN about the case for war in Iraq? We are, it seems, destined to repeat past mistakes.

Politics is littered with false prophets whose usual mistake is to extrapolate past and present ideas and events into the future. This can work in the short term but, sooner or later, some totally unexpected event or idea trips up these intricately woven visions. The events of September 11 provide a recent example, and we are all still dealing with the aftermath.

The years immediately after September 11 witnessed a profound swing towards semi-authoritarian rule and, at the governmental level at least, there was a feeling of solidarity and oneness with the US's response. However, the legacy of September 11 is now fading fast. As I write, the eight world leaders who attended the G8 Summit in Britain and posed for a 'family photo' are either history or soon will be. Schröder (Germany), Berlusconi (Italy), Koizumi (Japan), Chirac (France), and Blair have all gone. Bush is on his last legs, and Putin won't be around much longer either — at least constitutionally. Western leaders, almost without exception, are losing their grip.

In many cases, this is because voters have become disillusioned with the war on terror — which has had precisely the opposite effect from that intended. Voters are feeling less safe and secure than ever, due to everything from the shadow of terrorism and globalisation to their inability to effectively influence national or international politics.

The end result is falling membership of political parties (down 50 per cent in the UK since 1980), low voter turnout at elections, and a general collapse of confidence in both politics and politicians. In theory, this situation could be reversed with the election of a new US president and a fresh set of other world leaders, although, if anything, the level of anxiety is likely to increase due to the effects of globalisation and technology. Anti-globalisation and anti-US sentiments could also fuel a swing to the left in many developing nations, which, together with the rapid rise of authoritarian Russia and totalitarian China, could lead to a new world order and cold war dominated by patriotism and protectionism.

Fear, as the sociologist Frank Furedi has pointed out, has become a significant force shaping the public imagination across the globe, and in the future it will be used to justify everything from compulsory biometric identity cards to a global database. Our feeling of powerlessness is also driving an insecurity that makes us swing from one panic to the next, even when the probability of our fears materialising is almost non-existent. Clever politicians know this, and use fears about crime, immigration, education, jobs, and climate change to fan uncertainty, causing many to vote for the devil they know (the incumbent) rather than the devil they don't.

Nation states are also becoming irrelevant. Issues that matter are generally either local or international. National sovereignty is also under threat from the increasing mobility of workers and tax systems that encourage global corporations to move their profits elsewhere. There is also the question of what government and countries are ultimately for. For example, if governments increasingly withdraw from providing essential services and public infrastructure projects (education, health, transport, and so on), and national security is increasingly delivered through multinational organisations, what exactly are we paying national politicians to do?

Ultimately, I'd expect global voting on all major issues (for example, the US presidency could be voted on globally), and citizens will become more involved partly through convenience (electronic voting in supermarkets), but also because the internet — and future metanets — will make special interest groups and non-governmental organisations (NGOs) immensely powerful. In other words, the internet will effectively become the second chamber in most democracies, with leaderless movements and self-forming networks becoming a major threat to local control and regulation. In Australia, for example, the grassroots GetUp organisation has more signed-up members than any of the country's main political parties.

It will be a similar story with war. The idea of interstate war is becoming increasingly old-fashioned, with most future threats coming from the spilling over of interstate conflicts or stateless organisations. States will also be less likely to go to war simply because very few people in developed nations will be willing to die for an idea in the future. There will be notable exceptions to this, but generally fanatics will have quite an advantage. The causes of war will change, too. Oil is currently top of the list, but in a few decades water will become a major source of conflict, as will food. If plants are increasingly used to make fuel (to replace oil), conflicts may arise over control of the world's grain markets, which are controlled by a handful of rich western nations (OPEC in reverse perhaps?). Equally, an undemocratic regime (possibly acting alone or in conjunction with a terrorist group) could bring the US (and hence the west) to its knees, simply by selling some currency. Almost 70 per cent of global currency-reserves are now in the hands of developing nations, many of them undemocratic and unstable. Indeed, most of the huge debt owed by the US is 'owned' by China, Saudi Arabia, and Russia, none of which is an entirely model democracy, to put it mildly. Iran and Venezuela also have substantial holdings of US debt.

A more pressing concern for governments is demographic trends and, in particular, the ageing of most populations. More people are more likely to suffer from age discrimination than racism and sexism, but government legislation almost totally neglects ageism in favour of other forms of inequality and human rights.

An age-old problem

Ageing populations and declining fertility-rates are well-known trends, but what is generally missed is that this means there will be a future military-recruitment problem. It's possible to solve this shortfall by recruiting more women into the armed services, but most countries are still uneasy about using women in combat roles. Another solution is the importation of soldiers (say, through temporary or long-term immigration). To some extent, the future shortfall will be made up by the increased use of technology, but in the short term these devices will still need human operatives, and the best-qualified people will be young people who have grown up using computer games and virtual reality. The only other solution I can think of is compulsory national service, which has been universally unpopular. Mind you, this will be less of a concern in the future because the major voting bloc will be older not younger people.

Population — and more precisely the unregulated movement of population — is a critical element in the future security of nations. It is already looking as if Europe is under threat from growing immigrant communities that have very little loyalty to their host nation. Nationalism will become a defining trend of the twenty-first century and there is a very serious possibility that Europe will disintegrate into the regions from whence it came. Equally, the impact of foreign nationals living abroad is a significant factor influencing the so-called 'soft power' of nations. Much has been written about China and India, in particular the sheer size of their populations, but what is often overlooked is the 60 million Chinese and 20 million Indians already living abroad who are subtly affecting their host nations.

Instability in the Third World, brought on by environmental destruction, could send further waves of migration into Europe or perhaps Australia, on a par with the movements that led to the collapse of the Roman Empire in the fifth century. The most likely areas to experience mass migration include Africa, the Middle East, and Central Asia, which are affected by water shortages, a decline in food production, rising sea levels, and radical Islam. The impact would first be seen at the edges of these areas, but would become more problematic as borders disappear and large urban populations become ungovernable.

Population may influence politics in other more subtle ways, too. Across the globe, people are having fewer children. The obvious problem this creates is funding retirement, but there are some other implications. Philip Longman, writing in the *Atlantic Monthly*, has pointed out that if a generation has fewer offspring, its genetic legacy is reduced.

This means that the beliefs to which a generation adhered will weaken over time. Moreover, the people who do decide to have children — especially lots of them — tend to be more conservative than those that don't. For example, in 2004, states that voted for George W. Bush had fertility rates 12 per cent higher on average than states that voted for the more liberal John Kerry. In other words, individualist and libertarian elements of the population will tend to die out while more traditional, patriarchal, patriotic, and even fundamentalist elements will inherit countries by default.

Another thing that current politicians don't get is that for an increasing number of people it's no longer about the money. Materialism is still in full swing in most countries, with about one billion new consumers about to join the party in China, India, and elsewhere. However, for many people approaching the top of Maslow's hierarchy of needs, money is starting to lose its appeal. We are working harder and longer than ever — and earning more money as a result — but we don't seem to be getting any happier. People are also starting to realise that identity and self-esteem are not shaped by what you own or consume, but by who you are and how you live. To some extent, the happiness phenomenon is really a search for meaning. But it is also down to the fact that people have too much time on their hands to reflect on the human condition. Thus the politics of happiness will move increasingly to centre stage, partially replacing the debate about the work/life balance.

The implications are significant. Traditionally, politicians have been elected on the basis first of security and certainty and, more recently, on their promise to make you better off. Tax cuts have been the currency of politicians for the last fifty years; however, this is shifting. In the future, voters will demand happiness. This is a ridiculous demand, and one that surely says something about the delegation of responsibility in society, but it's coming nevertheless.

Happiness is not something you can buy off the shelf, and it can never be a permanent condition. Nevertheless, that's what ordinary voters will demand in the future, and opportunistic politicians will promise to deliver it. Obvious implications will include a focus on 'green' and community issues, and various promises of free time and family-friendly policies. Of course, this trend could go out of the window in the event of a wildcard event such as a flu pandemic or a major war.

Another wildcard is globalisation or, perhaps more accurately de-globalisation. Most people assume globalisation is here to stay, but I'd argue that this is far from certain. Globalisation will probably last for at least another decade or two, but there are a number of worrying signs. First, the rise of China and India could result in economic protectionism in regions like the US and Europe, putting a few speed-bumps in the road to further globalisation. It's interesting to note that in 1990 there were fifty regional trade agreements around the world, but by 2005 there were two hundred and fifty.

Equally, most of our international institutions are fragile, to say the least, and nationalism is already clearly evident in regions as diverse as the former Soviet Union, Europe, and even Australia and the UK. Ultimately higher oil prices could also lead to higher inflation, higher interest rates, and economic turmoil, which could cripple the global economy. Globalisation could then come to an abrupt halt because goods, especially perishables such as food, may not be able to be transported cost-effectively around the world. Industry and politics would thus return to a pre-1914 (or perhaps pre-1950) model.

Whether or not globalisation ultimately remains a key megatrend or not, nationalism will certainly be a feature of the next 50 years. Europeans collectively complain about George W. Bush, but the fact is they usually want to be governed by his local equivalent. As a result, global provincialism is taking over from global cooperation as a dominant theme of modern politics. This is happening because globalisation requires presidents and prime ministers to allow wide-ranging socioeconomic reform if a country is to compete internationally. However, ordinary voters are usually rather attached to the old ways, especially when these brought international prestige (history influencing the future again).

Thus an instinct for identifying and preserving what makes a country, or region, special is a prerequisite for high office and popular support. This may appear ridiculously parochial or superficial to some, but it's increasingly what voters want. This view not only explains George W. Bush and his particular form of 'muscular Christianity', but it also explains why Gerhard Schröder was such an enthusiastic defender of the German lifestyle or why John Howard was so in touch with Australian values.

From whiter than white to greener than green

Another instance of nationalism can be seen in South America. Energy has always been a strategic resource there, and the same will be true of a handful of key resources in the future. Ten of the world's largest oil companies are 'nationals' — state-controlled oil companies. Moreover, many of the owners of the world's largest remaining oil fields are moving to the far left politically, and could potentially nationalise all energy and resource production within their borders. Venezuela is frequently quoted as a future trouble spot as it contains some of the world's largest remaining reserves, but Nigeria (which has the eighth-largest oil reserves on Earth), Libya, Bolivia, Peru, Ecuador, Angola, and Sudan are other countries that could potentially shut off supplies to foreign nations or become catalysts for future conflict.

All this is important because we are about to enter a critical historical period. Resources (everything from oil and water to uranium and grain stocks) are running low, so there will be a headlong rush by energy-dependent countries into the arms of countries that can satisfy this hunger until technology provides them with a more sustainable solution. The same will be true of other key materials, and future development will be heavily influenced by the cost and regulation of these resources.

Edward O. Wilson calls this 'the bottleneck'. This is the point at which population growth, economic development, and environmental destruction put maximum stress on both the planet and the human race. As a result, the resources trade will increasingly operate on a 'no questions asked' basis. In the long term, I believe that energy (and general resource-scarcity issues) will be solved through technology; but, in the meantime, energy (along with climate change and sustainability) will dominate the political agenda.

Most studies predict we will hit peak oil production by 2015, or perhaps 2020 at the latest. Then supplies will run out around 2050. This will be followed by peak gas and peak coal. As a result, nuclear power is firmly back on the political agenda, an inconceivable thought twenty years ago. Wind and particularly solar power are also firmly on the development and regulation agenda.

According to Richard Heinberg, a US academic and author of several books on the end of cheap oil, we should all be planning for another 1930s style economic depression. Another report produced for the US Department of Energy says that when peak oil does hit, we will experience abrupt and revolutionary change. I don't agree. The world's appetite for oil is certainly insatiable. Between September 2003 and July 2006 the price of oil increased by 300 per cent, but demand has not declined at all. Indeed, demand for oil is predicted to rise by 50 per cent between now and 2025. This is partly because countries such as China are voracious users of energy, but also because developed nations such as the US are still in denial about future availability. And if it does run out, we will certainly be in for a shock. Higher fuel prices will drive global change, but we will adjust.

The end of oil may lead to a renaissance in local manufacturing and consumption, and even to an end of the worldwide obesity epidemic. If you think the last point is a bit farfetched, consider this. In Cuba the average adult lost nine kilograms after 1992 because the collapse of the Soviet Union increased the severity of the US oil embargo and the country had to rely on 10 per cent of its pre-1992 oil supply. As a result, Cubans started to use gearless Chinese bicycles to get around, and this increased the fitness of the entire nation.

Will all this really happen? The answer depends on human ingenuity and whether or not technology can provide an alternative to crude oil. Personally, I think there are tough times ahead and that we will have to get used to consuming less of everything, which may not be a bad thing. Reverse globalisation would re-energise local communities and people would become more self-reliant and, just as people did during and immediately after the Second World War, maintain and repair things rather than just replacing them. There is indeed a strong possibility of an energy bottleneck to pass through first; but, ultimately, I believe future generations will be better off, not worse off, once the oil runs out.

The desire to be green will govern how governments operate, much in the same way as it will corporations. However, governments will also increasingly pass the buck onto ordinary citizens and use green concerns as a way of increasing revenue. The desire to be green started with countries (the Kyoto protocol is a prominent example), trickled down through companies and organisations, and has now landed firmly at the feet of ordinary individuals. The environment will create regulation, which will in turn force change.

For example, a broad coalition of politicians, environmentalists, and economists believe that green taxes (and carbon taxes in particular) are the solution to the growing problem of energy scarcity around the world. With many of the world's governments facing a budget deficit, green taxes offer a way of building a better environment (or appeasing the environmentalists, if you're of a cynical persuasion). Crucially, they also generate extra tax revenue, which electorates find difficult to argue against without appearing selfish. According to Dieter Helm at New College Oxford (UK), green taxes will be used by most democratically elected governments within the next five years. In New Labour speak (UK), this means there will be a shift from taxing 'goods' to taxing 'bads'.

There is also likely to be a shift from energy and transport-related green taxation to taxation based on pollution, chemical use, and waste production, especially packaging. Like I say, many of these taxes may be aimed at individuals and small businesses despite the fact that most of the pollution is produced by a tiny handful of large companies and countries. Research conducted by the *Guardian* newspaper in Britain says that just six companies in the UK produce more CO_2 than all the car drivers in Britain combined. Meanwhile, Australians are being urged to turn out their lights while the government simultaneously sells millions of tons of coal to China and refuses to ratify the Kyoto protocol.

The problem of climate change certainly seems to be urgent. Of the twenty hottest summers on record, nineteen have occurred since 1980, and since 1970 the number of category four and five hurricanes has doubled globally. Yet we still currently release 300 per cent more CO_2 than our oceans can absorb. India's CO_2 emissions are also likely to rise by 70 per cent by 2025, and between now and 2030 emissions from China are predicted to equal that of the rest of the world combined. Nevertheless, we seem to be losing our sense of perspective. The science surrounding climate change is complex, and the outcomes are still uncertain.

Why the planet doesn't need saving

However, it is still possible that some of this is part of a natural cycle, although if you say this in most polite circles you will probably be lynched. This is precisely what happened to Andy Revkin in the *New*

York Times recently when he had the audacity to suggest that the planet is not in peril.

A growing number of scientists (but still not very many) believe that the activity of the sun could be linked to the Earth's temperatures, perhaps explaining as much as 30 per cent of global warming. Moreover, periodic environmental crises have been part of the Earth's history for as long as the Earth has existed. In fact, there are a few people who think that the odd mass extinction is a good thing because it allows evolutionary processes to start again.

What we forget is that, from the Earth's point of view, we don't need ice caps, Brazilian rainforests, or any specific sea level. These things ebb and flow with the passage of time, and it is arrogant in the extreme to believe that the Earth belongs to us and therefore we should protect it. The Earth will protect itself and, ultimately, bounce back from anything we humans could possibly do to it. In other words, the idea that the Earth is somehow in our care is a complete nonsense.

However, 6.4 billion people do currently live on the planet, and while mass extinctions are perhaps of no consequence when they happen to other species, it matters very much if it looks like it may happen to us. Thus the climate/carbon/water debate is really about how future change will impact on those people who are too poor to adapt. The key consequence of climate change — and one that politicians should worry about — is how rising temperatures, rising sea levels, and increasingly severe and unpredictable weather will threaten the food security of millions and perhaps hundreds of millions of people. And, remember, this isn't just an altruistic point. If millions of people have their food or water supplies shut off, they will do what any sensible person would do — they will move to the areas where supply is more certain. Such mass migrations would have profound implications for the stability of the entire world.

Water, in particular, will become a serious problem over the next few years, although not in the way some people expect. It takes

11,000 litres of water to make a hamburger and 83,000 to make a medium-size family car, while the average person uses 135 litres every day (most of it wasted). Water, or more precisely the lack of it, will be a big problem in the future due to growing populations and urbanisation.

These problems may evaporate, but I doubt it. We have already seen Coca-Cola accused of stealing water in India, and Chinese provinces are already accusing each other of taking more than their fair share of rain by seeding clouds. Water theft is thus set to be one of the defining crimes of the twenty-first century. If the water crisis continues, half the world's population will be living in 'water stressed' regions by 2025, and countries such as Australia could be in very serious trouble.

What are the consequences? Bottled water could be singled out as ethically unsound because it involves removing water from one region and selling it in another — and in Australia's case this often means shipping it 10,000 kilometres, contributing to carbon emissions. In Canada some churches are urging congregations to boycott bottled water, citing ethical and social-justice reasons.

Equally, eating lettuce may become socially unacceptable in the future because growing lettuce is not environmentally sustainable — it uses lots of water (and, in some cases, heat) — with a resultant nutritional value of next to nothing. Farming irrigation uses 60 per cent of all water taken from rivers and aquifers globally, and while the world grows twice as much food as it did a generation ago, we use three times as much water to do it.

A single kilogram of rice requires 2,000–3,000 litres of water, while a kilogram jar of instant coffee takes 20,000 litres. Even a litre of milk needs 4,000 litres of water. People's attitudes to water will therefore shift seismically in some regions; and politicians, keen to jump on another bandwagon, won't be far behind. The pollution of rivers and lakes will thus move centre-stage along with dam-building and the ownership of pipe networks and water companies.

The water use of every industry from food to fashion will be in the spotlight, and science will be given the task of developing drought-free crop varieties.

Finally, it's worth mentioning the link between water and economic performance. Water could potentially be an Achilles' heel for China. Currently, 400 out of China's 600 biggest cities are short of water, and the country has below-average water resources per capita, all of which could potentially put a large spanner in its development model.

By the year 2010 the world's population will stand at 6.8 billion (up from 6 billion in 1999), but 95 per cent of global population growth will come from developing countries, most of them in the east. India will become a superpower (especially in services), but most attention will continue to focus on the potential of its manufacturing-based rival, China. China is important politically for a number of reasons, including its sheer size (geographically and population-wise), its economic growth, and its territorial claims. These factors make China a significant foreign-policy player and ultimately, perhaps, the world's number one superpower. Nevertheless, we shouldn't forget that China is currently a totalitarian state with, some might argue, the seeds of its own destruction already sown. Urban–rural conflict, rampant corruption, a bankrupt state-backed banking system, overdependence on the US economy, and environmental problems could all bring China down — and it's a similar story with Russia.

So what are some of the most likely scenarios for China over the coming years? One possibility, identified by the Global Business Network, is that China will play by the established rules and slowly move towards a recognisable western democratic model. This would involve China enforcing intellectual property laws and opening its doors to foreign companies on a totally level playing field. Ultimately, labour shortages could become a problem, but then China could simply contract labour to regions such as Africa.

A second scenario is that corruption and urban unrest will continue and the region will simply grind to a halt. A third possibility is that China will grow in economic and political stature, but only as fast as its Asian rivals. This would mean intense competition for resources and markets, or it could lead to a series of regional pacts and trade agreements much to the disadvantage of the west, although this in turn could spur increased cooperation between the US and Europe or between North and South America. Either way, globalisation — or at least the free movement of goods, services, and people — may be in trouble.

The fourth and final scenario is simply that China will keep on growing. With unrest quashed (or peaceably accommodated), the country could end up as the world's dominant superpower. Then, perhaps, China will stop buying US debt, the US economy will collapse, and the yuan will become the favoured global currency, displacing both the US dollar and the euro. I think this is a bit unlikely — although not impossible — because China and the US are mutually independent economically. As a result, it would be in neither country's best interest to allow the other to falter economically. Nevertheless, China could still end up wrecking the global economy upon which it also depends.

I would therefore expect the power shift to the east to continue, although a key question is whether China can pull off what Japan did so successfully after the Second World War. In other words, can China move from a manufacturing-based economy that essentially copies what is designed and developed in the west, to one in which innovation is at the very core? Moreover, is the shift to an innovative, entrepreneurially led culture possible without full political freedom? We'll see.

Edukation ain't wurkin

Education, along with crime, transport, and jobs is another classic swing factor in politics. In the future, this list of voter concerns will be joined, increasingly, by health, immigration, and the environment, but education will remain a top priority — not least because it will have to change fundamentally if countries are to remain competitive in the new globally connected economy.

Education will also change radically in response to new discoveries and understandings about how the human brain works. Developments in artificial intelligence will ultimately cause education to focus on those areas of human thought and activity that computers and technology are unable to efficiently deliver — namely, the development of new ideas and the empathetic interaction with other human beings.

Twenty years ago the school gates marked a clear separation between the influence of teachers and parents. Trust was implicit and transparency was unnecessary. Moreover, the values and influence of business hardly got a look in. Not any more. Due to increased competition for university places and jobs (the influence of globalisation) and demographics (more pressure on individual children due to smaller family sizes), parents are getting more involved in their children's education.

In some cases this has led to a renaissance of private education (also due to an increase in disposable incomes), but even in state-funded schools parents are demanding to be let inside schools and have a say in what's being taught and how. Parents are thus being given the email addresses of teachers and, in some cases, are suing schools when their expectations (such as exam results and career paths) are not met. For example, in the US there was a 25 per cent increase in the number of teachers buying liability insurance between 2000 and 2005.

A good example of the pressure on students — from both parents and educators — is a quote from the head of a preschool in the US. Andi (who clearly can't spell) is of the opinion that afternoon naps for four-year-old preschoolers should be stopped because, 'If they get behind (by wasting their time sleeping), by the age of six they have difficulty catching up'. Never mind that kids of four or five need ten to twelve hours of sleep a day, and heaven forbid that kids might be allowed a few hours just to be kids and develop a sense of curiosity and wonder. The pressure to perform starts as soon as you are born.

A home for incurable talent

The issue for some parents is their desire for education to be directly linked to the 'real world'. Subjects must therefore have a dollar value career-wise, and knowledge for its own sake is taking a back seat to vocational learning. Indeed, the stakes are now becoming so high that some parents are removing the element of chance altogether and doing most or all of their children's homework or school entry assignments themselves. This won't last for long of course because technology can already be used to identify the writer.

Another issue is what's been termed 'cut and paste' education. A survey in *Education Week* (US) claims that 54 per cent of students have plagiarised material from the internet. In the UK the Plagiarism Advisory Service (really!) says that 25 per cent of students regularly pass off downloaded material as their own. There are even websites such as Cheathouse.com to help students plagiarise.

Of course, where there's a threat there's always an opportunity, so teachers can upload suspect material to turnitin.com. That's assuming their students haven't got their retaliation in first by reporting their professors. Sites like Ratemyprofessors.com allow students to evaluate their teachers publicly. In theory this is a welcome development, but one wonders where the obsession with instant evaluation will end. Could children be rating their parents online in the future, or could private school fees be adjusted on a daily basis depending on the previous day's ratings from students and parents?

In the US the education 'market' is already worth close to US$750 billion, although only 10 per cent of this is 'edupreneurial' in the sense that it is for profit. In Sweden a third of all schools are now run by private companies, and the sector is also growing fast in countries such as the UK, Australia, Brazil, and South Africa.

There are many arguments against the privatisation of essential services such as education, but the one that will capture people's imaginations in the future surrounds the long-term social consequences of a system where the best brains are creamed off at an early age, possibly by corporate sponsors with little interest in the wider social impacts of their actions. For example, if education becomes too polarised between the public and the private, this will magnify the creation of a new establishment elite and underclass, with each group living, learning, and earning in separate bubbles.

One implication I'd certainly expect to see is the development of schools based on the look and feel of companies or hotels. Hence, they'll open earlier and close later to fit in with the schedules of busy working parents. They will offer breakfast and dinner, and in some cases temporary overnight accommodation. They will also teach discipline and values because parents will be too busy to do either themselves. Unfortunately, these schools will rarely accommodate any talent that falls outside the prescribed curriculum or agenda. Commerce, media studies, accountancy, and law will all be well catered for, but anyone with an aptitude for the study of ancient history will struggle to find a home for their talents.

Another big issue in education is how to teach boys versus girls. Thirty years ago a major problem was how to teach girls when 58 per cent of undergraduate students in the US were male. Now boys account for only 44 per cent, and they are failing across almost every benchmark.

There are various explanations for this, including the general feminisation of society, but a more likely culprit is continual testing for very narrowly defined outcomes. Another issue that affects boys is the decrease in physical education and sports. This is partly due to urbanisation and booming property values (there is less space available because it has become so expensive), and also because parents are withdrawing their children from competitive sport because it is either perceived as dangerous or they don't like the idea of their child losing at something.

Thirty years ago scientists argued that the differences between boys and girls were largely the result of nurture (socialisation). These days most scientists think the opposite. In other words, behaviour is hard-wired and largely the result of chemistry. So if in the future boys are proven to be very different biologically from girls, perhaps we'll see the old idea of teaching them separately come back into vogue. This idea may also become popular because of the lack of male teachers in the primary (early education) system, meaning that young boys will have fewer and fewer male role models in their lives. In the US 40 per cent of boys currently grow up without their biological father, thanks to high divorce rates and high levels of single motherhood.

Here comes the taxman

They used to say that nothing in life is certain except death and taxes. In the future there may be a question mark over death, but taxes will remain, although their form may change.

In 1994 Estonia became the first country in the world to adopt what is now known as a flat-tax system, essentially one rate of tax — in Estonia's case, 26 per cent for all individuals and companies. There is no schedule of rates and there are no exceptions. The idea proved so successful that a number of other countries have introduced the idea. Critics who initially said it would be unworkable have now moved on to argue that it is unfair because it is not progressive (that is, everyone pays the same). However, while the amount is fixed, there's nothing stopping a government applying a threshold (exception amount). The advantage of a flat-tax system is its simplicity. In the US the cost of running and regulating the current tax system is estimated at between 10 per cent and 20 per cent of total revenue received. That's a sum equivalent to something in the region of 25 per cent to 50 per cent of the US budget deficit.

Thus I'd predict that more and more countries will eventually move to a flat tax system, and ultimately a single rate will apply across the entire world. But until then we will see a continued shift towards indirect and 'stealth' taxes.

These may include tax cuts for people who move to unpopular or depopulating regions, low-tax or no-tax incomes for people working in certain industries or professions (teaching and aged care for example), and conscientious-objection taxes for people who don't want their tax dollars spent on defence or other ethically challenged 'investments'. Zero tax for government employees may sound like 'jobs for the boys', but this, too, does make a certain amount of sense. What is the point of a government (generally the largest employer in most countries) paying its employees and then going on to waste administrative time and effort collecting taxes from these very same people? Wouldn't it be simpler just to offer lower, tax-free salaries in the first place?

A final 'swing factor' is crime. In the US, the Justice Department is funding research to identify and track the leading indicators of lawlessness in order to build a crime-forecasting model. The idea is that if supermarkets can predict sales by the month, or time of day, or based on the weather, the police ought to be able to do the same. Some crime forecasters already believe, for example, that temperature influences criminal behaviour. If this is true then, in the future, crime waves will be anticipated, although there still would remain the problem of knowing who to look for and where to go. The question of 'who' may be solved in the future by DNA tests (although a more low-fi methodology might be to simply observe or track the children of well-known criminals on the basis that history, criminally speaking, tends to repeat itself through the generations). This is controversial stuff, even suggesting that the sins of the father trickle down due to environmental factors, so imagine the implications if someone eventually proves a genetic component to criminal behaviour.

A department of future crime

In the UK there is already a groundswell of opinion within the government to support the creation of a national children's database, and it is not too much of a leap to imagine that eventually every child in the nation (currently 11 million kids) will be tagged to record their precise location and their interaction with known offenders — who would also tagged. And if you think this is too far-fetched, consider this.

If you are charged with a criminal offence in the UK, a sample of your DNA is taken and added to a national DNA database where it stays indefinitely, even if you are subsequently acquitted. So far the UK database contains the profiles of 3,130,429 people, or 5.23 per cent of the entire UK population. In contrast, the US DNA database contains just 0.99 per cent of its population, while most other national databases contain the names of fewer than 100,000 people. In theory, this DNA fingerprinting is a very good idea, not least because the technology allows police to create a DNA fingerprint using a single human cell (taken from a print on a broken window, for example). In the future, police officers will carry handheld devices that can instantly upload these samples and test them against the database. These samples will then be used to create 3-D photofits of suspects, giving police officers accurate information on likely height, skin colour, hair colour, and even personality type.

Privacy campaigners are obviously concerned about this, but the database and associated technology will be so useful that I'd expect the database to be enlarged as part of a national biometric identity- card scheme. Eventually, every single person in the country will therefore be listed 'for their own security', at which point adding some kind of GPS or other location-tagging component would seem an entirely logical idea. The problem with this, of course, is that once a government starts to view all its citizens as potential suspects, there will be subtle changes to how everything from policing to law-making operates.

This, of course, assumes that in the future people will commit crimes in person. In the UK, domestic burglaries have fallen by 45 per cent over the last decade, while identity theft and internet scams are now almost as worrying to people as car theft and muggings. It must only be a matter of time before an underworld avatar successfully commits a street crime against a law-abiding avatar walking the street in some virtual world or other.

Globalisation is also a factor in the sense that some products are now so cheap that it makes little sense to steal them. As a result, the new items of choice for burglars are cash (a perennial favourite), chequebooks, laptops, and mobile phones. The other reason for this shift has to do with drug trends. There is a correlation between the types of drugs someone takes and the types of crime they commit. The drugs of choice are now crack and powder cocaine, the users of which tend to be addicted to street crime, which takes less skill and planning than domestic burglary.

So what else will we witness in the future when it comes to crime? First of all, there will be a rise in organised cyber crime, including cyber terrorism. The former will target hapless individuals, whereas the latter will increasingly target companies and critical infrastructure. We will also see the continued emergence of failed states, especially within Africa, the Middle East, and Asia, which will become a major threat to civil order. In Sao Paulo, for example, police recently stopped removing the *fevelas* (street gangs) to concentrate on geographical containment of the problem. Sao Paulo's rich have literally risen above all this by using helicopters to bypass no-go areas (there are now 240 helicopter landing pads in Sao Paulo, compared to just ten in New York).

Other cities with the potential to become 'feral' include Johannesburg, Mexico City, and Karachi, although much will depend on the success or otherwise of national and global economies. In short, if the economy is booming, most places will remain relatively safe and secure; but if the economy crashes, all hell could break loose, especially in areas where the very rich live in close proximity to the very poor.

The doomsday scenario here, obviously, is criminal gangs aligning themselves with terrorist groups, resulting in the military replacing the police. This could ultimately lead to entire cities being walled off, much in the same way that Manhattan was fenced off in the film *Escape from New York*. While this is a very remote future possibility, private guards already outnumber the police by three to one in the US, so to some extent it is already happening — rich individuals and households are fencing themselves off from the outside.

The final thing to mention is voting. According to Morris Reid (a US political consultant), more people over the age of eighteen voted on the TV program *American Idol* than in the US election the same year. In the UK, 50 per cent of Britons are unsure whether they'll vote at the next general election, but the Royal Society for the Protection of Birds now has more members than all three major UK political parties combined. As a result, politicians are now regularly elected by less than a majority of voters (Tony Blair was elected by a mere 25 per cent of the UK electorate back in 2001), and most people would probably vote for Bart Simpson if they had a chance.

The issue of voter apathy is a very real concern and entirely the fault of opportunist politicians who believe that politics doesn't need big ideas and that politicians can be economical with the truth. Success is simply a matter of conducting research to find out what the majority of people want and then making them believe that you want the same.

It's also our fault. The average voter is now almost fully disengaged from the national agenda. They are up to their eyes in debt and are fully absorbed by their own material circumstances. They are selfish, self-absorbed, and greedy, and will vote for any character who appears optimistic or nationalistic or both. And if your face is famous, so much the better.

Historically, politics has been about promising future riches, but recent studies suggest that it is not your personal level of income that matters, but rather your income relative to other people you know and, even more critically, your level of income instability. In other words, while people still crave what they don't have, it's the fear of loss that ultimately influences elections.

Twenty-five years ago things were very different. There were two opposing worldviews (market capitalism versus state socialism), and this tended to reinforce class divisions and angst. As a result, people were engaged with a battle of ideas. Nowadays there is an increasingly convergent worldview. Or at least there is in the west.

Am I optimistic about the future? Ultimately, yes. Nuclear war — involving the use of tactical nuclear weapons in a regional conflict, or a terrorist attack on a major city using a dirty bomb — is a remote threat.

Globally, serious poverty and inequality are starting to be addressed, and while there is a growing polarisation between the very wealthy and the very poor, most people around the world are becoming better off. The ultimate question to my mind is therefore whether we will continue with a participatory and centrist system based on the individual and free markets, or whether we'll shift to a new idea, perhaps one based on the supremacy of the collective group. Events, as they say, will determine what happens next, although I'd venture to suggest that our newly found connectivity will also have a profound impact on how politics and political decision-making operate in the future.

24 March 2047

Dear Sven

I've just come back from visiting a friend in a nursing home who has been complaining that some of the other elderly residents have been playing Pink Floyd and the Sex Pistols too loud again. Myself, I've just got back from a walking trip in the Antarctic. The trees are lovely down there at this time of year. Awful news about the floods in the Mekong delta though. The floods in the Yangtze delta were bad this time last year, but this seems far worse. This is really going to increase tensions between Asia and the west, and I doubt whether the US president will be re-elected, given the power of the Chinese and Vietnamese voting blocs. On the other hand, the US has invested a lot of money in bio-fuel refining in both of these regions, so the local warlords might act to restrain voter anger. All I can say is that I'm glad I live in Paris. The city has taken on a new lease of life since the new French Queen took up residence in the city, and everyone is so happy now that the European experiment is finally over. Mind you, they're still really upset about Hungary and the bomb.

Anyway, I must fly. Got to do my compulsory duty and vote on this week's referenda. Can you believe it? They want me to say whether we should bring back compulsory national service for urban D-graders and whether future voting should be weighted in favour of those with a 90 per cent+ score in politics.

Best

Novac

Five trends that will transform politics

City states   Countries, national politicians, and national elections are all under threat. People and jobs are becoming more mobile, and defence, economic policy, and law-making are being increasingly influenced by regional or international interests. Corporations are becoming increasingly stateless, too, and in the future loyalties may be directed towards one's company first and one's country second. Voters will try to influence international politics through global NGOs and single-issue action groups, although the most significant shift will be back towards city states because this is where economic power, media interests, and ideas will be most concentrated. By 2020 the GDP of Tokyo or New York will be roughly similar to that of Canada, a G7 nation.

Tribalism   Historically, international relations have been forged between nation states, but this is changing. Many conflicts are now between tribal groups inside states. Moreover, the very idea of the nation state is under threat, not only from globalisation (above) but from regional politics (below). Local issues are seen by many voters as more important than national ones, because at least with them they have a chance of influencing the outcomes. This will lead to the rebirth of regional politics, as local patriotism mixes with nimbyism. It will also lead to xenophobia, as nations escape into their glorious (and not so glorious) pasts.

Happiness   Materialism and consumerism are starting to lose their appeal. We are working harder and longer — and earning more money as a result — but it's becoming increasingly obvious that money can't buy you happiness, and that identity is shaped by how you live rather than what you own or consume. To some extent, the happiness phenomenon is really a search for meaning. But it is also down to the fact that people have too much time on their hands. A century or two ago, people were focused on survival and just didn't have time for such introspection.

Climate change and the environment   Is climate change the new Y2K? The threat is real enough, but the panic reaction isn't. Present solutions are simplistic (like the war on four-wheel drives) and focus too much on the small picture. Our weather may indeed become more volatile and severe, meaning more bad hurricanes and severe flooding in some regions. Extreme heat and lack of water may make other places almost uninhabitable, while rising sea levels could devastate low-lying cities. But the solution to this isn't symbolic aviation taxes. What we need is a paradigm shift in the global economy, especially in manufacturing efficiencies. We should also focus on the limited future availability of natural resources. Shortages could cause global conflicts, while environmental destruction may trigger the unregulated movement of millions of people from one country to another.

On the other hand, higher oil prices could mean fewer cars on the road, less obesity (as we walk or use bicycles more), and less consumerism. This may trigger a new sense of make-do and mend that will rejuvenate local communities and national self-esteem. Climate change plus a shortage of resources will also be a catalyst for innovation, on the basis that crisis and adversity are usually the mother and father of invention. We'll see new bio-fuel technologies, hydrogen power, starch-based plastics, and home-based micro-generation. Even the landfill problem will be resolved when someone realises that there's money to be made by digging up old refuse sites and converting old plastic bags and bottles into fuel.

e-Voting   You can bank online, bet online, date online, and watch TV online, so why can't we all vote online? In the future, you will. Initially, e-voting will involve electronic booths inside polling stations, but ultimately you will be able to vote at home, at work, or in the supermarket on everything from whether teenage fathers should be given compulsory training to whether successful marriages should be awarded tax credits. You will also be able to vote for the American president, even if you live in Poland or Patagonia. Global e-Action groups will also thrive. This won't necessarily change anything, but it will make politics more entertaining.

Chapter 3

Science and Technology:
the rise of the machines

We live in a society exquisitely dependent on science and
technology, in which hardly anyone knows anything about
science and technology.
–Carl Sagan

The history of human civilisation is, to a large degree, the history of technology. Hence the history of the next fifty years will largely be determined by what is invented by boffins in Bangalore and nerds in New York. More precisely, the history of the future will be heavily influenced by what we as societies allow to happen in terms of applying science and technology. There will be other key influencers, too, like climate change or the emergence of an idea that will challenge global capitalism, but it is technology that will dictate change and that will be at the forefront of any future paradigm-shifts in social attitudes and behaviour.

For example, computers will become more intelligent than people by about 2030. At this point, humankind will be faced with something of a dilemma. If machines become more intelligent than their makers, what's to stop them taking over? You could, of course, design machines with in-built controls (see Isaac Asimov's 'Robot Rules' in *I Robot*), but there will be a very strong temptation for humankind to see what would happen if you don't. The other intriguing, if not outright alarming, aspect of this issue is the convergence of computing, robotics, and nanotechnology, which could give rise to self-replicating machines. Add to this the possibility of not only downloading intelligence into a machine but consciousness, too, and you are faced with the question of whether it is better to live forever in a machine or live for a limited time as a carbon-based biped. Personally I think downloading human consciousness is impossible, but you should never say never. Ian Pearson, head of BT's Futurology unit in the UK, argues that by the half-century mark it should be possible to download the contents of a human brain into a computer. If the human mind is then aware of what's happened this would be the start of the human race splitting into two halves: the natural and the enhanced.

Singularity is the term futurists use to describe the point at which machines have developed to the extent that humans can no longer fully understand or forecast their capabilities. The idea of artificial intelligence (AI) goes back to the mid-1950s, although Asimov was writing about smart robots back in 1942.

The true test for AI intelligence dates way back to 1950, when the British mathematician Alan Turing suggested the criterion of humans submitting statements through a machine and then not being able to tell whether the responses had come from another person or the machine.

The 1960s and 1970s saw a great deal of progress in AI, but real breakthroughs failed to materialise. Instead, scientists and developers focused on specific problems such as speech recognition, text recognition, and computer vision. However, we may be less than ten years away from seeing Turing's AI vision become a reality.

A company in Austin, Texas, for example, has developed a product called Cyc. It is much like a normal 'chatbot' except that, if it answers a question incorrectly, you can correct it and Cyc will learn from its mistakes.

But Cyc still isn't very intelligent, which is possibly why author, scientist, and futurist Ray Kurzweil made a public bet with Mitchell Kapor, the founder of Lotus, that a computer would pass the Turing test by 2029. Kurzweil has based this prediction on ideas expressed in his book *The Singularity is Near* — in essence, arguing that intelligence will expand in a limitless exponential manner once we achieve a certain level of advancement in genetics, nanotechnology, and robotics, and the integration of that technology with human biology. The precedent here is obviously the speed at which computing has developed. Sony's PlayStation 3, for example, is thirty-five times more powerful than its predecessor, and has the computing power of a supercomputer dating from 1997 — and all this at a cost of only US$600.

But while Kurzweil sees computers doubling in speed and power and programmers working feverishly to this end, Kapor believes human beings differ so totally from machines that the test will never be passed, not least because we are housed in bodies that feel pleasure and pain and accumulate experience and knowledge, much of which is tacit rather than expressed. Other experts such as Bill Calvin suggest that the human brain is so 'buggy' that computers will never be able to emulate it. Ultimately, though, this might not be the point; as some have suggested — such as James Surowiecki in his book *The Wisdom of Crowds* — the internet is already fostering an unanticipated form of AI, a highly efficient marketplace for ideas and information known as 'collective intelligence' or the 'hive mind'.

In the same way in which Adam Smith suggested that buyers and sellers, each pursuing their own interests, would together produce more goods more efficiently than under any other arrangement, so too online suppliers of collective intelligence — like bloggers

— can create more knowledge with less bias and over a wider span of disciplines than any group of experts could. At least, that's the utopian theory.

If in 1982, for example, anyone had suggested that hundreds of thousands of ordinary people located across the world could together create anything of real value they would have been seen as either a hopeless romantic or a complete lunatic. Nowadays, user-generated content (UGC) is all the rage, especially in new media circles, and empires like YouTube and MySpace have been built almost entirely on UGC. Then there's *Wikipedia*, the online collaborative encyclopedia with the modest aim of one day being the greatest and most comprehensive repository of human knowledge ever built.

If you don't know already, *Wikipedia* is 'open' in the sense that anyone can contribute, and the resulting content is made freely available to anyone who wants it. It has a benign ruler (a foundation) but no leader. It's huge, too. There are presently 4 million articles on Wikipedia in 120 languages. By contrast, *Encyclopedia Britannica* online has around 100,000 articles. Wikipedians (the content providers, essentially) agree collectively what is and isn't allowed, and multiple users create, edit, and link the pages, all of which tends towards content improvement. Interestingly, none of this was really supposed to happen, at least not in this manner.

The original idea behind *Wikipedia* was for experts to contribute content, but it turned out that the experts weren't in the least bit interested. Now you might expect that using amateurs instead of experts to supply, agree on, and edit content might be a good recipe for anarchy and online vandalism, but a recent study by the journal *Nature* found that the quality and accuracy of *Wikipedia* articles was almost indistinguishable from that of *Encyclopedia Britannica*. And vandalism is almost non-existent because the community stops any anti-social behaviour as soon as it starts. To my mind, the really interesting thought is what the consequences of *Wikipedia* might be. For instance, delicious philosophical questions such as 'What is truth?' can now be answered by a democratic community rather than an expert elite.

'Truth' is now whatever *Wikipedia* says it is. Moreover, 'truth' is whatever *Wikipedia* says it is right now (which, by implication, may change tomorrow). As a counterpoint, Jaron Lanier, who coined the term 'virtual reality', has predicted that collective intelligence — or digital Maoism — will have the same deadening and anti-creative effect as political collectivism. In other words, the wisdom of 'idiots' will remove any opinion that does not fit with its own; if the online majority decides that 1+1=3, that will be the 'truth'. Either way, it's important that we recognise what computers can do already (more than most people realise), and then think about how this may eventually change — and change us. Do we want knowledge to be owned by an anonymous online collective? If we don't, we should be saying so now before it's too late.

An obvious achievement of the internet is the retrieval of 'spot knowledge', the antidote to memory loss which enables us to clear the mind of minutiae to focus on things at a higher level. But while some dream of a life where embedded reminders mean we never have to worry about forgetting — and forget about worrying — others wonder what will happen to our cognitive functions if first-stage thinking is all but taken care of for us. The use of the internet to bring people together could also be useful in the future because questions like 'Should we use technology like space mirrors to solve global warming?' could be addressed to most of the planet, thus taking key debates far outside the scientific community.

But I'm moving off-track. *Wikipedia* is media not science. Or is it? Perhaps the point here is that it's both. Everything is converging and everything is increasingly connected, intimately, with everything else.

If the convergence of computing and communications led to the information age, then perhaps we are on the cusp of another dramatic shift. Engineering and computing started to converge some time ago, and other disciplines are following suit. For example, natural sciences such as biology are merging with physical sciences such as engineering. In automobiles, engineering is merging with areas such as computing, while computing itself is being greatly influenced by biology and neuroscience.

Equally, products are converging. TiVo allow users to time-shift their TV viewing habits. Similarly, Apple's iPod, like Sony's Walkman before it, allows users to shift their music listening to any place they like. This makes me wonder whether in the future you could be in two places at the same time or physically travel backwards or forwards in time.

This is pure science-fiction, of course, but science and technology are allowing us to look back and forwards in time, for example to identify future genetic time-bombs inside our bodies.

A more controversial idea, perhaps, is that free will does not exist, and that our personalities and actions are largely shaped by our genes and are 'fixed' by our ancestry. If proven, this would be an explosive idea because individuals could claim that nothing was ever their fault. Society could also look inside a young person and forecast with some degree of certainty how that person's life would pan out in the future. In other words, we would, like the Department of Future Crimes, know what people would do before they did it. This would also open up a Pandora's Box, where people's personalities could be altered through genetic fiddling. Even more explosive is the thought that there is a genetic component to intelligence (and other traits) and that this varies by ethnic group and sex. Even the merest hint of this idea is enough to incite violence, so imagine if there was a total collapse of consensus about all people being the same. The end of free will would also destroy the rule of law.

But I'm sidetracking again.

A scientist in Cambridge, UK, has developed a prototype computer that can 'read' users' minds by capturing and then interpreting facial expressions, such as concentration, anger, or confusion. In experiments using actors, the computer was accurate 85 per cent of the time, although this dropped to 65 per cent with 'ordinary people'. The technology raises a number of privacy-related issues, not least of which is the collection of highly sensitive personal data. Toyota is allegedly already working with inventor Professor Peter Robertson to link the emotional state of car drivers with various safety controls and mood-sensitive features. Other customers might include insurance companies wanting to crack down on dishonest claims, banks targeting identity fraud, teachers trying to teach (does the student really understand?), or governments wanting to identify terrorists or social-security cheats.

In the future, car companies or local councils could even tailor road maps or road signs to a driver's level of aggression. What intrigues me most, however, is whether you could link mood sensitivity to products such as radios and TVs so that they tune into 'happy' music or programs. There is also the fascinating possibility of online retailers tailoring their home pages, product offerings, and even product descriptions to the emotional state of individual customers.

A future challenge for scientists is thus to create software that develops in response to its environment, building neural nets that hold past experiences that will build into something resembling basic consciousness and intelligence.

So what else can we expect to see come out of the future? One interesting area that's close to my heart is forecasting. In the future, traffic forecasts will be as common as weather forecasts. There will be pollution forecasts, disease forecasts, and war forecasts.

War forecasting is already a growth industry, with a number of key players in countries such as the US, Germany, and Australia. One of the leading systems used to predict military outcomes is a piece of smart software called the Tactical Numerical Deterministic Model (TNDM), produced by a military think-tank in Washington DC. TNDM is the mother of all battle simulators, and can predict the outcome of future conflicts (especially casualty rates and duration). The accuracy of TNDM is largely due to the mountain of historical data and factors available, including everything from rainfall and river widths to foliage cover and muzzle velocities. The result is a mathematical model that predicts outcomes, including, you might think, the likelihood of presidents winning another term. Models like this will become increasingly common, thanks to the ability of smart devices to collect vast amounts of data in real time and to tag this information with time stamps and geographical locations.

RFIDs, sensor motes, and 'smart dust' are some new ways that such data will be collected in the future. Smart devices like these, some no larger than a full stop (0.15 mm square and 7.5 microns thick), will increasingly connect what is happening in the real world to mathematical models, which in turn may be used to alter or influence reality. For example, if the seas suddenly get too hot or there is a tidal surge in a remote region, we'll know about it. In other words, natural stuff, and dumb stuff, will increasingly be connected to smart stuff. Surprises and mistakes will, to an extent, disappear — although, in reality, they will simply be replaced by new mistakes and new surprises.

Some of these sensors will be part machine. Wasps, spiders, or houseflies may carry small cameras and wireless devices so that scientists can detect abnormal activities. Add a dose of nanotechnology (that is, the manipulation of structures at an atomic or molecular level) and things could get very interesting and very frightening indeed. It's another nail in the coffin for privacy. If everything becomes intelligent and displays its location to a central network, everyone will be 'bugged'.

The good news, perhaps, is that your clothes will contain sensors so they will never get lost, and they will 'talk' to your washing machine to ensure that they are not damaged when they are cleaned.

Equally, technology is getting smarter in the sense that it

can second-guess what you want or remind you to do things. Unfortunately, at the moment, you have to program most devices yourself for them to second-guess what you want. In other words, you have to adapt your behaviour to the technology. However, the next generation of devices will simply 'watch' and 'listen' to what you say and do (and where you are), and adapt themselves to you. For instance, mobile phones will 'watch' who you call, and when, and then remind you to do certain things at certain times. In theory this could be quite useful, because you will be able to interrogate your phone about when you last called your mother. Such 'reality mining' will undoubtedly be of great interest to sociologists and epidemiologists (and marketers), who will study how our social networks are created or how diseases spread; but, again, are we giving too much away? Controlling science and technology is already emerging as an area of great concern to the general public, and there is a growing suspicion that things are already running out of control.

Moreover, unlike twenty-five years ago, when most people trusted experts such as scientists, they now feel that many scientists are in the pay of powerful business and government interests, and can therefore no longer be trusted.

New technologies and ideas are nearly always resisted at first; the stronger or more disruptive the idea, the more resistance there will be at both a direct level (physical actions) and indirect level through the creation of myths. The mobile phone, for example, is one of the most successful innovations of recent times, and yet its ubiquity has done little to dispel safety fears surrounding its use. Similarly, the invention of the telegraph created a widespread belief that signals would interfere with the weather, while the introduction of trains and automobiles was predicted to create a variety of physical and mental disorders. I was talking to an eighty-six-year-old gentleman recently about mobile-phone masts, and he pointed out that exactly the same objections were raised when lamp-posts were first introduced. The point, as Philip Zimbardo (Stamford) says, is that we all need a balance between the past, the present, and the future. With too much (or too little) of any one type of thinking, we fall prey to a variety of conditions such as depression.

Rage against the machine

In my experience, the nostalgia bug tends to kick in around the age of forty. Before this, everything new is shiny and exciting. Afterwards, everything used to be better in the old days. Older people (and especially people aged over sixty — which will be 22 per cent of the world's population by 2050) tend to loathe technological change. Some very old people also struggle to remember who they are, although this problem is becoming more common with all age groups thanks to the growth of multiple identities online.

The average office worker has between six and twenty passwords that he or she is technically supposed to be able to remember. Now imagine trying to remember all that at the age of seventy. One solution is pictorial passwords (especially faces) or fingerprint IDs. Another solution is simply to drop out by refusing to buy kettles that know when you're getting up or fridges that re-order milk when you run out, whether you want some more or not.

Many of these devices are also liars in the sense that they don't really save you time, or else they make your life even more complicated than it was before. Dishwashers are a case in point. Everyone I know has a dishwasher, but I swear it takes longer to stack and remove the plates than if you washed all the dishes yourself. Plus you can't take the plates out for two hours once a 'standard' cycle has started, and what do we do with all the time we're supposedly saving anyway?

Another way of dealing with too much change is not to grow up. Psychological neoteny is a theory that the increased level of immaturity among adults is an evolutionary response to increased change and uncertainty. This makes a certain amount of sense. Humanity has long held youth in high esteem, originally because it was a sign of fertility and health, which were important for hunting and reproduction. In fixed environments, psychological maturity was useful because it indicated experience and wisdom.

However, some time in the latter part of the twentieth century child-like youthfulness started to have a new function, which was to remain adaptive to a fast-changing environment. In other words, if jobs, skills, scientific ideas, and technology are all in a state of flux, it is important to remain open-minded about learning new skills, and the best way to do that is to retain a child-like state of receptivity and cognitive flexibility.

Another fascinating new idea is continuous partial attention. Interruption science is the study of why people get distracted and how best to interrupt people. In the late 1980s, NASA needed to find ways to deliver important information to busy astronauts. If an important communication is not distracting enough it may get ignored, while anything too distracting could ruin a multi-million dollar experiment. In other words, the timing and style of delivery of communications is vitally important. NASA found that text-based communications were routinely ignored while visually based communications seemed to get through.

So how is this relevant to people with their feet firmly planted on planet Earth? The simple answer is that many of us suffer from too much information, thanks to faster computers and connectedness. We are constantly subjected to a torrent of interruptions, ranging from email to mobile phone calls. Indeed, a recent survey found that employees spend an average of eleven minutes on a task before being distracted by something else. Furthermore, every time employees were interrupted it took almost half an hour for them to return to the original task, and 40 per cent wandered off somewhere else. In other words, information is no longer power — getting and keeping someone's attention is. We are so busy watching everything and multi-tasking that we are unable to focus on or finish anything except after hours or at home.

Given that computers and the internet are largely to blame for this, it's not surprising that computer and software companies are taking the issue very seriously. Part of the problem is that our memory tends to be visual, and computers only allow the display of limited amounts of information on a screen. Some people solve this problem by sticking low-fi sticky notes around the sides of their screen. Another way might be to say no — to unsubscribe and unplug parts of your life. Or technology could change the way that information is delivered. For example, if a computer could understand when you were busy (via a camera, microphone, or keypad monitor), it could rank emails in order of importance and then deliver them at the most appropriate moments. Information could also become presented in the same way that aircraft instruments are laid out, so it can be glanced at easily. In the more distant future we may even figure out a way of getting rid of computer screens altogether and embedding information we can glance at in everyday objects, or we might deliver important information using pictures, sounds, and smells. Indeed, we do this already. I have spent years talking to companies about important trends, and most of the time the information zips in one ear and flies out the other. Last year I decided to do something different. Instead of words, I tried pictures — a map on a single sheet of paper, to be precise. The response has been extraordinary.

But my mind is wandering again. Back to robots. Robots have been a central feature of the future for as long as people have been making movies. Over the past four decades, popular culture has obsessed over the idea of machine intelligence enslaving its creators, yet still we push on building machines that emulate our own appearance and movement.

It's the same with aliens, but both genres of science fiction are really about what it means to be human and what we fear most about ourselves. The robots and the little green men (nearly always men, interestingly) are a sub-plot. So what are some of the coming attractions in terms of robots over the next twenty years or so?

Robotic assistants will slowly make their way out of the toy cupboard and off the lawn into our offices and living rooms. The cutting edge of robotics is probably military applications, but the ageing population offers up an alternative future.

Maybe robots, in an ironic turnaround from the script, will become carers and companions for the elderly — therapeutic robots delivering aged-care solutions. This, of course, brings us back to some interesting ethical debates, especially when humans start to profit from the addition of bionic arms, legs, and eyes (modelled on dragonfly eyes, probably), but in the meantime we can just lie back and stare in wonder at snakebots that slither down drain pipes, robotic lobsters (military applications, apparently), and robogoats that look for disaster victims on steep mountain sides.

None of this is very far off. In 2005 the US military deployed armed robots in Iraq. The robots, which looked like small radio-controlled tanks (what a let-down!), were operated by human soldiers up to a kilometre away. Each robo 'soldier' was equipped with cameras, laser sights, thermal vision, night vision, and either a machine gun or a rocket launcher. The Pentagon has been dreaming about the use of robotic soldiers for thirty years, and has just budgeted US$127 billion to create what is euphemistically called 'future combat systems'. This is the biggest military contract in US history, and it surely says something about the migration of the robot from a kid's room to a conscience-free combatant.

Meanwhile, in Japan a computer scientist has built what he claims to be the world's most humanlike (and attractive) android. In anticipation of the day when software can emulate human intelligence, Hiroshi Ishiguro has created a human-looking interface to house a computer. The android, modelled on a famous Japanese newscaster, has been painstakingly created to appear human — not only in looks, but in mannerisms and movements, too. The creator has found that some people, especially children and the elderly, have taken it for a real human being. Ishiguro feels that the creation of a human-looking interface is important for communication. However, while people can accept robots that look like robots from central casting, they are quite disturbed by those that look similar to humans but not similar enough.

I think it was the writer Bruce Sterling who once said that in the future all products would be cuddly, and he might have been right. It seems we are threatened by things that look too much like ourselves; if things become too high-tech I expect we will all do a handbrake turn in the middle of the road and rush headlong into the arms of things that are warm, soft, and familiar. But that's quite a way off.

Future technologies will include airborne networks that allow airliners to fly without pilots (inconceivable now, but acceptable in fifty years); silicon photonics (using silicon chips to emit light to speed-up data processing); quantum wires (using carbon nanotube wires to carry electricity); biomechatronics (mixing robotics with nervous systems to create new artificial limbs); bacterial factories; metabolomics (a new medical-diagnosis tool using metabolic information); and nanoelectronics (for example, using nanostructures to store more and more data in smaller and smaller areas).

We'll also have wireless battery recharging, new quiet materials (the future is a loud place), electronic camouflage, disposable computers, smart mirrors (that show you what you might look like next year), 3-D printers, customised materials (where the structure and properties of a material can be designed millimetre by millimetre), organic computers, space-ladders, holographic displays and storage, home-use DNA stamps (to identify what's really yours), wearable computers in all shapes and forms, voice-based internet search (for example, 'Show me film clips of car chases'), personalisation ports in all devices (so you can change them to suit your particular needs), a fully sensory internet (all five senses delivered over the Web), and a high level of machine-to-machine communication. Phew.

There will also be 'meta-materials' that can be programmed to react to light or electromagnetic radiation in controllable ways. This will allow the control of light flows over or around certain objects so that nuclear power stations (ugly) or military bases (secret) could simply be made to 'disappear'. In other words, they're there but they're not.

Getting even more futuristic, we might see robotic pest control, smart bullets (that follow bad guys around corners), sky shields (curtains or mirrors in space to stop harmful sunlight), joy-makers (use your imagination), accelerated schooling (everything else is speeding up), scramble suits (so people can't intercept personal communications), neuronic whips (a weapon that stimulates the nerve endings to cause extreme discomfort), randominoes (dominoes that randomly generate new numbers), mindwipes (had a bad day at the office? — simply delete it with a pre-moistened wipe), disintegrators, short-wave scalpels, child-care robots, space tugs, oceanic thermal converters (a device that uses the sea to generate energy), face-recognition doors, spray-on surgical gloves, napcaps (hats that send you to sleep), stress-control clothing, gravity tubes (a way of removing gravity in a specific area), sleep surrogates, quiet paint and self-repairing roads.

Another emerging field is epigenetics. This is the study of how particular genes act based on chemical and environmental factors. It's significant because previously scientists thought that genes (and the DNA from which they're made) were 'fixed' — in other words, DNA is destiny. But perhaps not.

The new theory is that environmental factors can influence how a specific gene acts. Moreover, the so-called 'junk DNA' that makes up 98 per cent of all DNA possibly isn't junk at all and can influence cell function. If true, this is revolutionary because if there is a 'criminal' gene or 'genius' gene it could, in theory, be turned on or off, thus making the world a safer and smarter but potentially more boring place.

Despite the focus on applied science over pure science, it is still one of the very few areas where ideas in their purest form are still prominent. We have discovered a lot over the past 2,000 years (1.8 million other species, for example), but there is still more to be discovered. Indeed, for every door we open in the future I suspect we may find another that is firmly locked. Moreover, the history of science shows that ideas are periodically reshaped by revolutions in thinking, and we are more than overdue such an upheaval.

So what ideas or events could produce another seismic shift?

The big one, to my naive mind at least, would be either the discovery of a parallel universe or the discovery of life elsewhere within the galaxies. It wouldn't even have to be very intelligent to totally transform how people think back on Earth. There is a wonderful quote from futurist Richard Neville that the question of whether or not UFOs exist is the wrong one. What if the real question was, 'Why do people keep seeing them?' What if their 'existence' was a 'cry from the collective unconscious, a plea for magic in a materialistic age?' Good point. As someone else (I forget who) once said, 'Any suitably advanced technology is indistinguishable from magic', so I think we will be seeing a lot more magic in the future. We will also be seeing a lot more religion because, despite arguing logically and scientifically that it's all a fraud, we will need religion as a counterbalance to our increasingly virtual and technological lives. I'm sure that the mere mention of alien spaceships and God will stop many readers in their tracks and confine me to the very edges of something or other; but, to be honest, that's fine. Actually, mentioning religion brings me to another thought: perhaps, in the future, science will be the new religion. What do I mean by this? Simply that historically science and God have been opposing forces. But as we discover more about the universe, science itself will become the higher intelligence that most of us believe in.

There is still the problem identified by Richard Neville that science lacks the ceremony and ritual that forms part of most organised religions. There are no cathedrals either.

Personally I'd just love it if a spaceship landed in Central Park in my lifetime, largely because it would call into question every single idea that has ever existed and would, presumably, topple mankind from his — or her — egotistical assumption that we are somehow special and at the top of an evolutionary tree. It would also be great in terms of watching how the individual religions cope with the fact of something else out there. One suspects that Buddhists would be pretty Zen about it, but I'm not sure about some of the others.

There will also be a lot more controversy in the future, some of it increasingly hostile. For instance, I fully expect the debate about climate change to become increasingly polarised between believers and sceptics. Equally, there will be a widespread panic about the next pandemic, with a small number of sceptical scientists claiming that a repeat of historical pandemics is unlikely because of changed conditions.

Other possible upheavals would be a collapse in consensus about one of the major ideas of nineteenth- and twentieth-century science. There are lots of contenders to be debunked, but surely the most high profile must be the theories of Darwin, Einstein, and Freud. Again, I will probably be labelled as a nut for even suggesting that a theory such as natural selection could ever be overturned, but this merely demonstrates the strength and power of conventional wisdom and the sheer force required to displace such ideas. As Arthur C. Clarke observed, 'If an elderly but distinguished scientist says that something is possible he is almost certainly right, but if he says that it is impossible he is very probably wrong.'

It is our relationship with machines that will be the defining characteristic of the twenty-first century and where we draw the line between what we want 'them' to know or do will set the direction for the next thousand years. For example, do we want machines to feel pain? If we are to imbue machines with a basic emotional capacity or understanding, surely they must be able to feel pleasure and pain? This idea immediately transports us back to the supercomputer HAL in *2001: A Space Odyssey*. It's a very important question and one that is difficult to answer with any half-measure. If machines are given the powers of life and death — robotic soldiers or surgeons, for example — surely they must be taught to understand right from wrong? It's also a case of all or nothing; you can't really give a machine a bit of emotional understanding. If you want a machine to feel pride — a very advanced emotion indeed — then you also need to install happiness and desire. And for happiness to function properly you also need to feel sadness and regret. And if we do all this we may end up with another HAL — a machine that's so messed up emotionally that it can't function properly. One of the really great things about machines (now) is that they don't think. They just do. And even if they do think they only really think about what they are doing, which leaves the gates wide open for humans to have empathy, imagination, creativity, and ideas. At least that's what I keep telling myself so I can sleep at night.

31 December 2049

Dear Ian

Thanks for the birthday present. To be honest I'm a bit old for a joy-maker, but I'm sure I'll put it to some good use (maybe I can wire it up to my old car and we can go for a joy ride, ha, ha). At least it's better than the emotionally aware bathroom scales your brother got me. They're driving me mad. Anyway, I just can't believe that you'll be fifty next year. Any idea what you want? I thought perhaps one of those new Monopoly holographic editions? By the way, did you see the story about the new jetliner that goes from London to Sydney in two hours? Apparently it just shoots up into the edge of space and sits there waiting for the Earth to rotate before dropping back down. Hope the seatbelts are good. Personally I'm still working on the space ladder project. We've cracked how to make the cable using carbon nanotubes, so now it's just a matter of putting the cable into a geosynchronous orbit and tethering it to a counterweight in deep space. Anyway, thought you'd like the retro communication. I even managed to buy a real stamp off AmazonBay, which apparently FedPost will still deliver.

All for now — busy as ever.

Cheers

Richard

Five trends that will transform science and technology

Nanotechnology   Nanotech is the hyped technology of the new millennium. It's unlikely to disappoint either because it's a disruptive technology. Nanotech will affect every industry from aerospace and construction to energy and medicine, and will create products that we cannot possibly imagine. However, public debate about it will be almost invisible until there is a major high-profile nanotechnology accident.

Biotechnology   We've had Dolly the cloned sheep (c. 1996), and since then we've had cloned mice, cows, rabbits, horses, and dogs. A human clone can't be far away, although it's unlikely that it will come from a US or western laboratory. A cloned human will certainly grab the headlines, but a more threatening prospect is perhaps the idea of genetically enhancing humans to strengthen or remove certain traits. There is also the alarming prospect of tests to judge personality or future actions based on genetic make-up and hereditary factors. In the future, everything from careers to relationships will involve genetic issues. Anyone for genetically engineered mosquitoes? How about one that glows in the dark so you can see it coming? Or how about genetic enhancements and tests for unborn children?

Emotionally aware machines   Much has been written about artificial intelligence, but personally I think AI in any meaningful sense is a long way off. Having said this, can you imagine the implications if an internet of the future did actually become aware of its own existence? Ohmygawd. As for a more foreseeable future, a more immediate driver of change will be emotional intelligence — or emotionally aware machines. In the future we will see cars that link the emotional state of the driver with various safety controls and mood-sensitive features, computers that can tell whether we are in a good mood, and voice-recognition systems that can tell if we are lying. How about therapeutic robots or radios and TVs that tune into happy programs when you're feeling sad? Or what about online retailers tailoring their home pages, product offerings, and even product descriptions to the emotional state of individual customers?

Ethics   Science, and to a lesser extent, technology, has always operated within a political context, but until recently it was more or less left alone. Not any more. Science, and to an increasing extent technology, will come under the microscope as society debates, not whether something is possible, but whether its consequences are desirable. Top of the list of gatekeepers will be government, with its own national and international agenda based on political philosophy, the economy, and defence. Privacy will also become a key issue once people realise that computers are everywhere and that almost no place on Earth is free from surveillance.

Robotics   Robotic soldiers anyone? They're coming, but should such machines feel pain or regret? And if (when) there's an accident, who should be held responsible? Would you trust a robot to administer a general anesthetic and perform general surgery on you? Or what about when someone makes a robot your child loves more than you? Robots have been around for years, but the convergence of a handful of trends is about to transform the field. First, the cost of computing power (processing and storage) is dropping fast. Second, distributed computing, voice, and visual-recognition technologies and wireless broadband connectivity are similarly becoming cheaper and more available. Personal robots will be cleaning floors, dispensing medicine, and keeping an eye open for intruders, while industrial robots will operate dangerous machinery and handle dangerous materials. On a smaller scale, robots could carry your bags from the supermarket, replace guide dogs for the visually impaired, or replace care-workers in hospitals or nursing homes. Whether a machine will ever fully replace human or animal contact is a big question, to which most people currently say no. However, attitudes may shift over time.

Chapter 4

Media and Entertainment: have it your way

In the future, everyone will be world-famous for fifteen minutes.
–Andy Warhol

I'm sitting reading a newspaper while waiting for a bus, having just bought a newspaper and cup of coffee from a local petrol station. Out of nowhere a rather scruffy-looking man aged about sixty approaches me. He mutters something and points to a small white table-tennis ball on the ground that has rolled underneath the wire fence behind us. I get up to hear what he's saying, and notice that his right arm is wrapped in a sling. He says that the ball is his, and asks me if I could get it for him. My initial reaction is that my bag, which contains my notes for this book, is about to be stolen by an invisible accomplice while my attention is focused on retrieving the tiny white ball. However, it turns out that there is no invisible man and that all he really wants is his ball back — because he uses it to exercise the hand he injured in a recent fall. I give him the ball, together with a rather limp smile, and bury my head in the newspaper so as to avoid any further eye contact. As usual, there is practically nothing of interest to me in the newspaper and I mutter something to myself about one day producing my own.

When I was growing up in Britain in the 1960s we used to get a newspaper delivered at home. We also had a black-and-white TV with only three channels. What's more, the channels all closed down around midnight and didn't start again until lunchtime. I have a feeling they even played the National Anthem at the end of each day's programming, although this could have been a dream brought on by eating too many Sherbet Spaceships and drinking too many bottles of fizzy Tizer. In other words, it was a case of 'you get what you get and you don't get upset'. My media diet was force-fed and I had no control or input over the one-size-fits-all, any-colour-you-like-as-long-as-it's-black-and-white media. If I mention my early media experiences to a teenager today, they think I'm some kind of digital dinosaur who has lost his memory. In the last forty years we've witnessed the birth of multi-channel TV, digital TV, twenty-four hour programming, VHS, DVD, cable TV, satellite TV, all-news channels, MTV, CNN, colour newspapers, weather channels, TiVo, Sony Walkmans, iPods, and the emergence of video on demand, or what's been described as Martini media — 'anytime, any place anywhere'. To anyone under the age of twenty-five, this multi-channel digital universe is just normal.

I don't say this to whinge about being born too soon; just that a lot has happened in the last forty-five years, and there is no reason to suppose that the next forty-five years is going to be any different. Indeed, as a general guide to what's going to happen to media over the next ten, twenty, or even fifty years, just look at what's happened over the last ten, twenty, or fifty years and then at least double it to allow for the effects of technological innovation and globalisation. Having said this, many of the fundamentals won't change. Despite what doom merchants are saying, there will still be mass media and storytelling. It's just that the mass media will be different media, and the stories will more personal. People will still want to find out what's going on in the world and they will still want access to entertainment to escape from that knowledge. Will algorithms replace newspaper editors? Possibly, but a more likely scenario is a trend towards quality and towards physicalisation, both of which will be a reaction to the almost infinite amount of digital drivel that will be produced by the likes of you and me.

In the future, we will still be watching movies in movie theatres and watching TV at home. We will also still be reading newspapers, magazines, and books made from dead trees, and we will still be surfing the internet. If you want to, that is. If you don't, you'll be able to do any of the above anyhow you like, or switch off completely.

Your own little Youniverse

In the future, it will be easier than ever to turn on, tune in, and drop out — because, while mainstream media channels and events will continue to exist, so too will a plethora of micro media appealing to every conceivable interest, belief, prejudice, and opinion. The top-down model, whereby media owners hold the attention of millions and then sell that attention to other people such as advertisers, is being replaced by companies and individuals who attract the fleeting attention of large, promiscuous audiences or by niche operators who capture the hearts and minds of very tiny audiences.

In other words, the media universe is becoming polarised between very large and very small players. Moreover, the content produced by these totally different types of media company will also be polarised between two extremes, with the larger companies clustering around proven formulas and the smaller operators pushing the boundaries with original ideas. Both will obviously aim to appeal to as large an audience as possible, but only one will be able to survive when the audience is tiny. Equally, anyone stupid enough to get caught in the middle will be history.

Newspapers are a good example. In the future, most newspapers will be free — you will only pay for functionality, personalisation, and physicalisation. A ridiculous suggestion? Perhaps not.

Fifty years ago 80 per cent of Americans read a daily newspaper. Today the figure is close to 50 per cent — and falling. Globally it's much the same story. Between 1995 and 2003, worldwide newspaper circulation fell by 5 per cent. In 1892 London had fourteen evening papers; now it has just one (or two, depending on your definition of a newspaper). Also in the UK, a staggering 19 per cent of all copies of newspapers delivered to retailers in the first quarter of 2006 came back as returns, and three national newspaper titles had return (non-sale) rates approaching 50 per cent. If these trends continue, the last physical copy of a newspaper will probably roll off a press sometime in the year 2040. Only they won't.

As someone once pointed out, if newspapers were invented tomorrow they would be greeted as a miraculous innovation. They are dirt cheap, paper-thin, easy to annotate, and don't use batteries. You can read them in the bath, outside in the sun (especially if they are stapled so the pages don't blow away), and when you've finished with them they can be thrown away and safely recycled. Unfortunately, they also go out of date the second they are printed, cost a fortune to distribute, and their user-generated content is limited to the letters page and some classified advertising. And therein lies the problem.

Despite fearless former predictions of paperless offices and a leisure society, we are all working longer and harder. As a result, we are time-starved, and the family breakfast (along with the home-delivered newspaper) is being replaced by fly-by breakfasts while we listen to up-to-the-minute cable TV. Either that or it's a drive-by milkshake from McDonald's while listening to the car radio, or drinking a cup of Starbucks' finest while reading an online newspaper in the office. Indeed, there is a direct causal relationship between media use and the speeding-up of breakfast, longer working hours, and the decline of public transport.

We are all becoming digital nomads. We read, listen, and watch what we want when we want. We no longer have the time (during the working week, at least) to read newspapers, and readers are shifting their eyes and ears to online information sources delivered via everything from mobile phones to iPods. Online news is especially useful because the content can be controlled and personalised. If you're of the active (or exhibitionist) persuasion you can comment on the news, too, through your own blog or send your own homemade documentary to YouTube, which is currently the eleventh-largest country on Earth in terms of population. People don't even trust newspapers these days. Only 59 per cent of Americans believe what they read in the newspapers, compared to 80 per cent who did so in 1985. (Amazingly, 36 per cent of US high school students also believe that newspapers should get government approval of news stories prior to publication, but that's another story). In short, what used to be a passive one-way conversation is turning into an active relationship. Content flows both ways, and consumption has time-shifted and place-shifted.

According to research by ComScore, Six Apart, and Gawker Media, 50 million people visited blog sites in the US in the first quarter of 2005 — about 30 per cent of all US internet users, or one-sixth of the entire US population. By the time you read this it will be more. What's more, they aren't all reading about 'social-lights' like Ms Hilton; the most popular sites were about politics (sorry, Paris).

Meanwhile, in Australia, research conducted by McNair Ingenuity suggests that 21 per cent of Australians have read a blog in the last six months. This figure increases to 38 per cent for eighteen- to twenty-nine-year-olds, but 6 per cent of Australians aged over seventy are reading them, too. In terms of writing a blog, the figure is much lower; but, nevertheless, 10 per cent of eighteen- to twenty-nine-year-olds have done so, with 3 per cent posting a podcast on the internet, too.

So, with this self-publishing or 'citizen journalist' trend in full swing, are newspapers old news? Not quite, as newspapers are already using innovation to improve their products. Some of the best new ideas include compact formats for commuters (in the UK, *The Times* and *The Independent* were available in a choice of two sizes for a while), kids' newspapers (*Play Bac Presse* in France), and newspapers written entirely by readers. *OhMyNews* in South Korea is created by over 30,000 'citizen reporters' and is read by 2 million South Koreans, while in the US the *Wisconsin State Journal* (the state's second-biggest-selling paper) asks its readers to go online every day between 11.00 a.m. and 4.00 p.m. to vote for the next day's lead story. Consequences include the appearance of sports stories on the front page.

In other words, we are entering what some exuberant commentators are calling the new participation age, when the traditional boundaries between creator and consumer are becoming eroded or are disappearing altogether. It's still unclear at this early stage what a fully blown reader-produced newspaper would look like, but it's certain that the amateur genie is already out of the bottle. Whether this is good or bad depends on your point of view. Some people claim that this democratisation of the media is the best thing that's happened since Gutenberg, whereas others see nothing but hyperactive half-wits writing on water. For example, 'citizen journalism' gives no weight to expertise. Wikipedia.com — the 17th-most-visited site in the internet — is written by millions of anonymous amateurs. In contrast, Britannica.com — ranked around 5,000 — is written by over 4,000 named experts, including 100 Nobel Prize winners.

One of the biggest questions arising from this type of open innovation is, who owns openly created content? This question will drive new business models and radically transform the relationship between media owners and their audiences. The other big question is, how do newspapers create revenue from content when readers expect it to either be free or sold at very low cost?

A second significant innovation is the growth of free newspapers. Most newspapers create revenue by double-dipping. Readers pay to buy a newspaper and then have to pay again if they want to place a classified advertisement in it. The theory is that this advertising (along with display advertising) supports subscriptions and newsstand sales, but it won't for much longer. One of the largest and fastest-growing newspapers in the world is *Metro*, a free newspaper currently published in 69 editions in twenty-one countries and eighteen languages. Another version of the same idea is *Loot*, which costs money to buy, but offers free classified advertisements.

Other interesting developments in the media include a magazine created by Nokia and MTV, produced almost entirely by their customers, who send in content via text and picture messages. Moving even further into the digital future, sites like Craig's List are giving traditional media-owners something to think about. Classified revenues from accommodation to cars and jobs are moving online, as is time-sensitive information such as stock prices and weather forecasts. The *New York Times* recently announced it was cutting back its stock market price tables because so many readers were accessing the information online, while the *Washington Post* has announced it has hired the creator of Chicagocrime.org to create 'mashups' (websites or web applications that combine content from more than one source) for the online edition of its paper.

So who will be delivering tomorrow's newspaper? The answer, apart from the usual suspects, is you and me. Newspapers will still be published by mainstream media companies, but brand-owners such as Wal-Mart or Tesco could also produce their own titles. Companies such as Nike and Procter & Gamble are already creating their own content, and this trend will continue as content becomes effectively infinite, and everything from walls and tabletops to cereal packets and clothes turn into video screens and interactive information displays.

I, for one, don't believe that newspapers will die, any more than I think that people will stop reading books. Part of the reason for this is historical (once established, habits and customs can take more than a generation to die), but it's also psychological. Newspapers are a ritualistic purchase, and loyalties can run deep. If you ask people in focus groups why they read newspapers, some people can't tell you. 'Because I've always read it' is a typical answer. I once did some work with United News and Media in the UK, and found that quite a few people read the *Daily Express* and the *Daily Mail* because their parents and grandparents did. Whether such loyalty extends to Generation Y remains to be seen, although early indications are that they don't — but perhaps this has as much to do with a lack of relevant Gen Y content as it does with delivery formats and platforms. Time will tell.

Sticking my neck out, I'd even go as far as to suggest that there could even be a newspaper renaissance around the corner. Many local titles are thriving because they are personalised. The news is local and so, too, is the advertising — which is something that people are making a song and dance about in new-media circles. For example, in the US, Fox Network is customising its TV ads so local neighbourhoods can receive tailored TV commercials. Newspapers know their readers extremely well and most also understand what's going on in their local town or city. For this reason alone, there are at least a few decades of revenue left in the old newspaper business model; over-caffeinated young journalists shouldn't start writing their own obituaries just yet.

The other reason that newspapers could make a comeback in the future is the ubiquity of online media. There is now so much digital content that it's becoming almost valueless and invisible. Physical media, by contrast — especially newspapers, magazines, and books that are written, edited, and designed by professionals — cut through this clutter.

In other words, the big news story is that, although the way media is created and consumed is changing, we will not totally abandon our old ways. In the old days (sometime last century), media content such as news or entertainment was created by 'professional' media organisations and then distributed to a supposedly grateful audience who consumed it how, where, and when they were told to. The news was on at 6.00 p.m. and 9.00 p.m., and if you missed it that was just too bad. These days, primetime is all the time, and anyone and everyone can create their own media. Viewers, listeners, and readers can then choose what they want to see and hear, and decide how and when they want to access it.

But while there is a symbiotic relationship developing between so-called mainstream media companies (for example, newspapers, radio, and television networks) and social media (for example, bloggers, podcasters, vloggers, and online social networks), the relationship is unequal; so-called 'free content' is rarely free. Indeed, much social media content that is not worthless is often stolen from a mainstream media company, for example, which paid to produce it in the first place. Hence the real cost of citizen journalism could be the death of the very sources on which it depends. Who then will hold governments and corporations to account?

Famous for fifteen minutes

If the cost of creating and distributing digital media content is now practically zero, in the future it will be even less. This means that anyone with an idea (and, hopefully, a rudimentary grasp of spelling) can become a one-person pundit on any topic that interests them. Of course, the trouble is that this is precisely what's happening. Most of this new-media content appeals to an audience of just one — the person who created it. For example, 99 per cent of the blogosphere is composed of the illiterate rantings of wannabe Paris Hiltons. Equally, the majority of content on sites such as MySpace and Facebook is produced by teenagers proving to themselves and others that they exist. I'm sure video clips like the one about how to eat a Jaffa Cake are of interest to somebody, but mostly it's just exhibitionism that appeals to its maker and a handful of voyeurs or stoned college students with an interest in post-modernist irony.

It's the same story with a trend called life-caching. This is a fancy way of describing insecure kleptomaniacs who hoard things and won't throw them away. Examples of life-caching include websites where you can upload every detail of your daily existence — text messages, emails, voice messages, photographs, video clips, and so on. This used to be called scrap-booking; but, as you'd expect, it's gone high-tech. Why do people do this? Again I think it's a cry from the subconscious saying, 'I was here'. But perhaps this is not as silly as it sounds, given that people are genuinely worried about things such as terrorism and whether they'll live long enough to show their holiday photos to their friends in person.

Of course, there is an ironic twist here; when we do want to get rid of these digital files we often find we can't because they've been spread virally around various networks. Conversely, the stuff we do want to keep forever gets lost because the technology to read these digital files goes out of production. Will we have a digital afterlife and digital funerals in the future? Probably.

Nevertheless, buried beneath this mountain of garbage is the occasional diamond. Some of the leading blogs have regular readerships that would put a national newspaper to shame; and if it's specialisation that you're after, online conversations could be for you.

The Daily Me (or Me Media) has been talked about for years as a way of personalising media content, and the internet is finally making this a reality. So if, for example, all you want to read about is English football or Arab politics, you can get it. Anywhere. And it's not just print media or online discussion groups that can deliver this either. One of the big trends on TV is the fragmentation of digital channels to the point where, pretty soon, there will be a TV channel for everything. Is this a good thing? On the face of it, it would appear so. After all, under the previous 'command and control' regime, user feedback and dialogue was almost non-existent. It was a one-way street, where audiences were consumers not creators. But ordinary individuals are now participants, and they can contribute democratically and directly to the sourcing, analysis, and ranking of stories.

In the future, we will see more and more people collaboratively creating and filtering content, but we shouldn't get carried away with the idea. The fact of the matter is that, despite this technological and participatory utopia, most of us are lazy or tired or both. Putting aside young voyeurs and exhibitionists, most people have neither the time nor the skill to create anything even remotely worth reading or watching. Hence demand for quality content will increase, not decrease, in the future.

Moreover, we should guard against this participatory trend being taken too far, because originality has always gone against the grain of conventional thinking. 'Professional' media and expert opinion have an important role to play in the future, and we would be extremely foolish to allow a benign dictatorship of experts to be replaced by a dictatorship of fools.

What's next at the movies?

Cinema is another good example of how things will change while the fundamentals will not. Back in the early 1980s, prophets of doom were predicting the death of cinema due to a new-fangled invention called the video recorder. This was an early example of time-shifting, in that the audience was now supposedly in control of what they watched and when they watched it. However, it didn't turn out quite like that. Sure, people recorded their favourite TV shows and rented movies to watch at their convenience; but, instead of replacing cinema, it enhanced it.

I've still never met anyone under the age of twenty who can program a video recorder to record anything. I'm not exaggerating. A couple of years ago, a friend of mine bought a new DVD recorder and, being a man, instantly threw away the instructions on the basis that a child of three could operate most pieces of consumer electronics these days. Unfortunately, his son, who was three at the time, did indeed operate the said piece of equipment and set the child lock, which he has been embarrassingly unable to unlock for the past three years. I'm sure he could go online and download the instructions; but who, quite frankly, has the time to do that these days? It would be cheaper to just buy another DVD recorder, or wait until his son is eight or nine and ask him to un-set it.

As life speeds up, people want to relax more. Crucially, as more and more people start to work for themselves or live alone, they will want more physical interaction with other people. So, while it's convenient and time efficient to rent a movie and watch it at home, it's not as much fun as going out to a cinema and talking to your friends about the experience afterwards. Live shows (one form of physicalisation of otherwise digital content) will therefore become more popular than ever in the future. You will even be able to buy social-network cinema tickets that tell you whether or not your friends are watching the same movie, or that introduce you to people with similar interests. Of course, you will also be able to watch feature-length movies on your phone; but most people won't, for the same reason that most people don't cook their dinner in a washing machine.

What will change in movies is this: cinema audiences have been falling for more than fifty years. In 1946, 4.067 billion movie tickets were sold. By 2005, this figure had fallen to 1.4 billion tickets. The primary reason for this fall is the emergence of new distribution formats such as the VHS and DVD. More recently, the emergence of alternative forms of entertainment have eaten into movie attendances, too. One estimate suggests that the computer-gaming industry is now larger than Hollywood in revenue terms, while profits are also being eaten away as retailers such as supermarkets aggressively cut the price of movies.

Moreover, movie production-costs have skyrocketed. The average US movie now costs close to US$100 million to make, and the window of opportunity for marketing and distribution it is limited to one or two or three critical holiday periods each year. I was talking to a vice-president of a major film studio in 2006, and he said that even the old idea of an opening weekend had now shifted to one of ten minutes. If an audience doesn't like the opening, they are immediately on their phones sending text messages to their friends, saying, 'Don't bother.' Add to this the increasingly unrealistic wage demands of movie stars, and it's clear that Hollywood itself is looking more like a disaster movie with every year that passes. However, while things are going to get worse for a while, there is ultimately a light at the end of the movie projector.

First of all, digital projection will save the movie industry an estimated US$1 billion simply by removing the need to make and send physical prints of films to movie theatres. Second, the co-creation and amateur-production trend is hitting movie production, just as it's hitting television and other forms of media. For example, machinima is the word given to people (usually young, tech-savvy computer-gamers) who make their own animated films using off-the-shelf game software like *The Movies* from Lionhead.com. Add to this trend the availability of zero-cost distribution networks such as YouTube (or MySpace for amateur musicians), and you can see how low-cost movies could rewrite the book for Hollywood. Don't get me wrong; I'm not suggesting that big blockbuster movies with expensive special effects and famous actors are history. It's just that, like everything else, the industry will polarise between the very big and the very small. The dilemma for the larger players will be how to recoup their $100 million investments when the movie is pirated or copied the day after its release.

Perhaps the answer to this question is not just producing movies, but creating ideas or properties that start in film and then are extended into other areas such as books, magazines, music, toys, games, theme parks, and even food. Hollywood knows this, of course, but it needs to think about the implications more seriously. For example, it's not totally inconceivable that a film could be sold as a download for 99 cents — or given away completely free — to sell something else that cannot be copied. A good example of this is the BBC TV series *Walking With Dinosaurs*. First, the series was an illustration of the convergence between entertainment and education ('edutainment'). Second, the broadcast series became a DVD, which became a live show, which became a soundtrack (selling 5 million copies) and a book (selling 10 million copies).

A new page for books?

How about books? The book hasn't changed much in 500 years, so if there's anything immune to technological innovation surely it's the book? The private library is largely a thing of the past, and book retailing has undergone a revolution, but surely we won't be curling up in bed with a handheld device anytime soon?

The book-publishing industry is about to undergo a fairly seismic shock. Again, books will still exist as we know them, but in the future there will be a whole host of new alternatives in terms of what we read and how we read it. The revolution is already underway. For example, fewer and fewer people are reading fiction. What people are reading instead is non-fiction — primarily, other media content dressed up to look like a book. We have lifestyle magazines masquerading as books, TV shows impersonating books, and even movies playing the role of books. There is some good news, as well. Popular science, current affairs, and history are all becoming more popular as some readers (not many, it must be said) struggle to understand the modern world and where we may all be heading.

However, it's not the content of books as such that will change most fundamentally, but the way that books are produced and distributed. In the near future, the creation of a book may not include an agent or a publisher. Instead, authors will self-publish using software and online services such as Blurb. Blurb is in some ways like a PowerPoint template in that it offers writers a set list of layouts and typefaces, but at least the end-result looks like a real book. Once you've added your pictures (cheap as chips these days), you simply send the completed document off to Blurb's contract publisher and, hey presto, you're in print. What's really extraordinary is that if you just want a copy or two to send to your mum and dad you can do this — for about US$30 a copy.

There's clearly a pattern emerging here — the democratisation of media. Whatever you want, you can get it; and, if you want to do it yourself, you can do that, too. The downside, of course, it that it is yet another example of the explosion of media content. In 2004 there were 1.2 million books published in the US, but a mere 2 per cent sold more than 5,000 copies. Traditionally, this would mean certain death for the other 98 per cent of titles; but, thanks to technology and companies such as Amazon, this is no longer the case. Some 60 per cent of Amazon's book sales now come from titles outside their top 120,000 titles. Allegedly.

So if you self-publish a book on vintage needlework from Kurdistan, there's sure to be a niche market out there somewhere for it, and either you'll find it or it will find you. At the moment, this probably means listing with Amazon or Barnesandnoble.com, but in the future you'll be able to use an automated publishing machine (like an ATM but with a 'P'). Using one of these vending machines, you'll be able to search for any book ever written (including books out of print), and it will be designed and printed in front of your eyes (you choose your own cover design, typeface, font size, and paper weight). Alternatively, you could simply download the soft-copy version onto your e-book reader or iPod.

You'll also be able to buy e-books in 99-cent instalments, much in the same way that Dickens produced serialised novels in the nineteenth century. Again, there could be a downside to this in that publishers will be tempted to sell smaller, easier-to-read (dumbed-down) versions of classic texts. But is that really a problem if the original versions are still available?

The idea of downloading books onto a computer or handheld device has been around for ages, and a handful of people regularly read books and comics this way. However, the idea has never really spread to the mainstream, largely because of the difficulties associated with reading large amounts of text on relatively small or illegible screens.

In Japan this is changing fast as young people download e-books onto 3G phones. Not surprisingly, the most popular downloads are manga comic books, the animation 'cell' format of which fits well with mobile-phone screens. Serialised fiction is proving popular, too.

As you'd expect, most readers are aged under thirty, but women make up a surprisingly large segment of users (as much as 70 per cent, according to some reports). Pricing is generally bundled up into a monthly membership fee that allows users to download books from a digital library.

Will e-books take off elsewhere in the world? Companies such as Sony and Philips clearly think so, and have launched products that aim to mimic the look and feel of 'real' books.

The technology these devices use is E-ink, which mimics actual ink by using a series of tiny pixels. Interestingly, the technology does not need any power to display the type unless the 'page' is turned, so up to twenty books can be read before the reader needs recharging. I'd expect Apple to launch something similar, not least because the iTunes music-store model could easily be adapted to literature.

What about advertising? Given how much the advertising industry goes on about creativity and strategy, it's ironic that the big agencies have been so slow to embrace the brave new world of new media. Perhaps this is because many prefer to kid themselves that they are in the movie business, or perhaps many are still in denial about losing the strategic high ground to management consultancies.

Advertising has already started to shift away from traditional media such as TV and newspapers to online, and this migration will substantially increase. This is not to say that lavish sixty-second TV commercials and full-page newspaper ads will disappear entirely; but most of the expenditure will eventually move online, where it will be highly targeted and customised. It will also be highly accountable.

Thanks to the internet, everything can be tracked and the return on investment can be calculated precisely. Does this mean the end of brand advertising? Probably.

In the future, advertising' will become more short term and promotionally focused, while image will be created elsewhere — for example, by the design of product and service experiences. However, even here there is a link between what goes on online and what happens in-store or in the product-development department, because behaviour and opinions can be tracked so easily.

As with other forms of media, customers will also want to control advertising. This means filtering what they are exposed to. In many cases, this will mean paying to turn it off entirely (70 per cent of people in the US say they like the idea of technologies that block advertising, and almost 30 per cent say they would accept a decline in their standard of living to live in an ad-free world). Conversely, I'm sure that other people would be willing to pay to have advertising target them personally. Both will be true.

People will also shift the timing and location of messages to suit themselves rather than the advertiser. Hence, search marketing will continue to grow; but so, too, will location-based marketing, once the technology catches up with the concept. Implicit in location-based marketing is localisation — so global ads will be tailored to

local contexts and customs — but it also means reaching people at
the 'moment of truth' when they are alongside whatever it is you
would like them to buy. Hence ads for soft drinks will 'magically'
appear on your mobile phone as you walk past a vending machine
on a hot day. It also means placing 'real' car ads inside virtual street-
racing games when your virtual car is off the road, or triggering a
short animation on a washing-powder pack when you pass by the
packs in the supermarket and they recognise you as a lapsed user.

However, it would be a mistake to assume that the internet will
take over from old media entirely. The internet is primarily a place
where people go to find information or entertainment, or other like-
minded individuals. This means that advertising will be repackaged
to look like information or entertainment, and it will be used to
facilitate conversations between the people who know about things
(such as brands) and the people who don't. Hence user reviews and
rankings will become increasingly important.

But can the internet ever completely take over from the
more traditional forms of media? Ads in magazines still have
a future because people are in a different headspace when they
read a magazine and there is an opportunity to seduce them with
photography that will never look the same on the Web. Newspapers
are often similarly superior in a design and usability sense, too.
Equally, radio ads aren't going anywhere because radio, unlike
the Web, is truly mobile in that it can be consumed while you are
doing other things. Radio also has a unique quality in that it holds
something back. Television, and to an increasing extent the internet,
are a full-frontal assault on the senses. They both shout at you. By
contrast, radio whispers. To listen to radio you need to turn your
imagination up.

Given that attention will be in such short supply in the future,
radio should therefore do very well. However, this doesn't necessarily
mean that radio stations will survive because they are, in a sense,
intermediaries. In the future, we may simply deal directly with the

actual maker, which may well be you and me.

Even TV, which people say is dying, will not disappear. It is undoubtedly true that TV is suffering from a plethora of new competition, ranging from computer games to people just not being home as much as they used to be, but you can't blame everything on everyone else. You can't even argue persuasively that attention-spans are so short that nobody will watch a two-hour movie. Sure, people won't watch two hours of rubbish; so if you want them to watch rubbish, you'd better make it short rubbish.

People will still watch TV, and when there's something worth watching they will watch in the tens and hundreds of millions — even if it takes two hours. The problem therefore, in a sense, is the lack of quality content. Make it and they will come.

I never tried it because I know I wouldn't like it

The future of media is that it's all about you. But the downside of such personalisation is that if media is 'narrowcasted' (created, filtered, or targeted by or to small groups), this will have the effect of reinforcing existing prejudices. In other words, people won't get both sides of the story. This is bad news for individuals because we will learn more and more about less and less. Empathy and understanding won't be big in the future.

It's also bad for society because media conglomerates will continually race towards the moral low ground in an attempt to reach what's left of the mass market. And it's bad news for everyone because fewer and fewer of us will be able to see the bigger picture.

Rupert Murdoch is exactly right when he says that media will become like food that we snack on, but I think the correct analogy is junk food. Media will become so ubiquitously available and so sliced and diced to capture our limited attention-spans that it will be of almost no value beyond comfort eating to relive boredom.

The ubiquity of media is a real challenge for media companies because the excess supply of digital content will put pressure on prices, in the sense that people will treat digital content as either a low-cost or no-cost product. This is a very real problem for businesses such as newspapers that invest heavily in journalists, editors, and photographers, only to see their products copied and repackaged and given away for free by bloggers. One solution is to restrict supply — which is already happening in the sense that ownership of some of the key media properties is converging into the hands of a few very powerful organisations, but it is also simultaneously fragmenting in that there are more channels, so restricting access is almost impossible — at least online.

Speed isn't everything

Another solution to monetarising digital content is to think about what people will pay for in the future. The answer to this question is still far from clear, but it's likely that it will include time, space, and the truth. What do I mean by this? Simply that if people are busy and stressed out, offering them even speedier products, even if they ultimately save time, will just make matters worse. What people will want are products that help them relax and that help them to find and interact with other people, including their friends and family.

This means that high-touch, not high-tech, will become increasingly important, so the opportunity for media companies is to become the starting point for journeys of exploration and self-discovery. A mundane example of this is Disney, which started off as a movie company but now embraces theme parks, hotels, cruise ships, publishing, and even food.

In other words, if you are a trusted media brand there is no reason why the brand cannot be extended and leveraged into other related fields ranging from television, movies, newspapers, magazines, and books to cafes, holidays, cameras, and cars. What would a car from Walt Disney look like? I've no idea, but it would be interesting.

Equally, how about a newspaper from the BBC, video cameras from CNN, or greetings cards from the *New Yorker* magazine? That last one has already been done, but I'm sure you get my drift.

Let's get a little more specific. I read the *New York Times* every day, but I've never paid for it because I read it online. I'm also interested in the Middle East, and I trust the *New York Times* to give me a fairly clear idea of what's going on. So what could they sell me? Well, for starters, how about a magazine containing their best coverage on the Middle East? Or how about a *New York Times* branded book? I'd also attend any talks they organised, and might even go on holiday with them if one of their Middle East correspondents was going along, too, or they had special access to people or places.

Tomorrow's headlines

Media organisations have also become obsessed with speed. This is partially to do with funding — there isn't any, so their aim is to get the raw news footage straight onto the screen as soon as possible without worrying about any analysis. This works, up to a point (it provides a certain level of realism), but accuracy and commentary are born of tireless fact-checking, investigation, and reflection — all of which cost money. This doesn't matter to some people. Indeed, there is anecdotal evidence to suggest that younger generations actually prefer speed to accuracy, but truth does matter. After all, journalism is founded on asking questions, not on reprinting press releases; there's not enough of the former and too much of the latter.

What are media companies for? What business are media companies in and what services do they provide? These are some of the critical questions that anyone involved with the media must ask themselves, and I can promise you that some of the answers they give today will not be the answers they will give in the future.

One of the best descriptions of media companies is that they attract and retain people's attention — ideally on an industrial scale — by using some form of technology. In the past this was relatively easy. These days, thanks to various social and technological shifts, it's not. However, we are still only at the very beginning of the second millennium, and the media as we know it is still wearing short pants. There is no doubt that the technological revolution ahead will impact on the media harder and faster than many other industries, but many of the fundamentals will remain unchanged. For example, most of the change that is happening already has to do with content delivery. It is about how and when people receive information. It is about format and devices. Content, although now co-created, co-filtered, and partially disengaged from traditional networks of distribution, isn't changing that much.

In the future, media companies will still be in the business of attracting attention, but it will be more about quality than quantity. Audience numbers will matter less to advertisers than information about where they are and when they're there. Equally, readers, listeners, and viewers will pay for quality information and entertainment that's personalised or physicalised. Media companies also need to attract people's imagination — not only in the sense of attracting talent, but also in capturing their audience's imagination through the interplay of words and pictures. In other words, the role of the media will still be to tell us stories.

10 March 2047

Dear Wendy

I've just been sitting at the bus stop reading the ten-minute newspaper I downloaded from my local Amazonbucks store while buying a coffee. A rather suspicious man approached me, but my newspaper recognised him as a regular reader and we joked about the fact that we've both selected the same story to appear on the front page this morning. The story was about the demise of *The Globe*, a recently launched e-paper that was supposed to be written by and for the planet. Unfortunately it was plagued with technical difficulties and attacked by a plethora of local e-papers created by non-profit citizen journalists. The final straw, apparently, was a lawsuit brought by a sixteen-year-old phone-cam paparazzi who claimed the newspaper had stolen one of his pictures. Bored, I clicked on the button underneath the story about a new restaurant and booked a table. Amazing what this new e-paper can do. After arriving at my office, I downloaded some vintage episodes of M*A*S*H to watch on my EyeView contact lenses over the weekend and refreshed my newspaper with a five-minute copy of the *New York Times* (Democrat viewpoint version with Republican argument overlays).

Cheers

Russ

Five trends that will transform media

Shifting   Media will be shifted by users to suit their particular requirements. For example, video-on-demand (or mobile video) will alter the way people watch TV, much in the same way that podcasting will change the way people listen to radio. Both put the audience squarely in charge of programming. In the future, people will watch, read, and listen to what they want, when they want, on any device they want, and content will be designed, edited, and personalised for specific physical locations and situations.

Time-starved   In the future, thanks to the acceleration of technology, we will be busier and have less spare time. We will also be stressed and sleep-deprived, so if you want to connect with an audience you'd better make it quick and easy. This will lead to an increased demand for snack-sized formats and content available in a variety of sizes or lengths. Equally, the old model of edit first and publish second will be reversed, with content being published first and edited second (filtered by the audience). Long copy and rigorous analysis will become a specialist demand available on a pay-per-view basis, with journalists being paid the same way. Conversely, there will be also be a flight to quality, with people seeking out quality content regardless of format, length, or even language. All of this will also create a high demand for quality search, editing, and information and entertainment 'sifting'.

Infinite content   The supply of content will become effectively infinite. The 'million channel universe' will include not just traditional media content created by traditional media companies, but a whole new set of content created and distributed by new players such as telcos, internet search firms, and device manufacturers. Everything from walls and tabletops to cereal packets and soft drink cans will be transformed into screens and interactive media content. Meanwhile, the plummeting cost of content creation and distribution will tap into a new generation of talented (and talent-less) writers, commentators, photographers, and filmmakers, but it will be increasingly challenging to attract an audience's attention and to build brand loyalty against this infinite noise.

User-generated content   Is user-generated content (UGC) the shape of things to come, or is it just that certain members of Generation Y have too much time and computing power on their hands? UGC will transform the entertainment industry, particularly gaming and other areas that tap into or rely upon social networks. The Web 2.0 trend of co-operation and aggregation will also continue to impact on the production of media content, although co-creation will largely be limited to local news, and lifestyle and entertainment 'news'. Hard news, in contrast, will remain the domain of highly resourced professional media organisations, although amateur users will filter and sift content, and occasionally rival their influence.

Personalisation and physicalisation   You will have paid under $40 for this book. If you asked me to show up and read parts of it to you in person, I'd charge you several thousand dollars. If you wanted me to personalise what I say, you'd be talking significantly more. On the other hand, if this book were online it would be free. So what's going on here? If the cost of creating and distributing digital content becomes practically zero, content will be ubiquitous and largely valueless as a result. Personalisation and particularly physicalisation, on the other hand, will be highly sought after. We will watch movies at home, but we will pay more to experience them in a cinema. Add to this a general flight to quality, and media such as quality local newspapers and live experiences could do very well in the future.

Chapter 5

➡

Banking and Financial Services: everyone is a bank

The trouble with the future is that it usually arrives before we're ready for it.
–Arnold Glasgow

Jon Merriman is the CEO of an investment bank, and is one of fifty people in the US with a radio frequency ID (RFID) tag inserted in his arm. Mr Merriman's firm is an advisor to VeriChip, a maker of ID implants for pets and RFID-enabled medical bracelets. If Mr Merriman ('Chip' to his friends?) is ever involved in a serious accident, doctors are just a scan away from all the necessary information. The chip contains everything from bank account information and social security records to medical files and locational information. I'm quite tempted to follow suit myself.

According to the research company AC Nielson, by the year 2020 only 10 per cent of financial transactions will be in cash. The rest will be digital — a mixture of micro-payments, contactless payments, stored-value cards, and plastic. This will be good news for governments, because about 25 per cent of all cash in circulation worldwide is used for illegal purposes, so any restriction on its availability will be beneficial. Cash is anonymous and difficult to trace; e-payments are not. Equally, a cashless society will appeal to business because it will speed up transactions, saving banks and other organisations a bundle of money. Indeed, the only people who will be against the idea of a cash-free society will be some ordinary, law-abiding citizens who rather like the look and feel of paper money — much in the same way that many people prefer real newspapers and books to their online equivalents.

This, in a nutshell, is the future of money. We will see the emergence of countless new payment options, and there will be a battle between the old and the new, with many of the newer options foisted upon people without their consent. Some people will fully embrace digital transactions through the use of various devices ranging from computers to mobile phones. At the extreme, some people will insert chips into their jaw or forearm. These chips will be used to gain access to safe-deposit boxes, to make payments, or to prove that you are indeed who you say you are. For this group of tech-savvy extroverts and security-conscious paranoids, banks and national currencies will become increasingly irrelevant.

The other side of the coin will be the traditionalists. These people will be keen to hang on to physical money and will fight to retain control of currencies that are symbolic of national identity and pride — a battle then between the global and the local, and between high tech and high touch, and no cash prizes for guessing who will win this battle in the longer term. By 2050 there is every possibility that we will have one global digital currency, whether we like it or not.

To get an idea of just how strong the rejection of a single global currency might be, you only have to look at Morgan Stanley in the UK, which offers a credit card decorated with your national flag of choice (English, Welsh, Scottish, or Irish). And if you think that's taking tribalism too far, American Express has launched the 'IN' card which is only available to people who live 'in' Los Angles, New York, or Chicago. The cards link rewards and offers to local products and services.

In the future, even this will be surpassed as banks offer cards with designs downloaded by the individual customer (as ANZ bank already does in Australia), tied to even more localised products and services. Not only that but, rather than tie things together geographically, banks and credit-card companies will start to realise that each generation and demographic actually consists of a series of 'tribes'.

These tribes have very similar interests and beliefs, so we will start to see financial products and services aimed at, for instance, the computer geek community, the music crowd, petrol heads, and bookworms.

Hot money

As usual, the early signs of change are here already if you take the trouble to look around. Anecdotally, I know of people in the UK who are so tired of carrying around coins that they are starting to give or throw them away. This is clearly a signal of prosperity, but it's also one of convenience. The average person now carries two to three times as much weight in their pockets and briefcases as they did two decades ago, so personal weight-loss programs will soon have to appear unless someone invents a lightweight alternative, or micro-payments become more widely accepted. Coins and banknotes could also disappear almost overnight for another reason. In all the recent talk about the consequences of a global pandemic, it appears to me that one important implication has been missed: bank notes and coins tend to be dirty, so people will refuse to handle them if they think they could be a conduit for disease. In Japan, some ATMs already heat banknotes as a precautionary hygiene measure; in an age of anxiety, 'hot money' could be a very cool idea.

Travelling to other countries like South Korea you get another glimpse of the future of money. Here, hundreds of thousands of phones are already fitted with devices that can turn a mobile phone into a wallet simply by flashing the handset at a 'dongle' located at cash-points and tills. Small transactions, such as buying a drink or a train ticket, are instantaneous, whereas larger transactions require a four-digit security code. Why is this happening in South Korea? Simple — the country has the highest use of broadband and the second-largest mobile data-services network in the world.

Back in Japan, the use of electronic money is also growing rapidly, with over 43,000 retailers installing systems to accept payment by mobile phone. This means that you can shop for everyday items with your phone or send money to family and friends via a text message. Phones can be charged with up to US$500 and, because the money is not connected to either a phone bill or credit card, security concerns are neatly sidestepped. Interestingly, the number of coins issued in Japan (around 91 billion) fell for the first time recently, and it's much the same story elsewhere. In the US, electronic payments (including credit and debit cards) surpassed cheque payments for the first time in history in December 2005, while in Australia the use of cheques has fallen through the floor. Indeed, there are certain road tunnels and parking meters in Australia that you can only use if you have a vehicle equipped with a contact-less payment device (known as an e-tag) or have a mobile phone.

The idea of electronic micro-payments has been touted as 'the next big thing' for years. Until very recently, though, there was a big problem with very small payments — there was nothing worth buying. But Apple changed all that. iTunes has doubled the percentage of Web transactions under US$5, and while micro-payments still represent only 2.8 per cent of all e-commerce, the percentage is growing rapidly. Online micro-payments for digital content is currently worth between $15–$30 billion in the US, and it's predicted this will increase to US$60 billion by 2015, partly due to the convergence of online and mobile channels.

Another indication of change is McDonald's. Until quite recently McDonald's only accepted cash worldwide. Now it accepts credit cards in the US and is testing ideas such as the MasterCard PayPass system in some of its restaurants. Such e-payment schemes use the same technology as the e-tag, and mean that customers not only buy things without getting out of their car but they don't even need to find their wallet. The obvious beneficiaries of 'drive-through' payment include other fast-food joints, but the technology could also spawn a new generation of fast drive-up and drive-through retail outlets, including petrol stations, convenience stores, and perhaps even banks.

None of these ideas would appear in the least bit futuristic to a twenty-three-year-old computer gamer (Deathifier to his friends) who once spent £13,700 on a Treasure Island that didn't exist. The island in question did exist in a role-playing game called Project Enthropia, and as a result Deathifier made a real-life killing by selling virtual plots of land on his virtual island to other gamers to build virtual homes. He's not alone either. In 2005, Jon Jacobs (Neverdie to his friends) paid £57,000 for a virtual space station — presumably so that he could sell virtual tickets to virtual space travellers in the future. According to one estimate, the value of this virtual economy in real terms is about US$800 million, and the market shows no sign of slowing down. Indeed, we'll probably see virtual bankers, virtual insurance agents, and virtual financial planners within the next couple of decades.

The serious point here is that life is blurring between the real and the virtual, and financial services are no exception. People are already exchanging real money for virtual goods and vice versa, so why not invent new products and services for this market? Several US-based retailers (including a real bank) have opened virtual branches inside virtual games, so why not open a bank-run virtual currency-trading exchange where gamers can exchange their 'World of Witchcraft' EU gold or 'Second Life' Linden dollars for real gold or US dollars? If that's a bit too weird for you, how about a real credit card that earns the virtual currency of your choice when you buy a pair of real jeans or an iPod? It could work the other around way, too — a real card personalised with a picture of your avatar that earns points every time you spend real money on virtual goods (like virtual clothes or real estate for your avatar). Such loyalty cards and points schemes are good examples of private currencies, and we will see more of these in the future as the cost of running such currencies falls. The makers of Entropia Universe are planning to issue 400,000 players with ATM cards so that they can view their virtual cash; this is surely a sign of the shape of things to come.

But the future of money will not be entirely digital. People are happy to make small payments, or to apply and receive loans digitally, but they are less happy transferring large amounts or making digital investments. This is human nature. When ATMs were first introduced in 1967 there was a widespread feeling that you would be mugged attempting to take your money out. Even today, only around 5–10 per cent of people feel confident about depositing money into ATMs because they are worried their electronic transactions will be snooped on and that banks will sell this information to others or flood them with junk mail. Given that over half of Americans say that a company has compromised the security of their data, this is not entirely fantasy either. Somehow, physical banks and human beings are just more reassuring, which is one reason why neither will entirely disappear in the future.

As I've said before, the more life becomes digitised, virtual, and remote, the more some people will crave emotional intimacy and human interaction. In banking terms, there has always been a need for trust, and one of the best ways of developing such trust is through a human relationship. This isn't something that people need every day. Most of the time, cost and convenience are the key drivers, but this changes when the stakes are raised.

For example, many people prefer to deal face-to-face for a large amount of money going out of their account or over a decision with long-term implications (such as a mortgage or a pension). This may be generational, but I'd suggest that even the youngest customers will rush into their nearest bank branch the moment the economy turns sour and they're worried about losing their jobs and missing their mortgage repayments. In other words, in the future, people will use a variety of channels to do their banking, and will visit physical branches less often, but the 'value' of branch visits and the intensity of human interaction will increase. As a result, banks will invest heavily in new sites and refurbishments, and particularly in ways of making the banking experience faster, friendlier, and more convenient.

People in physical branches also have a bright future for another reason — banks are expensive to establish and even harder to get right. So, done well, they are one of the best barriers to preventing competitors from entering the market. But apart from the continuance of physical banks, what else can we expect to see in the future? The answer to this question will be shaped by various product, service, and process innovations, but critically it will also largely hinge on external events, most notably the health of the global economy. In short, if globalisation and the long boom continue, so too will general prosperity, and this will drive interest in and supply of all manner of financial innovations, especially those delivered online. However, if the global economy slips into recession, or if interest rates climb or inflation takes hold, there is a likelihood that countries, companies, and individuals will act defensively to protect what they have.

Developed countries have traditionally been in favour of open markets for very selfish reasons — they want to sell more things to other countries. But as countries like China and India become the dominant economic superpowers, western countries will move towards more nationalist and protectionist policies. This will, in turn, spawn a return to local community and a flight to trusted brands and institutions. In short, people will stick with what they know and trust; wherever possible, this will mean people not machines.

The biggest threat to the economies of countries such as the US, the UK, and Australia will not come from external threats, but from within (the so-called endogenous threats). These include developments such as domestic housing bubbles or the EU slipping into deflation (or stagflation) caused by an ageing and unproductive workforce. In a fast-paced, globalised world, the love of the new dominates. But in a downturn, security will be paramount, and new entrants and foreign banks will be rejected in favour of long-established local names. People will also spend more wisely, and saving will enjoy something of a renaissance — not that most people are even on speaking terms with the concept of putting something aside for a rainy day any more. However, even this is a threat. Most modern retail banks and other financial institutions are built for lending, or at least there must be a balance between borrowing and lending. If there were to be a significant upswing in savings, and lending all but stopped, there would be some very serious trouble ahead.

In Australia, the average level of household debt is now equal to one-and-a-half year's annual average salary. In the United Kingdom, household debt will hit 150 per cent of annual income by 2010, which means household debt will increase from something in the order of £1 trillion to £1.6 trillion, give or take a few pounds. That's about £7650 per household in Britain.

At this rate, fifty-year or intergenerational mortgages and loans will become commonplace, and more than a quarter of homeowners will be paying off home loans after they retire. Likewise, if the US were a corporation it would have been declared bankrupt years ago, but it's in nobody's interest to upset the global status quo. The US borrows 75 per cent of the world's savings and imports 50 per cent more goods than it exports. As a result, US Treasury bonds to the value of around US$600 billion are issued every year. Most of this debt is financed by Asian countries such as China and Japan; but if either country were to pull the plug, the US dollar and bond markets would crash. This would lead the US economy into recession, and other countries like China would almost certainly be sucked in, too. So, as Larry Summers (Treasury secretary under President Clinton) once put it, we are all benefiting from a 'balance of financial terror' — a system of mutually assured financial destruction. That's assuming the US doesn't do something to antagonise China, so that they just pull the plug regardless.

I want it and I want it now

Why is there so much debt around? The UK currently holds around 60 per cent of all credit cards issued in Europe, and has around 75 per cent of total European credit-card debt — about £50 billion — or £1140 for very adult in the UK, the last time I looked. In the US, the figure for credit-card debt is close to US$800 billion — a 400 per cent increase since 1990. Historically, this would have been seen as a burden: something to feel ashamed of, and potentially even a threat to individual freedom. However, things have changed and will continue to do so for the foreseeable future. Over the past three or four decades we have shifted from a saving to a borrowing culture, and these days people often talk about their level of personal debt in the same way that others brag about the size of their salaries, which is not surprising given that one tends to be indicative of the other these days.

The problem, of course, is that many of the people with gigantic loans are living right on the edge. When interest rates rise by a couple of per cent they will be in very serious trouble — or perhaps the banks and other financial institutions that lent them the money in the first place will be. Personal bankruptcies in the UK are already at an all-time high, and even if there isn't a major crash these debts will last for a very long time. More worryingly perhaps is the attitude of Generation Y to debt. Under-twenty-fives are the fastest-growing group filing for bankruptcy in the US, partly because it's seen as 'cool' and partly because of the bills caused by 'must have' technology such as mobile phones and iPods. Peer pressure to own these devices is strong, but so too are the marketing tactics of the banks and especially credit-card companies that are targeting teens with 'unmissable opportunities'. And they are not discriminating between those who can afford debt and those who can't either. As a result, the amount of debt 'owned' by poor families has increased considerably.

In the US the level of debt owned by low-income households has soared by over 180 per cent over the last decade, while the figure for older people was close to 150 per cent over the same period. This is not a debt mountain; it's an avalanche waiting to descend. In the UK the government has already announced that it will pass legislation to apply 'wealth warnings' to all literature and advertising about credit cards and loans, and this will be just the beginning. In the future, these warnings will appear on the credit cards and statements themselves, and there will be tighter controls about lending.

Transparency and regulation will increase across other areas of financial services, too, which will significantly increase operating costs for financial institutions and will put many smaller players out of business. And don't expect the customer — however stupid and short-sighted — to take responsibility for their actions either. We will see a significant increase in litigation against banks, credit-card companies, and insurance companies because 'you made me have it' and 'I didn't think that interest rates would go up that much.'

This will make the financial services industry akin to the tobacco industry today. Once upon a time, it was used-car salesmen and politicians who were the least trusted people. In the future, it will be bank managers, financial planners, and mortgage advisors who people distrust the most.

One feature of national economies in the future will be that each country will exhibit differing degrees of prosperity and hardship depending on its geography, resources, and population.

For example, in some areas of Sydney real estate prices will be up, while in others they will be down. Why the discrepancy? The reason is globalisation. There will continue to be a huge demand for resources, but other areas of the economy will be flat. Equally, some skills will be in high demand while others will be unwanted. In other words, the high growth of certain sectors and cities will mask what is effectively a recession down the road. Can the two opposites co-exist? The answer is yes, although whether such co-existence will be peaceful is another mater. We haven't seen tax riots on the streets of London for several decades, but there is no reason they won't appear again.

There will therefore be several futures, but trusted brands and genuinely independent advisors will prosper in all of these future worlds. Can the big banks pull this off? Possibly, although community banks, building societies, credit unions, and local savings and loan companies are in a much better position to do so, given their scale, history, and more personal relationships with customers.

But what about when artificial intelligence really kicks in and you can speak to a fully automated, highly intelligent machine about the best loan or insurance policy? Would you trust it? The question is similar to whether or not you would allow a robot to perform surgery on you or whether you would climb aboard a plane flown entirely by computer with no human presence whatsoever. In a sense it's an academic question because, as usual, it's already happening — it's just that you and I don't come into contact with these 'machines', and even if we do they have not yet reached the stage where they can interact on a true human-to-human level.

Machines are already picking stocks and calculating risk-reward characteristics of share portfolios. In fact, they are probably buying and selling shares (or whole companies) for your pension fund as you read this. In theory, using a machine to assess which of 2,000 home loans is the best for you is no different. Algorithmic financial advisors will have several advantages over their human predecessors, too. First, they can work on your behalf twenty-four hours a day, seven days a week, 365 days a year, and they don't get tired. Moreover, they are dispassionate, cannot be distracted and, most importantly of all, they don't fall in love with the things that they buy. Of course, this also means they only have the ethics given to them, but the thought of a totally automated process is quite attractive.

Of course, there's a downside to this increased automation and digitalisation of cash, and that's identity theft. According to Forrester Research, over 60 per cent of online shoppers are 'very' or 'extremely' concerned about the theft of credit-card numbers during online activity. ID theft is now a US$56 billion problem in the US, and it rose by 600 per cent in the UK between 2000 and 2005. Electronic information is rarely totally secure and is often linked, so that anyone who penetrates a network can steal everything. Ironically, of course, the solution to this is more technology. Early ideas include verbal signatures, body double accounts (temporary bank accounts with 'fake' IDs designed to expire after a single use), biometric ATMs, and two-way identity verification where both parties ask the other to prove who they are before revealing sensitive information. The banks are also getting into the same game; Citibank has set up Identitytheft911.com.

But it won't all be high tech. Some of the innovations we'll see will consist simply of adding new channels so that, for instance, you'll be able to take out a loan to pay for an expensive meal in the restaurant itself. In Australia there are already newsagents selling home loans, and we'll soon see vending machines selling stocks and shares. Also in Australia one credit union (MECU) sets the loan rate to buy a car on the basis of the vehicle's environmental impact, while in Japan one bank links the amount of interest paid to the level of waste produced by an individual, business, or community group.

This last idea is extremely interesting because in the future we will see the growth of alternatives to individual loans. This means more bartering and exchange, but it also means using social networking to link people together to take out community loans or to club together to buy large quantities of the same product at a group discount.

People are also starting to use credit cards in different ways. Thirty or forty years ago, my dad only used his credit cards for holidays and for other large purchases. These days I always seem to be stuck in a supermarket queue behind a twenty-something trying to use a credit card to buy a loaf of bread and a bottle of milk. To be fair, the younger generation has never seen a recession. What they have seen instead is their parents make a considerable amount of money by using debt to buy property, so you could argue that their attitude to debt is not their fault. But it is. It's also the fault of parents and schools that teach next to nothing about money and financial planning; and, ultimately, I suppose it's the fault of the government, too.

One solution to this, especially for teens and tweens, will be the development of credit cards that lock off certain geographic locations or product groups. So, for instance, if your teenage daughter has a mobile phone and iPod addiction, you'll be able to give her a credit card but she won't be able to use it to buy either.

Things really aren't looking that good for Gen Y. First they have inherited a planet that is becoming fuller, dirtier, and more dangerous (or so we're told). Then they are told that they may have to tighten their belts because Gen X bankers have only done cursory checks before lending them money.

The way lending operates will have to change in other ways, too. Fifty-year or even seventy-five-year mortgages are one option. Another way forward will be the family loan. In the UK around one in fifty households are termed extended financial families (EFFs). By 2014 this is expected to have risen to one in twenty. What are EFFs? They are simply more than one generation living together under one roof. Typically, EFFs comprise grandparents, parents, and children.

This is nothing new, of course.

A few hundred years ago this was the typical household, and is perhaps yet another example of how we will be going back to the future. Why are EFFs increasing? The most obvious reason is the high cost of real estate, but pension under-funding, increased healthcare costs (people are living longer remember), and higher education costs are other factors.

Dad, can I borrow your salary?

Another spin-off from the high cost of living in the future will be that more and more parents will provide security, a deposit, or even part of the monthly payment for their children's homes. Some lenders like Wizard in Australia (part of GE Money) have already responded to this need with products linking the assets and income of more than one generation. Another means to a similar end is giving money to your children in the form of regular payments instead of a single lump-sum. Indeed, the very concept of inheriting money or property will become foreign to many young people as parental assets are increasingly used up to help with loan payments.

At the extreme this can also mean having kids who simply refuse to move out of the family home because it is too expensive to rent or buy real estate, or because doing so would seriously dent their disposable income. In Japan these kids are known as 'parasite singles' because they do not contribute financially to the running of the parental home, while in Australia the term 'boomerang kids' describes kids who leave home but keep coming back due to their accumulation of debt.

According to a survey by the University of Michigan, 34 per cent of adults aged eighteen to thirty-four receive money from their parents and 50 per cent receive non-cash gifts in the form of time which adds up to 367 hours of unpaid work per year. Cash payments are usually for housing, utility bills, and expenses.

Until ten or twenty years ago, parents assumed that the financial obligation to their children (typically US$191,000 up to the age of seventeen) ended when they graduated from high school. Now the financial support can easily go on for another seventeen years and can cost an additional US$42,000 because people are spending longer in education (which costs more than it used to), are getting married later, and are entering the workforce later than they used to. However, as *New York Times* writer Anna Bahney has observed, the reason may also be because children these days are taking the 'scenic route from adolescence to adulthood'.

So what are some of the other consequences of these shifts? One fairly fundamental implication is that today's children will never enjoy the same standards of living their parents enjoyed. This is a generalisation, but most things that used to be 'free' now cost money, and everything that costs money now will be considerably more expensive in the future, thanks to global market-pricing and the increasing scarcity of resources (including skilled workers). Theoretically this could make for a very bitter and unhappy generation, but I don't think it will. If anything, material possessions will become less important in the future, and people will be judged by who they are and what they do for the rest of society rather than by what they earn or what they possess.

Already 83 per cent of Australians think that society (which presumably includes themselves) is obsessed with money, and around 25 per cent have recently sacrificed income to improve their quality of life. However, this figure really needs to increase to 51 per cent because individuals judge their happiness in relation to other people. Thus, if the majority were to change their behaviour, the minority would follow suit, especially since most people fear loss much more than they crave gain.

At least I hope this is what happens. Money is the thing that most people worry about most often. According to one Australian survey, financial worries come in way above relationships, employment, security, education and terrorism. Thirty per cent of people also think that they are overexposed to interest rate rises. In the UK over 20 million people find it difficult to pay regular bills, according to the Post Office. Maybe the way to remove these worries is to give everyone a lump sum at birth. People could have access to an amount every month until they die, which would be like living life in reverse — you have lots of money when you are born and when you are growing up and when you really need it, but receive less as you get much older and don't really need it. I know this is a silly idea, but there's a sensible idea somewhere in there trying to get out.

Another reason I don't think it's all doom and gloom is human ingenuity and technology. One of the biggest debates in countries like the UK, the US, Germany, France, and Japan is how to fund an ageing citizenry. They are concerned by the fact that, because people are living for much longer, healthcare and retirement costs are escalating, and there are fewer young people to pay for all this. For example, in Germany and the US the level of public debt needed to finance old age is currently 65 per cent of GDP, but this will rise to 200 per cent by the year 2050 unless someone comes up with a clever solution or longevity starts to move in the opposite direction, which is quite possible.

One option is to extend the retirement age, and this will happen — not once but several times in most countries. Some countries may even abolish the option of retirement altogether or refuse to use state funds to support asset-rich, income-poor citizens. Personally, I think that technology will eventually come to the rescue and that productivity rates will soar as a result, thereby funding retirement requirements. I also think that people will simply adjust and learn to live on less with less. Real estate, for example, is not a god-given right, and many more people may decide to live in government- or company-owned, rent-controlled apartments. We may lease or borrow more products, too. Rather than lending to buy real estate outright, lenders may 'give' people property free of charge or at a low monthly cost but will then take some or all of the future capital gains on the property. Indeed, perhaps we will see a return to a feudal model whereby property or land is owned by your employer and must be returned once your employment ceases. Of course, this could be a recipe for social unrest — as it was the last time it was tried — although maybe certain safeguards could be built in or perhaps tied to the length of your employment. One thing we will undoubtedly see is insurance against the possibility of living too long.

Back in 1840 you worked until you died (usually at age 40) or you relied upon your children. This was clearly unacceptable, so governments devised a system whereby the income generated by those working would pay for those not working. This intergenerational transfer of income worked fine while younger workers outnumbered older retirees, but a declining fertility-rate coupled with increased longevity has led to an imbalance. The current idea is therefore that older people should save up and pay for their own retirement, but this idea is itself flawed because people have no idea how long they will live. Enter the financial markets. We have already seen the issue of so-called catastrophe (cat) bonds and cat derivatives that bet for and against events such as hurricanes, so the thought of mortality bonds betting on how long people will live is a natural extension.

But how will the key socio-economic trends influence the stock market in the future? As I've said, one of the biggest trends is the ageing population. In most developed countries the number of individuals aged over sixty-five is set to double over the next twenty to thirty years. In the UK there are currently just below 10 million people aged over sixty-five, but by the year 2025 this will have increased to 13 million. The beneficiaries of this trend will include healthcare companies and developers building residential care homes and retirement real estate, but other sectors will benefit too.

For example, many older people will be both cashed up and

time-rich, so industries from gardening and DIY to caravans and exotic travel will enjoy boom times. But the biggest area to benefit is what's been termed the 'dream fulfilment' industry. This includes garages selling classic cars to older people who drooled over them when they were younger but didn't have the money back then.

So what will the bank of the future look like? The standard futurist reply would be to paint a picture of a high-tech playground. Either that or people would argue that banks in the historical sense will cease to exist as we all move online. For example, Zopa is a virtual bank. Essentially it's a peer-to-peer money-lending site putting individuals with money to lend in touch with people who want to borrow it. The company takes a 1 per cent fee from the borrower for facilitating the introduction, and takes a cut of the repayment insurance on each loan. Lenders set their own rate depending on the risk level they are happy with, and borrowers are given a credit (trust) rating based on an Equifax rating and, over time, past behaviour through the site. Actual risks are minimised because the loans are aggregated across groups of at least fifty similar lenders and borrowers (a spread bet, if you like), and also because each loan is subject to normal debt-recovery processes. Rates are set by the individuals themselves and can be changed instantly, so niches like ethical or local lending can be tapped with great precision.

Prosper is the US equivalent of Zopa, and similarly seeks to remove retail banks from the business of lending or borrowing money. Borrowers bid for how much interest they'll pay, while lenders bid on how much they'll lend and how low an interest rate they'll accept for a specific credit profile. However, unlike Zopa, Prosper allows an individual to front an entire loan, and places borrowers into groups, with the group leader being made responsible for verifying the authenticity of each member. This is a very interesting idea and one that is similar in some ways to the community aspects of Grameen Bank in India. At the moment, Zopa and Prosper are both novelties, but it raises the question of whether banking services need to be provided by banks. Banks make money by using your money, and the really clever ones even charge you for it. They do a lot more besides, of course, like offering wealth-management and financial-planning services, but there is no logical reason why all of these services cannot be done by specialists. Indeed, the very idea of financial supermarkets seems to be on the wane as intermediaries and monolines (specialist companies focused on one area of financial services) take an increasingly large share of bank business. But perhaps not in the future.

Ten years ago, applying to a supermarket for a credit card or loan would have been unheard of. Now Tesco Personal Finance (established 1997) has 5 million customers. A key argument in favour of supermarkets becoming banks is that supermarkets have a very high number of (theoretically) loyal customers visiting each week, and they represent value, quality, and convenience (for example, more branches and longer opening-hours than banks provide) — precisely the things that people are looking for in financial services. Theoretically, supermarkets are not a direct threat to retail banks because customers still turn to banks for more complex and higher-value products like mortgages. Or at least that's the theory. So far, supermarkets have been content with selling credit cards, car loans, and pet insurance alongside baked beans, but this might be changing. A case in point is Asda (now part of Wal-Mart), which is testing the sale of houses on its online notice board, while Tesco has recently introduced health insurance alongside its fresh fruit and vegetables.

So the big question is, will supermarkets start selling mortgages and pensions, too? The industry says no, but I'd predict yes. There is obviously an issue with supermarkets selling (or mis-selling) complex financial products, but perhaps they won't be so complicated after the supermarkets have got their hands on them. One thing that supermarkets are very good at is looking outwards at the needs of customers. Retail banks, in contrast, still tend to struggle with the idea that they are shops, and their product offerings remain far too complicated for the average bank customer (or employee) to understand.

What are banks for anyway?

So if everyone from supermarkets to car companies and phone companies is offering financial services, where does this leave banks? One answer could be as low-margin suppliers of white-labelled products and services for other companies, which is clearly a fast road to low margins, commodification, and oblivion. Another answer could be for banks to remodel themselves as 'wealthcare' companies — specialist independent advisors that help people to safeguard and grow their wealth.

One reason the game may soon be up for the banks is that ordinary people are finally working out how they play the game. After all, why should banks be charging me when they are sitting on all of my money? Surely it should be the other way around? Moreover, why in the age of instant communications does it still take four days to clear a payment through my bank?

Bankers' salaries are also starting to be seen by many people — and governments — as a sign of an inefficient system, running contrary to everything we are told about free-market enterprise and competition. Why in Australia, for example, does a policy called the 'Four Pillars' exist, preventing the big four domestic banks from merging? In theory this increases competition, but it could be having the opposite effect. Moreover, if big foreign banks continue to grow within Australia, a domestic merger may be essential for survival. On the other hand, a scenario where all banks are seen as 'greedy' is a real possibility, so either way governments will have to act to open up the financial services market, sooner or later.

This will mean the entry of large foreign banks from China, India, and the US, but it will also mean allowing people who live in one country to use a bank based in another. To some extent PayPal is doing this already, although it is simply acting in the area of transactional fulfilment. But why can't I have a credit card from PayPal or a chequebook from a Chinese bank if that provider is offering a better deal than my bank down the road? Monolines are also a threat to the banks, but I think the killer blow will eventually come from outside the industry altogether. Most radical innovation does not come from industry incumbents, and banking and financial services will be no exception.

For example, I firmly believe that Wal-Mart, Apple, Microsoft, Google, and Vodafone will all eventually hold banking licences. How would that feel in terms of competition? Wal-Mart has been processing money orders since 2001 and has been cashing pay-cheques since 2004. The world's largest retailer (responsible for 1 per cent of Chinese GDP) also houses local bank branches in many of its stores. In the UK, Asda, a Wal-Mart subsidiary, even sells insurance alongside the carrots and spaghetti. Will Wal-Mart go the whole way and open up its own full-service banks in stores or in stand-alone locations? If it does — which I believe will happen within the next decade or two — it will not be a first. Sears Roebuck tried the idea back in the 1980s, but the experiment ended in tears. Part of the problem is moving outside a store's core competencies, but another reason is the need for trust. Supermarkets are trusted — up to a point, and many people are happy to buy holiday insurance or perhaps get a small loan from a retailer — but they somehow lack credibility and expertise when it comes to much larger financial matters. However, this is simply a temporary branding problem. Eventually you will undoubtedly be able to buy a fifty-year mortgage alongside the thirty-second noodles.

If supermarkets are competitors to banks due to convenience, scale, and the sheer volume of customers who pass through their stores, companies like Apple are a threat for another reason — style. For instance, what colour would you like your bank to be? iTunes is a classic example of business-model innovation meeting stylish industrial design, so what if the company created a stylish gadget that securely contained all of your financial records along with instant access to 10,000-or-so financial products from around the world?

The device could be used to make phone calls, but it could also contain digital cash, which would make your wallet — and the need to carry coins — redundant. It would come in a choice of sixty colours and finishes, and you could even customise aspects of its functionality and appearance. Want one? I certainly do. Would I still use a bank if I had one? Unlikely, although if the device was a joint venture between Apple and, say, GE Money, I'd have the option of talking to a real banker or visiting one of their physical branches if I so desired.

All of the information contained on the device would automatically be backed up by the company in case of loss; and since the device would be equipped with GPS technology, it would also be able to assess risk for insurance purposes in real time because it would know where I go (at what time and for how long). It would also be intelligent, so it would learn about what I buy, and this information — along with the locational information — could be used to send me highly personalised information or promotions. For example, the device would know that I like old cars because I've used it to pay for a subscription to *Classic Cars* magazine; so if I was walking past an old-car showroom it could send me a video message of what was inside the showroom alongside loan rates for investment vehicles.

Would a bank launch such a device? Highly unlikely. But a Telco, a tech firm, or a start-up working with a Telco or a tech firm probably will. Realistically, such a device won't appeal to everyone, but even if it captures half of Generation Y that would probably be enough to give the banks a headache that could last for a generation.

Would you like insurance with that?

How about insurance? Will this industry change the same way as banks in the future? I think it will. The technology that's transforming banking is also capable of transforming insurance in the sense that GPS-embedded devices and RFIDs will allow insurance companies to price risk in real time. They will know where you are and thus be able to cost insurance by the minute, opening up a whole new market of instant cover insurance. For example, if you're worried about boarding a particular chairlift while on a skiing holiday, you could buy additional insurance to cover the five-minute trip instantly through your mobile phone. Equally, cars could be sold with insurance embedded into the vehicle. Payments would be made on a per-kilometre basis depending on time of day, location, speed, and traffic conditions.

The annual cost of compensation in the UK stands at £10 billion, mostly billed straight to the taxpayer. Insurance claims have been rising at around 15 per cent every year, largely due to an increase in litigious attitudes. But many of these claims are bogus, and anything that can reduce the amount that insurance companies pay out or help them assess risk more accurately will be welcomed.

Insurance will also be personalised in the sense that it will be tied to our individual actions. Three insurance companies in the US, the UK, and South Africa already do this — the idea being that the healthier you are, the smaller your insurance premiums become. PruHealth UK offers 'vitality points' to customers who join a gym, give up smoking, improve their body-fat index, or read books about keeping fit. Discovery Health in South Africa and Destiny Health in the US offer similar 'cash for health' policies. Given that car insurance companies have been offering discounts to safer drivers for years, it's surprising that nobody has thought of this before. So what's next?

Perhaps governments will link personal income-tax rates to an individual's health or lifestyle — if your waistline goes down, so too does your annual tax assessment. Somehow I think I preferred it back in the old days when I could go to the pub without my employer, the government, my doctor, social services, or my health-insurance company knowing I was there.

In theory, our modern world, with its anxieties and new risks, will be a bonanza for insurance companies, although too much risk could sink them, too. For instance, the level of terrorism in Iraq means that insurance for foreign journalists is now so high it's almost unaffordable, while global climate change and severe unpredicted weather could hit insurance companies very badly indeed.

Insurance isn't going away any time soon, and neither are banks. Indeed, the insurance business will grow significantly in the future in response to new risks and fears, although quite what companies and individuals will be insuring themselves against is far from clear. Equally, while banks and credit-card companies will be damaged by the digitalisation of cash and the increase in mobile payments, micro-payments, pre-pay, and contactless payments, I don't foresee banks being disintermediated entirely. Banks will hold onto larger transactions simply because big-ticket payments require risk management, and default and dispute systems, which are generally too expensive and complicated from a compliance point of view for non-banks. Nevertheless, digital money will turn parts of the financial services industry on its head because the banks and credit-card companies will no longer be in sole charge of chequebooks, credit cards, ATMs, and branches.

4 July 2036

Dear Li

Yesterday I walked into a branch of Wal-Mart bank and was waiting in the queue when someone I've never met pulled me out of the line, greeted me by name and offered me a decent mug of mint tea! (How did they know?) Somehow they guessed I needed a car loan and led me off to a rather groovy lime green sofa where they gave me all the essential information. I was also asked to talk into a voice recorder to make sure I filled out the form truthfully. This is now mandatory on all loans.

There was no queue at the 'Gold customer' ATM so I verified my identity at the palm print verification panel and iris scanner. The machine recognised me and greeted me by name, so I withdraw about 500 GCUs (the new global currency unit). I usually wire this straight to my phone but this time I decided to play safe and hid the digital cash inside the tag in my shoe. I was then sent on my way clutching a leaflet about loans with my name on it, featuring a photo of the 246 GTS I'm thinking of buying. It also lists an interest rate and repayment table personally tailored to me. There was an advertisement playing on the wall for car loans as I was leaving the bank. It was interesting, but I was in a hurry, so I swiped the ad and took it home.

See you next year

Suzie

Five trends that will transform financial services

Mobile, pre-pay, and contactless payment   Convenience is
a mega-trend that will transform banking and insurance just like
every other industry. Plastic is convenient; but once digital cash gets
moved into electronic devices, things really will be transformed.
Objects holding digital cash will include mobile phones and cars,
but there's no reason for the list not to include clothing and even
the human body. The pre-pay and embedded-value trend will also
extend to private currencies and barter schemes.

Intermediaries   If recent history has taught us anything it is
that, despite the need for convenience, people like to buy products
and services from specialists experienced in a particular sector
or able to provide an independent overview of the hundreds if
not thousands of products that are available. Hence independent
brokers will play an increasingly strong role, as will global
monolines that specialise in just one area of the financial-services
market. In other words, independence, impartiality, transparency,
and specialist expertise will be big in the future.

Debt   There are some people who believe we have entered
an indefinite economic boom; hence, cycles of boom and bust
have ended. I don't agree. Eventually there will be a major global
recession (global because every economy is now hyper-linked and
interdependent). And when it does come, the severity and hardship
will be almost unprecedented because of the amount of debt built
up by individuals, corporations, and even entire countries. When
will this happen? Impossible to say, but we should all be planning

for it. Businesses that will do well in such a situation include local lenders and banks with physical branches. Why? Because customers will seek security and familiarity, ideally with a human face attached.

Regulation   Banks and especially credit-card companies do not generally discriminate about who they lend to, and individuals are not very smart about the amount of debt they take on board. When money is very cheap, this doesn't really matter. If interest rates go up, it does. As society becomes more risk-adverse and litigious, governments will seek to protect their citizens (and their own financial liabilities) by tightly regulating the entire industry. Big banks, in particular, will come under increasing scrutiny about their lending practices, and there will be calls for salary and profit caps in some extreme instances. Smaller operators will be deluged by a sea of red tape, regulation, and compliance requirements, and will find it increasingly difficult to operate profitably. Large companies will similarly see their margins eroded, especially since they will have to support an increasingly large number of channels.

Foreign and non-bank competition   Until recently, banks, insurance companies, and other financial-service companies had it easy. Innovations within retail banking were more or less limited to longer opening-hours, telephone banking and, very recently, online banking. Beyond this, the internet has had very little impact on traditional business models within financial services, but this will change in the future; brands such as PayPal, Zopa, and Prosper are very much the shape of things to come. Also, expect to see hyper-competition in the sense that every major global player will attempt to enter every developed market, whether the local players — and local governments and unions — like it or not.

Chapter 6

Automotive and Transport: the end of the road as we know it

Warning: objects in the mirror may be closer than you think.
–Ford Motor Company

In the future, we will all drive cars that fly. Fifty years ago, that's what most people thought we'd all be doing today. Strangely, the idea persists. A cartoon entitled 'predictions for 2007' recently featured — you guessed it — dozens of flying cars, although what people were flying towards or from was far from clear. The car is perhaps one of the top ten most significant inventions of all time, dating from roughly the beginning of the twentieth century. Will it survive another century? The answer, I'd suggest, is yes, because it has to, although its form and precise purpose may change beyond all recognition. Last century the car was important because it symbolised freedom and mobility. But ask a twelve- or eighteen-year-old today what symbolises these ideals, and they'd probably name the internet and the mobile phone. So perhaps what will happen in the future is that our freedom and mobility will become virtual. Physical movement will become an optional extra. The open road will be replaced by open source, and our need for speed and convenience replaced by virtual worlds and online delivery. But not quite yet. The combustion engine still has a few kilometres left in it.

The automotive industry, along with the oil industry, is a dinosaur roaming the Earth looking for what's left of its food supply. As with all large creatures, the industry is slow to move and adapt to changing environments and conditions; so I'd predict that, while changes will be made (bio-fuels, hybrid vehicles, hydrogen power, and ceramic batteries, for example), another industry will most probably reinvent the wheel in the twenty-first century — the high-tech industry. As cars move away from the internal-combustion engine and become mobile-technology platforms, car companies will become vulnerable because their knowledge of computers, batteries, and electronics is so far behind the high-tech industry. Then, again, perhaps we'll see a mega-merger between the old and the new, with a company like General Motors being acquired by Microsoft, or Toyota acquiring Apple, so as to deliver technologies to drivers via their dashboards.

Re-inventing the wheel

From a technological perspective, the car you drive today will be very far removed from the one you might have access to forty of fifty years hence. The shape will be slightly familiar, although the materials the car will be made of will be as foreign to most people as a Lexus would have appeared to someone in the 1880s. First of all, most of the panels will be constructed from biodegradable plastic made from the starch found in potatoes and rice. (When you've finished with them, you could theoretically bury them in your garden to simply rot down into garden compost.) The panels will also be made using nanotechnology, meaning they will remember the shape they are supposed to be, so dents will fix themselves. The colour will no longer be sprayed on in a separate and time-consuming batch process either, but will be programmable by the owner, much in the same way that an iPod operates. In other words, you will be able to set the colour of your car to change each week depending on your mood. The 'paint' will be self-repairing, in that if it gets scratched or chipped the colour will simply flow over the damaged area, making it look as good as new, and the exterior will wash and dry itself every time it rains.

There will be a safety override, too, so that if the weather turns nasty or there is an accident up ahead the car will sense this and automatically change itself from, say, silver, to a safer, more visible colour like white or yellow. Things will be pretty colourful on the inside, too. Given the amount of effort that carmakers have traditionally put into colour forecasting, it's surprising that the interior lighting of automobiles and other vehicles has received so little attention to now. Or perhaps not. Most people spend a lot of time and money discussing what colour to paint the inside of their house, but lighting is given virtually no thought whatsoever. In the future, the lighting inside cars will be fully programmable and, again, will automatically adjust according to the conditions inside and outside.

This means that if you select the 'sport' gearbox option in a luxury saloon the interior and exterior lighting may change to a safer and more visible intensity, but the car will also override these selections if it feels you are a threat to other road users. This means that, in the future, vehicles (and other machines, for that matter) will be mood sensitive and will adjust themselves to their owner's feelings. For example, if traffic conditions deteriorate (or you receive a phone call that puts you in an anxious or stressful mood), the vehicle will compensate with relaxing dashboard instrumentation, anti-stress lighting, and chill-out sounds. Either that or a spy in the sky will somehow recognise that you are a danger to yourself and other road users, and you will receive a message through your radio stating that, 'Your speed has been reduced for your own safety. Thank you for your co-operation'.

The opposite will be true, too, in the sense that military vehicles will use 'active' camouflage systems to disguise themselves from the enemy by projecting video or still images of the surrounding area onto themselves so as to appear invisible. More alarmingly, military vehicles and aircraft will probably change their interiors to 'combat mode' when an attack is imminent so as to make their operatives more aggressive and focused.

Back in civilian street, safety will continue to compete with its nemesis, speed, with car manufacturers falling over themselves to offer the latest in high-tech safety features, including collision avoidance. Historically, car safety has generally been focused on keeping the driver and his or her passengers alive in the event of a crash. This has meant higher and higher levels of crash and rollover protection, safety cells, airbags, and improved seatbelt technology. However, drivers have become so cocooned from the world outside that they have started to become a real danger to both themselves and other road users. Indeed, as someone once remarked to me, the safest car in the world wouldn't feature any seatbelts at all, but would simply have a sharp metal spike sticking out of the centre of the steering wheel. Thus there will be a shift towards protecting other road users, especially pedestrians, and the prevention of accidents, which will mean the mainstreaming of 'sixth sense' technologies such as lane-departure warning systems (43 per cent of all crashes are the result of vehicles straying into the wrong lane or off the road completely), skid-avoidance, automatic speed adaptation, and anti-sleep alert devices. However, drivers are already so overloaded with information that, unless this information is delivered by touch or smell, it's highly likely to be ignored.

Sleep is already becoming a major issue for the automotive

industry worldwide as more and more drivers become tired, thanks to the relentless march of technologies that are always on, such as email and mobile phones.

In New Jersey, judges can jail drivers who fall asleep at the wheel and go on to injure or kill others, and it looks as if sleepy driving will become the new drink-driving in the years ahead.

The problem, obviously, isn't people who are knowingly sleepy when they step into a car, but rather people who are more tired than they realise jumping into the driver's seat after an extra long day at work or perhaps after a weekend spent trying to recover from the week before. The problem is micro-sleeps rather than fully fledged naps. In Australia these so-called micro-sleeps often last for less than a few seconds, but are nevertheless responsible for an estimated 30 per cent of all road accidents. Solutions include infrared cameras to monitor eye movement, touch pads to monitor hand pressure on the steering wheel, and chassis technologies to monitor unusual directional movement. If a car thinks you are falling asleep there are already various things it can do to wake you up. These include blasts of cold air from the dashboard into the driver's face, audio alarms, vibrating seats, and our old friend, interior lighting. But don't hold your breath about any of this really working.

More low-tech solutions could include the mandatory requirement that all car journeys be shared. This is potentially a bit of a double-whammy solution because car-sharing has environmental benefits, too, but it's been found that people drive more safely when they are travelling with a passenger — especially if the driver is male and the passenger is female. According to German research, 44 per cent of men say they adjust their driving style when a female passenger is sitting in the car compared to just 29 per cent of women when a male passenger is sitting close by. Taking a scenic route has a similar effect, so in the future perhaps we will see cars that sense whether the driver is tired and then automatically divert themselves to country roads rather than motorways.

Road accidents killed 43,443 people in the US in 2006, and it is estimated that by 2020 road accidents will be the third-biggest global killer, second only to heart disease and depression, and overtaking both HIV and war. Unfortunately, this level of death and dismemberment is likely to increase due to several reasons.

First, drivers will face more distractions. The use of mobile phones is a well-known risk, and using a phone while driving increases your chance of being involved in an accident by 400 per cent (alcohol, by contrast, increases your risk by 200 per cent at a level of 0.06 per cent). This immediately begs the question of why talking to a passenger doesn't also increase your chances of having an accident. The answer is not completely clear, but it's likely to be because when people are on the telephone they enter something that Dr David Strayer (a psychologist at the University of Utah) calls the 'phone zone', a virtual-reality zone where people are momentarily transported to somewhere else outside their vehicle. Talking to a passenger, on the other hand, does not involve immigration to cyberspace and both parties are fully aware of each other's presence and the world outside. They also provide a handy second pair of eyes to notice potential hazards.

Phones and cars aren't going away for quite a while, so we can fully expect accidents due to mobile-phone use to continue despite the best efforts of the police and lawmakers. Indeed, the feeling among the general public is that using a handheld phone in a car is perfectly all right so long as you don't get caught. This attitude is similar to drink-driving twenty or thirty years ago, and it will probably take at least this long to stop people talking or texting while travelling.

I was recently driving at night down a major arterial road when up ahead I saw a red sports car with a strange glow coming from the driver in a parallel lane up ahead. Being somewhat curious, I inched forward in the traffic to see what might be causing the glow. After five minutes — in the rain, incidentally — I drew level and saw that the driver (the only occupant) was a smartly dressed woman in her late twenties. She was on the phone and smoking. But the light wasn't coming from her cigarette; it was coming from the laptop she had balanced on her legs, which she was occasionally typing into. I kid you not. I know nothing about actuarial tables of risk, but I'd guess that she was what you might call an accident waiting to happen.

Thankfully, she wasn't eating and drinking at the same time. In the US, eating while driving causes 30 per cent of all motor accidents, although only 57 per cent of drivers will admit to doing it. Often the problem isn't actually eating or drinking, but spilling your food or drink and trying to clean it up while still driving. In the US 15 per cent of all meals are eaten in cars, and the big fast-food chains typically generate between 50 to 60 per cent of sales from their drive-through windows, so this really is a big deal. Solutions, apart from obviously sitting down at a table for a meal, include the ubiquitous car cup-holder, and food and drink designed to be eaten or consumed on the move. Some automakers are even putting foldout tables into their vehicles, which are obviously not intended to be used by the driver, but there's nowt so stupid as folk, as my grandmother used to say. I've even seen a slow cooker that plugs into your cigarette lighter and cooks your evening meal while you drive home.

Of course, some of the best solutions to the growing problem of driver distraction and aggression will be very simple indeed. For example, 70 per cent of pedestrian deaths happen at night, so you'd think that a technology such as intelligent night vision would be a good idea. Two infrared cameras could be mounted at the front of a vehicle to sense 'warm' objects in the dark, and a computer could match these objects to a database of known shapes — such as humans. Distances would then be calculated almost instantly, and an alarm sounded to alert the driver to the impending risk. This is a very good idea, but an even better idea might be streets with absolutely no centre markings, no kerbs and no streetlights.

This probably sounds like a recipe for disaster, but it is actually a very serious experiment proposed by the Kensington and Chelsea Council in London. The theory is that if you remove all signs, drivers will become disorientated, and will slow down and start to think as a result. This obviously wouldn't work if the idea became common and expected, but in certain inner-city areas it could be a real winner. Add intelligent night vision, though, and it's back to removing the spike from the centre of the steering wheel.

So what else can car companies, councils, and lawmaker do to cut road deaths and accidents? The question is both real and urgent, not least because of the rapid growth in car ownership in countries such as India and China. In 1990 there were 1 million cars in China; by 2004 this had risen to 12 million; and by 2020 it's predicted that there will be 140 million. Moreover, China is also home to the world's third-largest road network, which wasn't even created until 1988. The result of all this is that there are millions of Chinese taking to the road for the first time, with low levels of safety awareness compared to other countries. The cost of road crashes in China is around $12.5 billion annually, which is more than the national budget for public health services or compulsory rural education, and road accidents kill an estimated 100,000 Chinese every year. And that's before car ownership explodes there.

But don't be fooled into thinking this is just a problem in emerging economies. In the UK, road accidents are currently the largest single cause of death for young men aged sixteen to twenty-four years of age, and the story is much the same in other countries, too. One idea that does seem to be working is that new drivers must drive with a qualified driver; but of course this can simply have the effect of killing more people, not fewer.

One answer is the sale of speed-restricted cars to learners or recently qualified drivers, although perhaps an even better idea is the use of a smart key or 'speed key', such as the one developed by Volvo. The idea here is that the (theoretically) responsible adult owner of the vehicle can program the maximum speed using a special key. In the future, similar devices will limit the maximum power or acceleration of vehicles, or even lock off certain geographical districts or destinations. However, like the key drivers have to blow into to test for alcohol before the engine will start, the device is open to abuse, either by an average twelve-year-old technical genius or by using another vehicle or key. A better idea might be the use of a steering wheel that can judge a driver's mood and adjust the maximum speed or acceleration accordingly. An idea similar to this already exists, whereby the steering wheel can test alcohol content merely by the driver touching the wheel. Too much alcohol, and the car simply won't start. But again there are problems: one can imagine two drivers trying to drive a car, one who's been drinking and one who hasn't, with one operating the steering wheel and one pressing the accelerator.

Other solutions include night-time bans on young or learner drivers and not allowing newly qualified drivers to carry passengers. Or what about simply passing a law that drivers under the age of twenty-five can only drive a single type of car, power restricted with added safety features? This would be unpopular, but possibly effective.

But, in the future, the problem may not be young drivers at all. Quite the opposite, in fact. Populations are ageing all over the world, and people are living longer and driving later than ever before. This ageing demographic will have a tremendous effect on how cars are designed and what laws are passed in the future. For instance, older drivers have problems with mobility, slowed reaction times, and poor vision. Hence better vehicular access (doors) and better forward, backward, and side vision will become an increasingly important engineering element, and the testing of older drivers will eventually become commonplace globally.

Ultimately, though, the solution to both older and younger driver safety will be to take the necessity of driving away from the driver altogether. Along with flying cars, self-driving cars have been a feature of the sci-fi future for decades. Cars that drive themselves first appeared in the 1950s, although the idea was never really progressed beyond the concept stage for a number of legal, social, and technical reasons. Nevertheless General Motors claims it is building such a car and that it could be introduced as early as 2008. Fat chance — although if what GM is really talking about is adaptive cruise control, it's a possibility. This is essentially a system whereby the car recognises that there is another car in front, and sets a safe speed and distance using a clever mix of cameras and laser beams. If the car gets too close, the speed is reduced or the brakes are applied. Equally, if the car starts to stray out of its lane, the power steering corrects the mistake or else the driver is alerted using beeps, flashing lights, or vibrations. Of course, as with any early technical solution, there are problems. First, the technology won't work when there's no car in front (so it's not much use late at night or on country roads). More critically, there are serious legal implications to this type of technology. Last but by no means least, people actually like to drive their cars. Indeed, the car is probably the last private space available to ordinary people, and it's highly unlikely that drivers will give up the freedom to get stuck in traffic unless they are forced to, legally or financially.

One way drivers might be persuaded to let go of the wheel is to allow them to do other things inside their car instead. Cars are already moving towards being mobile information platforms with iPod connectivity and video screens, although much of the latter is aimed at backseat drivers. There is clearly a strong latent demand for people to talk on their mobile phones, read newspapers, and check email while they are driving, so why not let them do it? Cars will increasingly shift from transportation devices to information platforms, and anything you can currently do at work will ultimately be available inside a car — whether it's stationary, in a traffic jam, or flying down the highway at 100 kmph.

Gaming is another thing that drivers would undoubtedly do from the driver's seat if allowed. Once the strain of driving has been removed and most, if not all of the control is handed over to the vehicle (think of the autopilot in planes), dashboard controls and windscreens could be used for other purposes. There are obviously numerous safety concerns with ideas such as these — not least the sense of allowing someone to play a racing game inside a stationary car and then allowing them to drive on a real highway moments later. Nevertheless, the technological invasion of the family saloon is well underway, and we shouldn't forget the many possible benefits.

Goodbye, freeways; hello, payways

Once you start to think of cars, roads, and even parking spaces as a network rather than as individual objects, you open up all sorts of possibilities. Satellite tracking will set safe distances between cars, tell vehicles about congested routes, identify passengers who wish to car-share, and also find parking spaces in real time, setting a daily or hourly price for their use depending on demand. This could include private parking spaces in cities that could be released into public use if their owners could receive online bids for their use. Roads will obviously all be priced, too, with charges varying from nothing to rather a lot, again depending on real-time demand. If you want to drive at peak hour or get somewhere really fast in a so-called 'Lexus lane' then you'll pay. If, on the other hand, you are prepared to pick an unpopular time to travel, you won't pay nearly as much or perhaps nothing at all.

A more likely scenario is a mixture of public and private roads (economy and business class, if you like). The idea of private toll roads is nothing new — they have been around longer than the motorcar — and to some extent tolls have always been based on the idea that the use of toll roads is not compulsory. There is usually a free road or route available; but if you wish to travel across private land or use a specially constructed route to save time, you pay. Governments love this idea because they are growing tired of publicly financing infrastructure projects such as roads, tunnels, and bridges. So, in the future, if you want to wait — in a traffic jam, for instance — you will be free to do so, but if you hate to wait and want to use the faster route you'll pay through the nose.

There are obviously some meaty political issues here, not least because the public will increasingly be asked to pay to travel on roads they technically already own; but, generally, where there's a whiff of revenue, central governments, local councils, and investment banks won't be too far behind.

Embedding technology in vehicles — or using satellite spies to see where everyone is — will have some other benefits, too. The most interesting consequence is probably insurance. Previously, risk was calculated and premiums set using fairly crude measures such as where the vehicle was kept and what type of person or persons drove it. In the future this information will also include real-time data on where the car is twenty-four hours a day, who exactly is driving it, and what speed or driving style they are using. This is potentially bad news for privacy campaigners, but it does open up the possibility of pay-as-you-go insurance, with drivers able to buy insurance by the day or even by the kilometre from their local petrol station. Norwich Union Insurance is already conducting trials of a similar idea in the UK, whereby risks are calculated in real time and payment is made monthly in arrears bundled up with other services such as route planning and emergency roadside assistance.

Another idea already taking off is the pay-as-you-go car. The notion that everyone needs their own vehicle is beginning to sound faintly ridiculous, especially in cities, where lack of parking spaces and congestion charging are making other forms of public or group transport more logical.

However, you sometimes need a 'proper' car, so a number of companies are starting to spring up offering car-sharing services of one type or another. In the US, companies like Zipcar and Flexcar are growing at breakneck speed, partly it seems because small companies and businesses are trying to cut costs, and car-sharing makes more sense than traditional car rental or taxis. In Switzerland, 2 per cent of drivers already use such schemes, while in the UK car clubs like Smart Moves are lending cars to people for as little as £15 per month plus an hourly usage and kilometre charge. Better still, again because of remote-monitoring technology, there are companies that simply scatter share cars across a city. Users then find them via internet search (probably from their phone) and open the doors with either a membership card or a barcode contained within an SMS message. There's no paperwork, either, because the companies already know where you are and where you drive, so bills are sent automatically via email.

In the future, such services will operated by retailers like McDonald's (the owner of one of the largest number of parking spaces in the world) and apartment blocks, where each apartment will come with a part share in a vehicle — or a range of vehicles — parked underneath the building. We could even see apartment blocks exclusively built for petrol heads or classic car buffs with the above-ground architecture suitably in touch with the owners' sentiments, and a range of machinery underground to suit the tenants' whims and passions.

In other words, usership will shift from the individual to the group, and ownership will in many cases give way to rental or what some people call fractional ownership. Ten or fifteen years ago, you couldn't rent a classic car for love or money. The same was more or less true with exotica such as new Ferraris, Lamborghinis, and Aston Martins. Now you're spoilt for choice. In the UK alone, there are more than twenty companies renting classics like Jaguar E-types for the day or Porsche 911s for the week.

This is partly because people realise that actually owning something like this can be a headache (they break down and need constant care and attention), and therefore partial ownership or rental makes more sense. In effect, this is timeshare for classic cars. At the upper end of the market, it can also make more financial sense to buy a share in a $500,000 car — which, to be honest, you'll hardly ever use because you're always at work trying to pay for it— than to buy what is generally a depreciating asset outright.

Speeding up and slowing down

However, there is something much more interesting than dollars and cents going on here, especially with the boom in classic-car ownership and rental. What I think is happening is that cars have now become so technologically advanced and packed with electronic features that they have lost their souls. Cars are an emotional purchase, and customers are longing for the past when cars (and the world) were easy to understand. There is a simple element of nostalgia going on here — people (especially men) in their forties and fifties are longing for the cars they dreamt about and couldn't afford when they were growing up. But there's more to it than that.

In the US one of the latest trends is teens buying 'grandpa' cars. Teenagers are purchasing cars like Chevrolets, Buicks, Oldsmobiles, and Cadillacs from the 1970s and 1980s, partly because they are cheap, partly because they are so 'out' they're 'in', and also because they are simple to understand and easy to fix. There are no on-board computers or sealed boxes of electronics, and mechanically minded owners can work on (and, crucially, customise) them themselves. Another explanation for the trend is the influence of TV shows such as MTV's 'Pimp My Ride', but I'm sure the main reason is probably a combustible mixture of low cost, simplicity, and nostalgia. There is even a new magazine in the US dedicated to tricked-out old motors (*Donk, Box & Bubble*).

Manufacturers like Ford are all too aware of this trend, but it's very difficult to make something simple. It involves uninventing technologies, so the idea of re-creating a perfect copy of a 1960s Mustang or Ford GT40 with re-manufactured mechanicals will inevitably end up as a new twenty-first century version packed with every gizmo and device under the sun.

Another good example of the power of nostalgia and simplicity is a small chain of fix-it-yourself garages in France. 'O' Garage is for people who own cars but don't have garages or tools. The garages are fully equipped professional workshops that can be rented for an hour, a day, or a week, and help is available on site if you don't know your wishbones from your brake discs. Given the boom in domestic outsourcing (that is, paying people to do things you are perfectly capable of doing yourself), this is a bit contrary, but I'm sure it's connected to a new need to get your hands dirty. As life becomes more and more technical and virtual, more people will crave simple physical tasks. So perhaps carmakers should throttle back a bit on the computer-enhanced engine-management systems, and design cars with an element that owners can fiddle with themselves.

I suspect carmakers are already onto this, in a sense. We've had retro car design for years (not quite the same thing I've been talking about), but there is a new trend on the horizon. According to *Car* magazine, the next big thing is local design. Ever since car companies went global (a long time ago) and started using computers rather than pencils to design cars, cars have started to look remarkably similar. Take the badge off a Hyundai and replace it with a Honda badge, and most people wouldn't notice the difference. Moreover, it's virtually impossible to tell where the car has come from, as they all look like the product of a world-design studio. This wasn't always the case. Once upon a time, a British car could only have been made in Britain, and the same was true with cars from France, Germany, Italy, and the US. However, global markets, CAD design, and worldwide focus groups changed all that. But not so in the future.

As with food and wine — and increasingly everything else — people want to know where things have come from. Provenance is important, and localisation is becoming a strong countertrend to globalisation. Hence, car-makers are rediscovering their roots, and in the future cars will once again look and feel like local products, even if they are made and sold internationally.

Suburban living

Another thing we'll see in the future — or, more precisely, won't — is tunnels. Put simply, the cost of tunnelling is going down. This means that cross-city tunnels and, ultimately, underground cities, will become increasingly common. This should delight futurists from the 1920s and 1930s who foresaw similar urban landscapes, and certainly gives new meaning to the phrase 'suburban living'. By lowering the air pressure in long tunnels beneath the streets, friction is reduced, which could also have significant benefits in terms of achievable fuel consumption and top speeds (the latter more for trains than cars).

Future urban design will dramatically influence the way we travel in other ways, too. First and foremost, there will be a slow shift back towards public or mass transport. This will partly be because of urban congestion, but also because of environmental pressure. Private car-owners will be edged out of cities due to a mixture of social stigma and taxation. The British government recently increased the level of road tax paid by owners of four-wheel drives, resulting in a dramatic drop in their second-hand value. Superficially, this is because four-wheel drives are petrol-guzzlers that pollute the environment. In the US, a direct-action group called the Detroit Project has even accused four-wheel-drive owners of promoting terrorism on the basis that they consume more than their fair share of oil reserves, thereby making the US more reliant on foreign oil — which in turn provokes US military action in the Middle East.

Meanwhile, the Alliance Against Urban 4x4s is hell-bent on harassing drivers of four-wheel drives, while the New Economics

Foundation (a UK think-tank) has described them as 'Satan's little run-arounds'. But is this so? A typical spin in a 4WD emits less than half the CO_2 produced by a dishwasher on an economy cycle — but we don't label dishwasher owners as 'selfish' or 'greedy'. Equally, the little electric cars that whiz around cities are not quite as saintly as most people think. In most cases, the electricity to power these 'green' vehicles comes from — you've guessed it — giant coal-based, oil-burning, or gas-burning power stations, so where's the logic in that? Better still, what about air conditioning? America has less than 5 per cent of the global population, but consumes 25 per cent of the world's electricity; and the use of air conditioning is responsible for a third of that energy use, or 8 per cent of global energy consumption. But nobody (yet) is proposing that air-conditioning users should pay additional carbon taxes.

Carbon offsetting is becoming one of the fastest-growing businesses worldwide. This is where numerous companies promise to offset your guilt by planting trees or investing in green energy schemes. But do these schemes work? The answer, it seems, is that nobody really knows. Official offset schemes — those sanctioned by the Kyoto agreement and used by companies and countries — are strictly enforced and time-limited. Private or individual offsetting schemes are not. Moreover, because most schemes (especially the tree-planting variety) are essentially an exercise in time-shifting emissions into the future (offset futures, if you like) nobody can be quite certain what will happen to these 'investments' over time. For example, back in 2002 the rock band Coldplay planted 10,000 trees to offset the production of their album 'A Rush of Blood to the Head'. Almost half of the trees died. Not only is this a problem, but planting trees can cause other problems. Outside the tropics, dark-leaved forest canopies can absorb more heat than the individual tress can offset, thereby making global warming worse. This is not to say that doing something is worse than doing nothing; simply that selling carbon-offsets as a quick solution is not helpful, especially when the real name of the game is not offsetting but cutting the emissions themselves.

We are already seeing direct-action groups targeting owners of certain types of car, and in the future you can expect to see this vilification intensify to include mass boycotts of certain car manufacturers because of the models they make. Indeed, companies may have to restrict access to certain vehicles or ensure that they are only used in certain places or specific ways. In the UK, another think-tank has seriously suggested that owners of four-wheel drives be forced to carry health-warning stickers on their vehicles, while Greenpeace activists have chained themselves to the gates of a Range Rover factory to demonstrate against 'climate criminals'. But again, why is this happening? Perhaps the attacks have more to do with middle-class anger and envy against the aspirant working class or the semi-idle rich.

What has also been overlooked in this battle seems to be why people drive these vehicles in the first place. Generally speaking, I'd suggest that most urban 4WD owners drive their cars because they feel safe in them and because the driving position engenders a sense of control. Taking a long-term view, neither of these desires is going to go away. As life becomes less safe and more uncertain, people will continue to desire mobile fortresses. The downside, though, is that if people perceive themselves to be safer, they may be inclined to take more risks — which brings us back to the safety issue once again.

Two of the fastest-growing segments of the car market in recent years have been small cars and four-wheel drives. Both are relatively safe, especially if they crash into each other, but the problem is that they frequently don't. Large cars crashing into small ones (and old cars crashing into new ones) are becoming a serious problem, as older or smaller cars will generally come off much worse.

One future solution to this is a world car in one size only, but I don't seriously expect this idea to ever be acceptable. A more likely scenario is restricting certain car sizes or types to certain locations.

So if you live in a city, perhaps you will be forced to buy an electric or hybrid vehicle with certain legally enforceable dimensions and safety features. If, on the other hand, you live out of town, your vehicle choice changes. Better still, perhaps drivers who repeatedly have accidents will be forced to drive certain types of car or be demoted to L-plates and small vehicles until they establish a safe-driving record.

Can't see the road for the trees

Thirty years hence, one can imagine a situation where drivers of petrol-fuelled cars will be forced to pay for the oxygen the engine uses as well as for the petrol. This is already happening, in a sense, with carbon credits being given to countries such as Brazil that own 'oxygen reserves'. The desire to be green has trickled down from countries through companies to the private car owner. There are now green car loans, green car hire companies, and even green car insurance. Most of this is gimmickry gone mad, but bio-fuels and hybrid cars (and, ultimately, hydrogen-powered cars) are all here already or are coming over the next few decades or so. Alternative energy is certainly a hot topic right now, and there is little or no indication that the bubble is about to burst. However, what's often forgotten is that the ideas are nothing new.

Rudolf Diesel, for example, displayed an engine at the Paris Exhibition of 1900 that ran on peanut oil, and Henry Ford was a fan of ethanol fuels back in the 1920s. The point here is that, contrary to predictions of doom and gloom, the car is not about to be killed off due to a lack of fuel. There will be arguments in the future about what the fuels should be, and many people will migrate from private to public transport. There will also be an increasingly vociferous debate about whether plants should be grown to fuel vehicles or feed people. But a lack of oil alone will not kill off the internal-combustion engine.

Whatever the detail (and whatever happens to the price of oil in the short to medium term), it's a very safe bet that the development of new fuels will be one of the largest breakthroughs in automotive innovation over the next fifty years. The reason for this is mainly political. The US, China, Japan, and most of Europe have become too reliant on Middle Eastern and Russian oil, and they need to create some level of fuel security through the invention or discovery of other fuels or reserves.

Asia is expected to account for nearly 40 per cent of global car sales and more than half of the world's car production by 2020. You should take this prediction with a pinch of salt because the figures are based on a simple linear extrapolation. Nevertheless, many car manufacturers are attempting to get into the market — essentially China, but also India and Indonesia — by launching small, ultra-low-cost cars there. At the forefront of this competition is Tata Motors, which aims to have a five-seater priced at just US$2,200 for sale by 2008. Such a low-cost vehicle could have enormous appeal in India, a country where over 56 million citizens earn just $4,400 annually. But it's not just about selling cars.

Tata is interesting because it plans to involve local mechanics as franchisers for partially or fully knocked down car kits, which can then be assembled and sold onsite. However, the extra production of oil and carbon emissions will cause problems if countries like China and India do indeed turn into the giant car markets that many car-makers and analysts predict.

Personally, I don't think that linear extrapolations of current demand can tell you very much about the distant future; it's quite likely that things will evolve in a way unseen by industry experts and analysts. China, for instance, may skip over the need for oil, and develop hydrogen power instead, thereby decreasing its strategic dependence on unstable regions such as Russia, Africa, and the Middle East. Alternatively, China and/or India could falter economically, resulting in millions of new vehicles remaining unsold.

What we'll certainly see in the more immediate future is a boom in car sharing, fractional ownership, electric bicycles (especially in India and China), and the reinvention of the humble pedal-bike, especially in Europe.

We'll also see the emergence of some very clever new business models applied to transport, most likely using the internet and other forms of mobile communication to connect people wishing to travel to roughly the same place at roughly the same time. Pricing and routes will become increasingly variable, dependent on demand, but equally there will still be a certain level of status attached to using a private vehicle. So, in other words, it's not the death of driving as such, but it's certainly the end of the road as we know it.

Being an optimist, I also think that it wouldn't be the end of the world if the oil ran out tomorrow and we were unable to find an alternative. According to the UK Department of Transport, over the period 1980–2004, people in all income groups became much more mobile. Road traffic increased by 81 per cent over the period; rail trips, by 43 per cent; and air travel overseas, from 18 million to 64 million trips. However, walking and cycling both declined over the same period (walking by about 20 per cent), which coincided with an increase in obesity among both adults and children. So perhaps the silver lining could be a stronger, fitter planet. This probably won't happen because innovation thrives on a crisis — so the end of oil will be a spur for all sorts of activity and imagination, but you never know.

14 April 2047

Dear Yofi

You won't believe this. I was at a garage in downtown Los Angeles at 2.00 a.m this morning with a group of eight men of all ages looking in awe at a 1949 Mercury Sedan. The vehicle's a museum piece, but that's not why we were there. The owner (Steve) was planning to do an illegal run up the highway running the car on petrol. As you know, petrol is pretty rare these days but you can still buy it from various illegal sources. The petrol for last night's run came from a guy outside of San Francisco who discovered how to extract it from vintage plastic shopping bags dug up from a Mexican landfill.

Steve started the car up. Man, that engine sounded unlike anything I've ever heard! You know how you can buy software to make those silent electric cars sound like old petrol engine sports cars from the last century? Well, let me tell you, they're a pale imitation of the real thing! The exterior of the car is made of metal and is painted bright red and inside it smelt gorgeous — a mixture of oil and leather. Five of the guys jumped into the car and slowly inched it out onto the yellow road. The road was confused because it didn't recognise the vehicle. But since it was dark and the car doesn't have positioning or speed indicators it couldn't be tracked from above, so the only thing they had to worry about was an automated police vehicle. They had about fifteen minutes before one of these would pass by. Steve floored the throttle (what a noise!) and blasted off into the night, much to the delight of those of us left behind.

Afterwards I went outside and sprinkled the contents of a small packet onto the roadway. Within seconds nanobots had assembled a fully functioning vehicle atom by atom. Just $999.95 from Tesco-Mart.

What a night!

Regards

Alexei

Five trends that will transform transport

Embedded intelligence   Cars can already be opened or started using fingerprint and iris recognition, so we'll see more technologies linking vehicle security to user identification. We will also see 'mood sensitive' vehicles that adjust their behaviour according to the mood of the driver or occupants. Cars will also become mobile-technology platforms linking data to other services such as healthcare. For example, if your car regularly detects an abnormal heartbeat or high levels of stress, this information could be sent wirelessly to your doctor. Obviously, privacy issues abound, but cars could become useful data-collection and delivery points.

Remote monitoring   Electronic data recorders are little black boxes that already covertly sit inside some cars and monitor your speed, acceleration and braking. When you have an accident the data contained within these boxes can be used by police or your insurance company to see who did what. Similarly, networkcar.com allows people to remotely track who's in their car and where it's going and at what speed. So, for example, you can find out where your husband really is or what speed your son is driving at. In the future all cars will be automatically tracked from space, making no journey entirely private. The good news in all this is that real-time data on where a car is and what it's doing will revolutionise the car theft recovery and car insurance industries and will drive various location-based services such as pay-as-you-go insurance.

Driverless cars   Don't expect this any time soon, but by about 2035 we will see cars capable of driving themselves with minimal interference from the driver. Cars will also travel in 'social groups' and correspond with other vehicles about conditions ahead or alternative routes. Of course, if drivers don't need to drive, this will open up a whole host of entertainment and information possibilities. Drivers (and passengers) will be able to turn sections of the car into mobile offices or part of their home, with video and music on demand, and email services and food and drink all on tap.

The environment   Climate change, urbanisation, and resource shortages — most notably, oil — will fuel a shift away from large petrol-engine cars to small electric cars and hybrid vehicles. There will also be a boom in cheap cars and bikes in emerging countries. Tax rates, licence charges, car-loan rates, and parking charges will increasingly be linked to vehicle type, and we will see even more anti-car and anti-driver sentiment and regulation in the future. This will be a catalyst for car-sharing schemes, green car rental, green car loans, and green car insurance. Conversely, though, there will also continue to be a demand for luxury cars and sports cars for at least the next decade or until the current global economic boom runs out of steam.

Reinvention of public transport   It would seem logical that, as urban roads and parking spaces fill up, there will be a growth in public transport. However, the car is so linked to ideas of individualism, freedom, private space, and personal identity that we are unlikely to give up private car ownership in the short term. For example, in the UK 70 per cent of people still drive to work. In theory, high oil prices should stop people from driving private cars, but that's what people said twenty-five years ago. From a sustainability point of view, the future must see the reinvention of public transport on a mass scale, but people won't embrace the idea until governments start thinking long term and build safe, clean, convenient, and affordable networks. This means services that link supply and cost to real-time demand, and it also means politicians actually using these services themselves.

Chapter 7

Food and Drink:
faster *and* slower

If enough people predict something it won't happen.
—J. G. Ballard

A little while ago I was sitting in on a research debrief concerning the attitudes and behaviour of twenty-somethings. The highlight, for me at least, was a video clip of a young man complaining about the time it took to get served in McDonald's. 'I mean, you go in there and place your order and sometimes you have to wait, like, almost two minutes … and they call it fast food.'

In 1950, some people were predicting that the world was going to run out of food. The Earth's population was exploding, and the result was going to be starvation on an unprecedented scale unless scientists could create synthetic alternatives to naturally farmed foods. Hence we would all be consuming techno-foods produced in laboratories and ingested in tablet form. Half a century or more later, though, and most of us are living in a world characterised by abundance, not scarcity, and the major public-health issue for the developed world is too much food, not too little. Part of the reason for this shift is technological. As a race, we have learnt how to apply scientific knowledge to farming, with the result that agricultural yields have skyrocketed and the cost of food has declined. For example, while the world's population has indeed exploded, doubling since 1950, cereal yields have tripled while the total amount of land under cultivation has hardly changed.

Of course, there are still hundreds of millions of hungry people, but this situation is improving, too. There are currently 800 million undernourished people on the planet, but this is expected to fall to around 600 million by 2025. Moreover, by 2050 the global population will level off at around 9 billion, taking some of the pressure off natural habitats being turned into farmland. Having said this, there are still problems ahead. As countries develop and people become richer, their diets tend to change. Out go cereals like rice, and in come protein-rich foods such as red meat, which are 'hungry' in terms of land use and water. One solution is to switch to fish, but here the situation is even worse. According to the UN, almost 50 per cent of the ocean's fish are already close to the limits of sustainability, and another 28 per cent are either over-fished or nearing extinction. How then will we meet the demand for fish, which is expected to increase by 50 per cent between now and 2020?

Some of this future demand will be met by fish farming (30 per cent of global demand is already met this way), but land-based fish management is proving unpopular for a number of environmental and political reasons. What we'll start to see, therefore, is the farming of fish in open oceans — gigantic cages of fish floating around the world's ocean currents, feeding on natural prey until they are large enough to be hauled up onto similarly huge factory ships.

Is 'fish ranching' a good thing? When compared with people not having enough to eat, probably yes; and while there are some very real concerns about semi-farmed fish mingling with the wild variety, people are ultimately more important than fish — or at least humans lives are more important than the genetic purity of plants or animals. It's progress; get over it.

Back on dry land we'll see some dramatic changes, too. 'Precision agriculture' is an idea whereby farmland is monitored and controlled metre by metre with seeds sown at exactly the correct time, and fertilisers and pesticides applied almost on a plant-by-plant basis.

Similar techniques exist for cattle, whereby individual herds can be monitored and controlled by satellites, and the history of an individual animal can be tracked from paddock to plate. RFID chips are one way to do this, but an even better way is to test for DNA. However, in the future, the dining tables will be turned. At present, RFID chips are a logistical tool used by supermarkets and their suppliers. In the future, customers will tap into these chips to monitor where their food is from and how it was produced.

DNA testing is not something the average person currently has access to, either. For example, there is already a test available called FoodExpert ID that can test for the presence of 32 common animals (including humans) in foodstuffs. The test can be used to test for food contamination such as the presence of pork in kosher foods or to identify meat cheats that bulk out chicken with beef waste. In the future, such tests will be available to ordinary individuals like you and me who just want to know what we're eating for dinner.

However, it's genetically modified (GM) crops that will really change the agricultural landscape in the future. So far, the reaction to GM crops has been quite hostile, especially in Europe; but many new technologies encounter resistance when first introduced, and it's highly likely that the arguments against GM will fall away once the benefits are widely understood and safety fears addressed. Entire books have been written on GM food, but suffice it to say that some of the products ultimately delivered by GM technology will be suitably futuristic. Apart from crops with built-in disease and drought resistance, it's likely we will see foods stripped of 'problematic' properties (allergen-free nuts, for instance) and foods with added health-related properties such as memory-enhancing vegetables for older people. Some of these so-called 'nutraceuticals' and 'farmaceuticals' will undoubtedly justify their existence, but one does wonder if the world really needs appetite-suppressing toothpaste and breakfast cereals that treat acne. Still, it's all food for thought.

Why have we become so interested in food all of a sudden? One reason is our increasing interest in personal and environmental health. Food has become a consumer issue tied up with everything from politics and globalisation to fashion, economics, and national identity. And it is this last point that's often overlooked. Recent debates about immigration and ethnicity have thrown the spotlight onto culinary heritage, and food has become mixed up with trends ranging from tribalism and well-being to nostalgia and nationalism. This means we'll see everything from food terrorism and the rise of food-related, single-issue action groups to backward-looking, nostalgic food products.

One development that's definitely coming is personalised food; but, again, this will come in two flavours, so to speak. At the serious end we'll see diets and foodstuffs tailored to our individual genetic make-up or medical history. If, like me, you have high blood pressure, it will be possible (perhaps even compulsory) to eat a range of ordinary (even indulgent) foods modified to treat this particular condition. Equally, nanotechnology will allow us to change the properties of an individual product at will, so you can increase the vitamin E content of an orange-juice drink after you've bought it.

At the silly end of the spectrum we'll also see nanotechnology being used to store certain ingredients or additives inside food products to be called up all at will. For instance, you may wish to change the colour of your soft drink or dial up the spice level of your ready-to-eat curry by firing a command off your mobile phone. None of this is going to happen next week but, sure as eggs are eggs, if you can dream it you'll be able to do it.

But back to now. What are we already seeing in food that we'll see more of in the immediate future? For starters, we'll be eating fewer meals at home and eating more snacks between home and work. In the US 15 per cent of meals are already eaten in cars and roughly 60 per cent of fast-food breakfast sales are made at the drive-through window. 'Grazing' — a buzzword in the 1980s and 1990s — is now being replaced by phrases like 'portability', 'eating-on-the-hoof', and 'drive-by-dining'. The reason for this is primarily that we're time-starved, but it's also linked to other societal shifts like the social acceptability of eating in the street while walking (unthinkable a generation ago).

As a result, we are seeing food manufacturers develop a host of new products in 'portable packs' to be eaten on the go, although whether food companies are creating demand or responding to it is somewhat unclear. Hence chocolate bars and other snacks are now available in cup-holder packaging so you can eat while driving (if the fat-laden crisps don't kill you directly, the car in front probably will). Meanwhile, 50 per cent of soup is now consumed outside the home, whereas a few years ago the figure was just 2 per cent. By the way, if you're wondering about driving while consuming hot soup, don't worry: the trend is primarily for office-based consumption. Speed and convenience (together with anxiety about health) will also drive plain-language labelling over the next few years, together with small-plate meals and single-course restaurants.

But a lack of time isn't just shifting consumption away from the home; it will also change how people shop for food and even what people eat in restaurants. We are already seeing growth in online supermarket shopping and home-food delivery, and this will increase in the future. As a result there will be two types of food shopping: the regular weekly or monthly repeat buying of items consumed day-in, day-out (most of which will eventually go online with automated ordering, shopping lists, and delivery), and impulse buying, where we shop for premium foods and meals in highly sensory, high-touch environments.

How fast our food gets will, of course, depend on where we are and what we are willing to pay for convenience. Fast-food companies such as McDonald's, Burger King, and Taco Bell are currently testing a product from Hyperactive Technologies that can predict what you eat based on the car that you drive. A camera 'reads' your car model as you enter the drive-in, and it compares this data with what drivers of similar cars have ordered in the past. An order is then sent to the kitchen, which starts preparing your meal before you've ordered it, thus saving you vital minutes. Clearly the model isn't perfect, but it's good enough to interest the fast-food companies because wait times have dropped by at least sixty seconds.

Interestingly, staff retention levels have also improved because kitchen stress-levels have declined. So how about a supermarket that 'reads' its customers the moment they walk into a store? This is quite likely. Tesco in the UK has 13 million Tesco Clubcard holders, so asking customers to swipe their cards when they enter a store would provide vital information about what they are about to buy. If you could then predict a sudden rush on white-bread sales within the next two minutes, shelf facings and special offers could be adjusted accordingly. And that's before you start introducing RFID cards that can be read remotely (no need to swipe them) or software that compares customer body size and shape (and clothing) to what similar-looking customers have bought in the past.

A trend sweeping the US at the moment, and certain to appear elsewhere fairly soon, is the do-it-yourself dinner shop. Also known as fix-and-freeze companies, these are stores where time-hungry customers concerned about what they are eating purchase pre-prepared ingredients for assembly in the store. Leading the field is Dream Dinners, which has grown from around fifty stores in 2005 to approximately 160 in 2006. Competitors include Let's Dish, Super Suppers, Dinner by Design, and Really Cool

Foods. While the names and menus may differ from company to company, the setup is essentially the same: customers go online to choose a range of dishes and book an appointment to visit the store. Once there, they assemble their meals from pre-cut colour-coded ingredients, customising them to suit their particular taste or dietary requirements. If they need help it's available, and meals are packaged and ready for the freezer, complete with full cooking instructions and use-by dates. The idea behind these self-assembly food stores is that they allow time-starved people to provide their family and friends with a nutritious hot meal at a lower cost than take-away or supermarket dinners. There's no time spent shopping; there's minimal cleaning-up afterwards; and because you only buy what you use, there's minimal waste. If you want organic, you can have it; and if you're really pressed for time you can cook up a whole month's worth of meals and have them delivered to your door.

There's another possible explanation for the success of these food stores. It could be argued that the social aspects of meal preparation (women usually visit the stores in small groups) are compensation for increasing loneliness or that the hands-on participatory nature of this type of cooking compensates for increasingly virtual and remote lives.

Strangely, something else we'll see in the future is less choice. One problem with abundance is that there's just too much of it, a point well made by Barry Schwartz in *The Paradox of Choice*. He argues that having too many options is paralysing our ability to make quick and meaningful decisions. One solution to this in a supermarket is simply to throw out any product that doesn't offer a real point of difference or to replace the countless 'me-too' brands with private-label alternatives. Another solution is to heavily edit or curate what's available. For example, Ranking Ranqueen in Tokyo is a small chain of stores in which everything is sold by lists. For example, the store only sells the 'Top Five Pasta Sauces', 'Top Five soups', and so on. Taken to the extreme, this will mean stores that only sell one type of cheese, although perhaps the variety might rotate from week to week. This, too, is already happening, and we are also starting to see restaurants that offer very little choice. Salt restaurant in New York gives diners the choice of just two main courses, and Clarke's in London generally offers just a couple of fish, meat, and vegetarian alternatives. This, of course, is an excellent example of how some trends go in cycles. If someone opened a restaurant tomorrow on the basis that high-flying city types were stressed out from making decisions during the day so they need a restaurant that makes all the decisions for them (no choice at all), I suspect that some people would regard this as an innovation. The reality is, of course, that this is exactly how things used to be. The menu was made up each day according to what was available at the market, and there was next to no choice because holding stock or preparing ingredients that might or may not get used was expensive.

So if there's anyone out there thinking of setting up a restaurant called Red or White, where the only choice is the colour of the meat and the wine, I suggest you do it very soon before someone else does.

One final point on restaurants is that in the future they will become much more savvy in terms of getting people to spend money. It's reasonably well known, for example, that playing certain types of music can change a person's mood. Classical music makes diners feel rich and sophisticated, and they tend to be willing to pay more for their meal as a result. Pop music, in contrast, makes people less willing to spend, although one suspects that everything depends on the age of the particular customer, the type of restaurant, and which specific piece of music is being played. This is all perfectly legal, although in the future food retailers may be tempted to push the boundaries. Food, after all, is very good at influencing mood, but I'm not just talking about the difference between eating proteins or carbohydrates or the mystical properties of chocolate. Adding tryptophan and valerian acid to desserts and petit fours, for instance, would make customers more relaxed and therefore happier about paying a large bill.

The relationship between mood and food is well known in food-industry circles and is slowly making an impact at the customer level, too. One of the first instances was the link between food colourings and hyperactivity in children, but we have only started to scratch the surface in terms of which foods do what and how they are sold as a result. A good example comes from a supermarket in the UK that noticed a spike in sales of foods such as broccoli at the same time every year. At first the supermarket couldn't work out what was going on, until it realised that the sales spike coincided with school examination periods. What was happening, of course, was that word had got out that broccoli was a brainfood, and anxious mothers were force-feeding it to their youngsters as a study aid.

Naughty but nice

Future developments will include other brain-enhancing foods (initially using omega 3 oils), foods that aid relaxation (such as chocolate with added amino acids), anti-ageing products, anti-tiredness foods, foods that send you to sleep, and foods that wake you up. We could even see dream-enhancing foods and foods designed to trigger specific childhood memories. People will also tap into moods by treating themselves with sensual self-indulgences. This will drive an interest in luxury food products and foods that are good because they're bad for you, if that makes any sense at all.

We'll also see more foods targeted at older people. One of the biggest trends affecting people in developed nations is ageing — particularly the increase in numbers of people over sixty, many of whom find it difficult to chew or swallow, or have very specific dietary requirements. As a result, we'll see more foods such as ice cream specifically developed for seniors, or crossover foods such as easy-to-eat vegetables and fruit purees that can be eaten by babies and seniors alike.

For people over about forty-five, food will increasingly be linked to well-being and medicine, which means body repair and longevity. For those under forty-five, eating will be about the control of body shape and appearance.

Thus we will see more products like Norelift (a French jam that contains anti-wrinkle compounds) and perhaps more faddish products like Bust-Up — a Japanese chewing gum that allegedly firms up and improves the appearance of your breasts (honestly, this exists). For anyone aged over forty-five, the name of the game will be not dying too soon, so foods that promise increased longevity or increased brainpower or memory will increasingly start to appear on supermarket shelves.

A future coloured by extremes

The future of food will thus be polarised between a number of opposites: the local and the global; the healthy and the indulgent; the futuristic and the nostalgic; the low cost and the luxurious; and the fast and the slow. For most people, convenience will be everything, and if that means never peeling a potato or washing a lettuce, so be it. If it means eating less healthily, that will slide, too. Eating will be replaced with a series of 'meal problems' and 'meal solutions', and the faster some people can shop, cook, and eat, the better. Sometimes what people eat will be healthy, but for the most part it will be 'comfort food' — something that helps you unwind, that gives olfactory and oral pleasure, and perhaps that reminds you of what you ate as a child before food got so complicated and dangerous. We will see people swinging from indulgence to health on a daily or weekly basis — sometimes even in the same meal. We will save up food credits from healthy eating or exercise and then 'spend' these points on indulgent foods or physical inactivity.

And what is 'healthy' anyway? Is it a slice of white bread made from GM wheat to reduce calorific absorption or is it a carrot freshly plucked from pesticide-free soil? I, for one, am confused. The answer, of course, is dependent on who is asking the question. For a sixty-year-old man with high blood-pressure, genetically enhanced foods could be future lifesavers; for a baby, Mother Nature does generally know best.

How people became suspicious of food

If you took all the overweight people in the world and crossed them with all the underfed people, what average-size person would result? I have no idea, but you can be fairly certain the average global size is increasing. According to the UN, 60 per cent of US adults (and 15 per cent of kids aged six to nineteen) and 30 per cent of European adults are already obese. World Health Organisation estimates suggest that 300 million adults are now obese (2005) up from 200 million in 1997. In the US, deaths from obesity are second only to deaths from smoking, and by 2020 75 per cent of Britons will be overweight. For food companies, the concern here is that food will become akin to tobacco, attracting spiralling legislation and lawsuits. So far this is a long way off, although theoretically all it would take to open the floodgates would be a piece of academic research proving beyond reasonable doubt that certain foodstuffs, or ingredient combinations, were addictive, and that the food and softdrink companies have known this all along.

Future hot potatoes

Assuming for a moment that obesity gets even worse in the future, what can we expect to see as a result? Fat taxes have been openly debated for a number of years. The idea here is that if you knowingly sell foods that make people ill or susceptible to illness, you should cover some of the costs associated with future treatment.

This is obviously tricky because how do you define healthy and non-healthy foods, and where do you draw the line in terms of normal and abusive use? Perhaps what is more likely is that certain foodstuffs will attract supplementary taxes or tax credits. Either that or healthcare will be restricted according to your food history.

In other words, you are free to eat anything you want in any quantity you like, but you cannot then have access to the same healthcare services as people who have been more restrained or responsible. Why, for example, should a forty-year-old vegetarian woman on a long-term self-imposed low-calorie diet (that drastically reduces blood pressure and cholesterol) have exactly the same access to medical services as a forty-year-old woman who smokes, drinks to excess, and lives on a diet of burgers and chips? In the future, she won't — or at least her insurance company will know all about her food-purchasing patterns, and will increase her health premiums accordingly.

Certain types of eating will be blocked off much in the same way that insurance companies currently prevent high-risk drivers from driving certain types of vehicle. How will they do this? Easy. In the future, most transactions will be digital using bankcards, credit cards, or digital cash stored in your mobile phone, and anonymity will be virtually impossible. Insurance companies will then buy (or be given) data on their customers' eating habits and behaviour, and will adjust their risk profiles accordingly.

We could even see food influencing town planning and house building in the future, with national governments and local councils teaming up with cartographers to produce 'food maps' showing how local food-availability influences consumption and health. These maps would then be used to zone certain residential areas as 'non-food areas', although politically this could be a hot potato. When I was growing up there was a sweet shop immediately opposite my school gates. As a result I have a mouth full of fillings. Will this be allowed in the future, and if so could children sue the shop owner for the cost of the subsequent dental work?

Another non-governmental solution to the obesity problem will be at the retail level. We have already seen supermarket loyalty cards in the US linked to FDA recommended daily allowances — your purchases are compared to recommended level of calories and vitamins, and any shortfalls result in a money-off voucher printed on the back of your till receipt. But whether retailers should be made responsible for the health of their customers is an interesting question. Perhaps a more likely scenario is a mobile phone that uploads information about what you eat (from the RFID codes on packs, or the barcodes on restaurant menus), and that makes helpful suggestions about what you are eating. Such devices could be quite useful because they would contain your food history. For example, your doctor may want to know how much alcohol you really drink or what your annual calorific intake is, while you might want to know how many days it's been since you ate a Caesar salad and where you bought it.

Why is food so controversial? Why are extremely fat and extremely thin people so media friendly, and what is it about food that we are so afraid of? Again, context is everything. In northern Europe, the US, and Japan (and the UK in particular), there have been a series of food safety scares ranging from CJD to BSE, and people are naturally sceptical about the ability of government and big business to tell the truth. Add to this distrust the fact that most food is grown on an industrial scale in artificial conditions, and it's no wonder that people are flocking to farmers' markets and organic butchers, and growing their own. In other words, it's about information and trust.

An appetite for information

People want to know where their food is from, who grew it, and under what circumstances. They may even want to know what the producer believes. In the US you can currently buy 'Christian

chicken' produced in accordance with the teachings of Jesus (I swear
I'm not making this up). Admittedly this is a bit on the fringe, but
it's simply an extrapolation of the same idea as kosher or halal foods.
This tribalism will also make itself felt in other areas. For example,
food will become more regional in the sense that, in the future, you
will no longer simply pop out for a Chinese or Indian meal. By 2020
such generic terms will be as meaningless as having an English.
Instead we will be eating Oaxacan instead of Mexican, Szechwan
rather than Chinese, and Tuscan rather than Italian.

Hence provenance will become increasingly important, not just
for the chattering classes buying organic Welsh lamb in Harrods,
but for soccer mums buying sliced white bread in Wal-Mart. In
other words, the type of information provided to the public on a
bottle of wine (who made it, when, where, and how?) will become
the norm on all other foodstuffs, too. This will mean a return to the
consumption of seasonal products because they will be local, which
means cheaper and more environmentally sustainable. If a product
has too many air-miles we won't buy it, and we may boycott the
company that makes it or transports it.

You can see the early signs of this already. Back in the 1960s and
1970s the slogan of US student activists was 'No War'. These days,
with wars raging in Afghanistan and Iraq, it's 'Eat Local' as students
boycott national and global brands in favour of locally grown
produce that supports the livelihoods of local farmers and that
stops (they think) global warming and pollution. Back in 2001, the
University of Portland, which dishes up 22,000 meals a week, spent
just 2 per cent of its food budget on purchases from local suppliers.
Now the figure is closer to 40 per cent, and 200 other US universities
have jumped onto the local-supplier bandwagon (over half of them
since 2001). Students are busy pushing organic, seasonal, slow food
and food-miles agendas to catering giants such as Sodexho and
Armamark Corporation. However, while these students are full of
idealism for eco-eating, they (and we) are finding out the hard way

the practicalities of global economics. Sourcing local ingredients from a multitude of small suppliers is time-consuming and expensive compared to hiring a single company with a global supply chain. But, like they say, principles aren't principles until they cost you money.

Buying an organic tomato in a supermarket is all very well, but if the tomato has been grown using child labour in Zimbabwe and then flown by a company owned by a corrupt politician from Harare to London it's not ethically produced, is it? Thus sustainable agriculture will move centre-stage and people will become genuinely concerned about the CO_2 emissions created by a lettuce. Part of the problem here is not only globalised production and air transport, but also the logistical operations of big supermarket chains that centralise warehousing and distribution. Thus a lettuce grown down the road can end up travelling half-way around the country before it ends up in your local supermarket. Hence retailers will not just emphasise the country and region of origin of food products; they'll devise a way of displaying food miles and other sustainability ratings, too.

At the other extreme, we will witness the continued growth of luxury food products that cost well in excess of what we and the particular food category in question have historically been used to. This could conflict with the need for local sourcing, but perhaps a compromise will be a renewed interest in rare wild foods found locally.

This regional and seasonal trend is great news for local food producers and retailers, and you can be certain that the larger food companies will follow suit, too. Some of this might work, like developing a local-products isle in the supermarket, or stocking fair trade products. However, while marketing departments that try to fake localisation or bolt on authenticity will be found out, authenticity is a complicated issue. For instance, when does a dish or ingredient gain or lose its 'authentic' status? Is fetta cheese made outside of Greece really fetta? (The EU doesn't think so.) Is a pizza really a pizza if it's eaten outside Naples? Equally, what does 'fresh' or 'natural' really mean, and should there be legislation to prevent the abuse of these terms? 'Organic' used to mean something, but these days it's increasingly just another offshoot of global agribusiness. In the UK the term doesn't even mean 'no pesticides' — only that they have been used sparingly. Animals are even suffering because organic rules prevent the continuing use of antibiotics.

The current debates about food miles and fair trade products will thus grow in stature, and food retailers will be forced by customers and local politicians alike to support local producers and Earth-friendly production, whether they like it or not. In the US, Heritage Foods (a poultry company) already provides detailed information about how their products are produced, and it provides a Web link so customers can visit their farm online. It would be interesting to see what their reaction would be if you turned up in person and asked to see the conditions first hand.

Another spin-off from the localisation and sustainability trend is the movement to grow your own food. It's interesting to note that in the UK the four largest seed firms recently reported that sales of vegetable seeds exceeded sales of flower seeds for the first time since 1945, when the entire nation was being encouraged to dig for victory as part of the war effort. Why is this happening? It's obviously connected to the need for traceability, but it's also indirectly connected with technology and busyness. As technology moves further into our lives, people feel disconnected from the natural world. Growing your own food is one way to connect with nature. Meal preparation is also an outlet for creativity and relaxation — which is why we'll see a rise in things like hobby baking, too.

Warning: the future contains nuts

Equally, we are in the middle of a food-intolerance epidemic. In the UK about 25 per cent of people claim they have a food allergy, sensitivity, or intolerance of some kind, and the figures are much the same in other westernised societies. For example, between 1997 and 2002 there was a doubling of peanut allergies in the UK, according to one study. Much of this may well be in peoples' heads as some kind of subconscious reaction or remembered experience to the various food scares of recent years, but some of it isn't. Whatever the reason, things are getting out of hand. For instance, my brother can no longer send his son to pre-school with a slice of homemade cake or bread. Such homemade foodstuffs are banned because they may contain nuts or might have been made using implements that came into contact with nuts. To my knowledge, no child at his school suffers from a nut allergy, but nobody is willing to take a chance.

A report commissioned by Norwich Union Healthcare in the UK found that 63 per cent of doctors have seen an increase in the number of patients reporting food intolerances. However, 75 per cent of the reported intolerances were psychological rather than physical. Nevertheless, scientists are engineering safe copies of popular foodstuffs so that people with food intolerances and allergies can eat 'normally'. The products are expected to be available in supermarkets by 2016.

One plausible explanation for the intolerance epidemic is to do with the high level of processed foods in the modern diet, while another lays the blame at our super-clean lifestyles that banish dirt (and resistance to illness). We are not only becoming suspicious of food, we are becoming anxious and even paranoid about everything it touches. Hence you can buy everything from knives and plates to workbenches and even garbage bags with anti-bacterial properties. Whatever the reason, it is highly likely we will see the kind of labelling that has previously only been seen on tobacco products on everything from milk and bread to ready meals. 'Warning: this packet of nuts contains nuts' sounds totally nuts, but it has already happened in some litigation-crazy countries.

The other reason localisation will happen is because of

globalisation and resource scarcity. In theory it makes a lot of sense for the food giants such as Unilever and Nestlé to source ingredients globally and then sell the same food products the world over. Unfortunately, this is not what people want. This homogenised approach will come under increasing pressure due to a number of factors. First labour costs will eventually equalise the world over and transport costs will skyrocket as oil and other natural resources become more scarce. Add to this a grassroots backlash against local jobs going abroad (eventually supported by government tariffs and protection) and we'll see food returning to where it came from a century ago. But not for everyone.

One of the broader trends we are starting to see with innovation and change is that instead of a new innovation replacing an incumbent idea often the new sits alongside the old. Thus, in the future you will have a choice about what you eat and where you buy it. If you want cheap, frozen, farmed fish or low-cost hamburgers made from rendered beef carcasses you can get it, probably in a supermarket, but you'll also be able to buy wild fish and organic beef all within a 2-kilometre radius.

A taste of the technology to come

As in other industries, technology will fundamentally affect not only how food is produced and bought in the future, but how and where we consume it. RFIDs, sensor motes, smart dust, and tiny flat screens and computers will help producers, retailers, and consumers alike keep a track on where things are from and where they are now.

Foodstuffs will be made safe — or at least appear safe — through the use of technology. In Japan you can already scan the barcode of some fruit and vegetables with your mobile phone to find out where it's from, and precisely which pesticides and fertilisers have been used on it. In the future, this will go much further. Identity verification will allow us to 'interrogate' frozen mince-meat in supermarkets, or download information at home about which herd the beef came from, the name and location of the farm, the diet of the animals, the application of pesticides and fertilisers, and the method of killing. Such 'tagging' is already commonplace with beef in countries such as Australia where 'paddock to plate' information is captured, but currently data is not usually shared with the end-user or consumer.

Another area where technology will be used is in speeding things up still further, although whether this is really good for us is another matter. People will want food that's easier to buy and to cook. This will mean designing ready-to-eat meals in packaging that goes straight from the shopping basket into the microwave. It will also mean pre-washed, pre-cut ingredients, clearer labelling, faster checkouts, and restaurants that know what you want before you do. It will also mean kettles that boil water a few seconds faster, appliances that cool things down quicker, and appliances that are networked and linked to devices such as mobile phones and laptops so you can switch on your oven while you're still at work.

Wine bottles will have built-in thermometers that tell you exactly what their current temperature is, or will play a short film explaining where they come from. Milk cartons and eggs will flash danger symbols when they are past their use-by dates, and cake mixes will speak to you to explain how to make them. Cereal packets will play short animations to keep the kids amused at breakfast time, and packaging 'networks' will allow packs to speak to each other and interact with other household devices and appliances.

Does this mean that the internet fridge will finally take off? Probably not, because there is no real customer need and the computer usually gets old and out-of-date before the fridge does, but some way of alerting people to what food you've got in your house, what you can make with it, and ordering what you need but don't have could be a winner.

In Japan, Mitsubishi sells a kitchen appliance with the snappy name of the Umasa Vitamin Zoryo Hikari Power Yasai Shitsu fridge.

It's the first fridge in the world that increases the vitamin C content of the food contained within through a process of photosynthesis. It's a good example of how technology will be used to increase the healthiness of what we eat.

They used to say that you are what you eat. If that's true, many of us will become paranoid schizophrenics in the future. Eating used to be a pleasure — it still is, for some — but many of us are becoming either frightened by or fanatical about food. Both are forms of food slavery. Food is becoming either something you try to avoid because you think it will kill you or make you fat, or else it's something deeply inconvenient you'd rather do without altogether if only you could. We are either junk-food monkeys eating whatever is convenient and within reach, or we are food bores constantly moaning about the water not being organic or that our boutique chocolate isn't made in accordance with Kenyan fair trade principles and the wrapper isn't recyclable. Not everyone thinks like this, of course. There are still people out there (large chunks of France and Italy, for example) who live to eat and still find the time to shop and eat properly, too. Elsewhere we eat, but we seem to need to justify what we eat and the time we spend doing it.

Once, during the week, people went home during lunchtime to eat. Others went to eat in the works canteen. Work stopped for a brief moment, and people sat and talked. Now we grab a bite on the run or sit at our desks alone and spill portable foods over our keyboards, like I've just done. And heaven forbid if you're tempted to have a drink at lunchtime if you're working. Don't get me wrong here; drinking eight pints of beer and then operating heavy machinery isn't a good idea. But a glass of wine over lunch isn't going to ruin your accountancy business. Does any of this matter? Yes, because the dictates of global capitalism have overridden a natural human necessity. We are feeding our bodies, but not our souls.

In the future, you will pay your money and make your choice. If you're feeling anxious about an increasingly uncertain and seemingly out-of-control world, you will escape into the supposed safety of your childhood by eating comfort foods like macaroni cheese or meatloaf, if you're a baby boomer. Your home will be a shrine to 'Aga nostalgia' (at least in the UK), and you will dream of moving to Italy to grow your own lemons and bake your own rustic bread.

If you're a microwave mum or a member of a hectic household, you'll eat a mixture of ready-to-eat meals and portable snacks suitably enhanced by science to offset their highly processed nature. Most of us will live somewhere in the middle, juggling time and a need for speed with financial constraints and concerns about individual and environmental well-being: a crazy, mixed-up world where nobody is quite sure what they should be eating, and suffering from feelings of anxiety, starvation, and gluttony in equal measure.

12 September 2026

Dear Theodore

How's things? I'm in a rush as usual. This morning I checked my AiPhone to see what was in my fridge and a series of flashing icons told me that all my milk and fruit was way past its use-by date. I sent a message to my cleaner to please remove it and ordered some more from myfridge.com. I grabbed one of the new WakeMeUp™ apples on the way downstairs and jumped into my Personal Electric Vehicle. It was still only 6.30 a.m. so I drove into my local MacBucks. My head was already full of what I was supposed to be doing later, so for a brief second I couldn't think of anything I wanted to eat. Fortunately MacBucks Intelligent Ordering System had already identified my PEV from my last visit and beamed my recent order history onto my windscreen. I scrolled down and decided on a free-range Ethiburger.

'Do I want a happy drink with that?' You bet. Lunch, as usual, was a protein slice at 4.00 p.m., most of which ended up all over my Web gloves. Actually, that was quite lucky because one of the sensors in the right glove picked up traces of ZXD131 and I immediately spat out the rest of the slice, adding the incident to my food history file and passing the matter onto my food lawyer.

The evening wasn't much better. It was my term to cook (I use the term lightly), so I decided to pop past the 5-Eleven gourmet convenience store to see what tickled my tastebuds (sometimes it's fun to turn everything off and just show up unannounced and see what they do!). Eventually I sat down at the table (I know, it's such a cool, retro idea) and tucked into a Yagga beefsteak from Canterbury (New Zealand). They're my favourite, especially since the whole country went organic ten years ago. Drinks? I had a bottle of Irish Zinfandel. When I waved the bottle in front of the computer it played a film about how the 2024 harvest went. I could even press a button on the bottle and order another!

Cheers

Ronald

Five trends that will transform food

Convenience and portability   Individuals will lead time-pressured lives in the future, and families will be time-starved and in a constant hurry. This means a further decline of traditional meal-times, especially where families sit down together, and an increase in eating on the move and between home and work. Food will therefore become faster and more mobile. This means it will be easier to buy, easier to cook, and easier to eat. In some cases this will mean designing ready-to-eat meals in packaging that goes straight from the shopping basket into the microwave. It will also mean pre-washed and pre-cut ingredients, clearer labelling, faster checkouts, and restaurants that know what you want before you do.

Seasonal, regional, and slow   While some people will crave food that's fast and cheap, others will pay to slow things down. This means locally grown food eaten in season. It also means all kinds of information about where food is from and how it was produced. For some people, provenance will mean buying directly from the producer, while for others technology will allow them to interrogate individual products or the companies that make them. Over time, the food-miles debate will move centre-stage, as will fair trade products and practices. For people with the luxuries of time and space, growing your own heirloom fruit and vegetables will make a comeback as the ultimate form of traceability.

Health versus indulgence   When people eat, they eat with their eyes. They also eat with their heads and their hearts, so while our logical side tells us to eat healthy foods, our emotional side tells us to eat things that we shouldn't — foods that are naughty but nice. Most people will therefore operate a kind of credit and debit system whereby indulgences will be offset by healthy foods or exercise. This can happen on the same day or even in the same meal. Foods will thus become increasingly polarised between those that are good for you and those that are not. Both are a reaction to anxiety in some form; and both, increasingly, will need to be within arm's reach, as convenience will generally trump both the desire for health and for indulgence. Food will similarly become polarised between low-cost and luxury items.

Nostalgia   As people become more stressed, depressed, and lonely they will try to comfort themselves by eating. In other words, people will use food to transport themselves back to what they believe were simpler, safer, more certain times. This anxiety will fuel nostalgic eating habits, ranging from simple comfort foods and childhood favourites to making bread and buying 'authentic' jam. This interest in 'old food' will also influence restaurant design, and we'll see the return of 1950s style drive-in movies and diners.

Food science and technology   The food industry will merge with the pharmaceuticals industry to create a host of new farmaceuticals, nutraceuticals, and functional foods. Products will range from apples that cure headaches to waters that suppress appetite. Equally, technology will deliver faster and more convenient food choices, due to everything from RFID tags to intelligent packaging 'networks' that allow packs to speak to each other and then recommend recipes based on what's in your kitchen. We'll also see wine bottles that play short films about their origins, milk cartons and eggs that flash danger symbols when past their use-by dates, and cake packets that explain how to make a cake. Medical records will also blur into shopping lists, as common conditions are treated with food rather than drugs. This will mean that food packaging will become more tightly controlled and legislated.

Chapter 8

Retail and Shopping: what we'll buy when we've got it already

Predicting the future is easy. It's trying to figure out what's going on now that's hard.
–Fritz Dressler

Jump in a Volkswagen and take a quick trip to the town of Rheinberg, Germany. It's home to a 4,000-square-metre supermarket created by Metro, the world's fifth-largest retailer. If you believe all the hype, you'll see the future of supermarket shopping here.

In this store — and there are a few others like it scattered across the globe — you'll find the latest retail innovations, including 'vegie vision' intelligent scales that can identify and price fruit and vegetables by sight, regardless of whether they're loose or wrapped in plastic. You'll also find computers that can be clipped to shopping trolleys and activated by inserting a customer loyalty card. Once signed in, you can download the shopping list you emailed to the store earlier, check your favourites list, print out personalised special offers, and get directions to the toothpaste aisle (which in theory could be any toothpaste isle to compare products and prices if the store allowed customers to link to other stores via Google maps, for instance). There are also information terminals scattered around the store to help you learn more about a particular product or to request a recipe for the fish you just bought. Needless to say, the store also uses RFID technology to ensure that the shelves are never empty.

Looking a few decades further into the future, in-store ads will target you the moment you pick up a bottle of Heinz tomato sauce. You may be pegged as a frequent Heinz buyer, and instantly offered a voucher rewarding your past loyalty. The ads — on individual sauce bottles — may even know how much sauce you have at home and remind you when to stock up, thanks to wireless links to cupboards and refrigerators. Indeed, everything you have ever bought will reside on a database somewhere, theoretically to help retailers track returns or model-buying habits and to adjust product availability in your local store.

But do you want Heinz, or for that matter the supermarket, to know that much about you? Some customers will, selling — or giving away — personal information in return for a fistful of discount vouchers. Others, like me, will guard their privacy jealously using cash — while it's still available — or fake loyalty cards to dupe the system and remain 'off network'.

Shops are already intelligent and they are getting more so. The Prada store in New York shows footage of models wearing certain outfits if you hold the clothes up to a nearby screen.

In the future, the store might greet you by name and you will be directed to a loyalty queue for a speedy checkout. Or you may not even have to check out: an RFID reader will scan your shopping bags as you walk out of the store, and the bill will be sent automatically to your credit-card company or bank.

Similar technologies will scan your body from all angles and produce a 360-degree 3-D model to help you find clothes that fit you precisely. Entering the data into a terminal will also instantly tell you whether certain items are in stock, or perhaps inform you of where products were made and under what conditions. Will customers really wear such high-tech innovations? Some will and some won't.

Retailers like Tesco have been collecting data on their customers for years using the euphemistically named loyalty card (surely the loyalty should be the other way around?). Indeed, one report has it that Tesco now knows more about every citizen in the UK than the British government does. The sheer amount of this data has created a bit of a problem for some retailers historically, but in the future it will become easier to analyse, resulting in personalisation of everything from special offers and advertising to product design, revolutionising how people shop. In the case of Tesco, this means listening to the needs and wants of very small subsets of the British population whose voices are usually drowned out by statistically representative samples of the majority.

For the younger crowd, technology will increasingly replace people, either through automated vending and robotic assistants or via smart kiosks and online commerce; not for all goods, but for anything that's a habitual or commodity purchase. Online stores will also blur the line between reality and cyberspace, with much of the 'brand experience' and browsing being delivered by virtual stores built in virtual malls or other online communities.

E-tail is obviously a massive trend, but in many ways online shopping is still divorced from the real world. Online supermarkets are usually just text-based lists of products — you can't walk through the store. Indeed, despite the convenience factor, online shopping has virtually nothing in common with its real-world equivalent, and in some ways this is an opportunity. For example, online you generally have to know what you're looking for, and most people shop alone. In the real world, shopping doesn't happen like this;

it's more of an event, an experience usually shared. And customers listen to the recommendations of friends and trusted experts. This obviously hasn't escaped the attention of some savvy internet retail entrepreneurs, and we are therefore starting to see the emergence of 'social shopping'. Examples include sites such as Crowdstorm, ThisNext, Kaboodle, Become, and Stylehive. These sites are a mash-up between search engines and social networking sites, and allow shoppers to browse and buy based upon other customers' recommendations.

In the REI store in Seattle (US), smart kiosks are used to supplement traditional customer service. Each REI store carries around 30,000 different products, of which staff can only be familiar with a fraction. Each kiosk, by contrast, carries information on 78,000 products, and has flawless product knowledge. In a similar vein, American Apparel and a host of other retail brands are building stores inside games like 'Second Life' to attract members of Gen Y. The American Apparel store is 180 metres of prime retail space. You can stroll upstairs and choose something you like, then touch a nearby information panel, which triggers a Web page displaying information about the garment — for example, what sizes and colours it's available in or perhaps information about where it was made. Of course, the store only exists in cyberspace, but that's where Gen Y are found these days — they are becoming harder and harder to reach using conventional stores or physical marketing.

Becoming a virtual retailer has one profound implication — the reputation of products, services, and individual retailers will be given a concrete value by customers. Retailers with a history of doing what they promise will be rewarded, while those who are new or have an indifferent history will be treated cynically or avoided altogether. You can see the shape of things to come already on eBay with its vendor-rating system, but this idea will increasingly flood into other areas, making it increasingly difficult to hide unpalatable truths or conceal poor products and experiences. This will be another example of the customer being in control.

By contrast, older people generally loathe new technology. Most seniors (over sixty-five) like dealing with people face-to-face, as they're always done; despite the emergence of 'silver surfers', most will remain resolutely offline whenever and wherever they can.

Technology and ageing populations are two of the key drivers of retail change in the twenty-first century. While much has been written about the former, very little has been written about the latter or about other changes in the population structure, such as the breakdown of the nuclear family or the growth of single-person households in urban and suburban areas.

I'll come back to technology in a while, but let's first deal with some of the implications of ageing, and the shift in attitudes and behaviour among all age groups.

Permanently large prices

Let's jump back into that Volkswagen and this time take a journey to the Austrian city of Salzburg. Here you'll find a store called the Adeg Aktiv 50+ food market, which is targeted squarely at the over-fifties shopper. (The average age in Europe is 37.7, but this figure is expected to rise to 52.3 by 2050.) Here you'll see better-than-standard lighting, non-slip floors, lots of seats, and large, easy-to-read prices. The store also features lower-than-average shelving (so it's easier to reach the top), shopping trolleys that easily attach to wheelchairs, and magnifying glasses on aisle-ends so that people who have difficulty seeing can read the packaging. The only thing Adeg Aktiv 50+ don't seem to have is a defibrillator in-store to revive older customers when they have a heart attack.

However, this retailer is clearly an exception; most stores are still firmly designed to attract younger shoppers. This is deliciously ironic because baby boomers managed to get retailers (and manufacturers) to pay attention when they were young and had money to spend. But now that they're old and have even more money to spend, retailers (and manufacturers) generally aren't interested because they are run by young people.

This is clearly another world compared to the virtual stores inside 'Second Life', but one thing older people increasingly have in common with younger people is that they often live alone.

In Europe something like 20–25 per cent of all households are single-person, while in the US the figure is even higher. This has future implications for everything from packet sizes to the type and frequency of shopping trips. Broadly speaking, singles tend to shop at the last minute — often on foot — whereas families tend to do weekly mega-shops using a car. Older singles tend to have more time and less money available than younger singles, whereas younger singles tend to have less time and more money.

Future migration back to cities also means that low-tech convenience stores, twenty-four-hour kiosks, and giant vending machines like the Tik Tok Easy Shop, Smartmart, or Shop24 may be more in touch with future customer needs, too.

You can already buy (or, in some cases, rent) iPods, shoes, movies, pizzas, and mobile phones from vending machines; and in Japan, the spiritual home of the vending machine and all things robotic, there's even a robot department store, although you'll have to wait a few years until the store is entirely staffed by robotic sales assistants. In the meantime, though, you can always get a robotic fix by visiting the Aqua City commercial complex on Tokyo's waterfront. Here you can already find D1 security robots patrolling stores and entertaining the shoppers.

What all these vending machines and convenience stores clearly have in common is speed. Apart from browsing for luxuries, daily shopping takes too much time, and any idea that can speed things up is welcomed with open arms — at least by certain sections of the population. In some instances things can go a bit too far, though. US golf clubs are hiring service representatives to firmly assist seniors who take too long to finish a round of golf, while some golf carts now feature GPS tracking so the club can monitor individual rounds and give slow people a 'nudge'. We don't have GPS in shopping trolleys just yet (apart from perhaps in Rheinberg), but I'm sure it's only a matter of time.

What we do already have in some stores are in-store nutritionists offering dietary advice to shoppers, 'keep-fit trolleys' (that help you burn calories as you shop), in-store massage to relax people waiting in queues, in-store poets, and personal grocery shoppers. There are also male or female crèche areas inside various supermarkets. If you think I'm kidding about male crèches, just take a trip to Marks & Spencer in the UK, who were recently seen testing such an idea in a number of their stores. As for the massage, I'd seriously predict that, along with other forms of instant stress-relief (at home, in-store, and especially at work), it will become a fixture in the future as people's lives speed up even more and become more stressful.

The male/female crèche idea is especially interesting to me. Conventional wisdom says that men don't like shopping unless they are a metrosexual or 'uber-male', and therefore should be put inside playpens while someone else (a female) does the shopping. But this misses the point entirely. Shopping to most men is either research or a game to be fought and won. Winning means getting the best deal, and foraging is usually done alone; women, by contrast, tend to browse in groups, shopping being a social experience as much as anything else.

The differences between men and women have not been lost on retailers and, as we find out more about how male and female brains work, we can expect to see more retailers designing their stores to appeal to one or the other — but very rarely both.

Women are well served when it comes to female-only spaces, but men are not. For women there are women-only floors in hotels (Switzerland), female-only department stores (Argentina), female-only health clubs, shopping centres aimed squarely at women (Venus

Fort in Tokyo), and women-only banks. There's even a convenience store called Happily (owned by AM/PM) in the Toranomon district of Tokyo, especially designed for women. All staff are women (except late at night for security reasons), and products are designed and selected 'for women by women'. One nice touch is a powder room featuring full-length mirrors, a dressing table, and a stool for women to rest their legs on while they change their tights.

Nevertheless, designers and developers still seem to be getting the basics wrong by building the same number of toilets in shopping centres when it's well known that women need at least twice as many cubicles as men because they take longer. But I'm going off at a tangent. Let's get back to some of the key drivers of change: in particular, the 'need for speed' and 'too much choice'.

In the 1980s and 1990s, shopping malls seemed to appear everywhere, and the Mall of America was supposed to attract more visitors each year than Disney World. Nevertheless, change is in the air. Nowadays many gigantic enclosed shopping malls are starting to look like dinosaurs because shoppers are just too busy and too tired to fight their way through huge carparks and endless corridors just to buy a pair of shoes. In the last ten years the number of women who consider shopping a 'pick-me-up' has fallen from 45 per cent to 21 per cent in the US, while in another survey 53 per cent of shoppers 'hate the experience'. In a similar vein, in 2000, US shoppers spent an average of four hours per month inside malls, but by 2003 this had fallen to 2.9 hours. Something is going on here. It could be that most shopping centres have no authentic identity or sense of self. I call them 'anywhere places' because the look and feel is the same in Boston and Bangkok. But I'm sure the main reason is that, while shoppers have more money to spend, they have less and less time to waste. This is slightly misleading because there are several quite distinct types of shopping.

The first is 'habitual shopping' for commodity items or essentials, where price and location are critical. This is 'unthinking' in the sense that the shopping list of products (but not necessarily brands) barely changes from one month to the next, although the definition of 'essential' will differ from one shopper to the next. Time-saving and convenience are critical, so much of this type of retail activity will move online, with substantial growth in home delivery and drop-off (at work, petrol stations, or transport hubs, for example). Customer service for this type of retail activity will be almost entirely irrelevant, as most shoppers will prefer to bypass physical interactions if it means saving time or money. However, it doesn't mean that customer 'servicing' (getting things right and responding efficiently when things go wrong) won't be important. It's simply that going above and beyond the call of duty will not be expected.

City-centre supermarkets (in many cases, inside apartment buildings and offices), convenience stores (some inside vehicles), and stores modelled on the sari-sari stores in countries such as the Philippines that sell small packaging sizes will, however, all be perfectly suited to the needs of the habitual shopper — so we'll see more retailers adopting these formats and channels in the future.

The second type of shopping is 'purposeful' (often referred to as laser shopping). Purchases are more infrequent than habitual shopping, and often involve replacing an existing product such as a toaster or fridge. Again, much of this activity will move to the internet, although this will be mainly to find information before seeing the product in the flesh. Again, speed will be of the essence, so using mobile phones to research and then purchase products will grow as fast as high-speed data networks allow. Indeed, by 2017 I'd expect as much as 80–90 per cent of all e-commerce within the fifteen- to nineteen-year-old demographic to be conducted by mobile phone. Already 80 per cent of Ford's customers use the internet to find out which car they want to buy, and how much they want to pay, before they even set foot inside a dealership. Similarly, around 75 per cent of mobile phone buyers in the US use the internet to research products. In other words, customers are seizing power and are now better informed about everything from prices and specifications to reliability and ethical issues. Nevertheless, seeing products in the flesh will still be critically important, even if the final sale is made online.

This has profound implications for certain kinds of retail because some physical stores will become places where people touch and feel but do not ultimately buy. In other words, we will see brand showrooms where you cannot buy products.

The mindset of customers is also shifting, in the sense that we are moving from a permanent acquisition culture — where you save up money and then buy something that you keep for a long time — to one based on instant gratification, where people sell things the moment they become bored with them. Thus stores may have to adjust to a model where customers can sell as well as buy new and second-hand goods, which are increasingly sold alongside each other. That's, of course, unless the auction culture remains almost exclusively online.

The third type of shopping — slow shopping — is more aligned with wants rather than needs, and is therefore more emotive and experience based. It also is very sensory, so we will witness a growth in the use of sensual (five-dimensional) branding, with retailers using smell, taste, and touch alongside the more usual elements of sight and sound. This is shopping as a leisure activity, with the fun part being the looking rather than the buying. Customer service is critical in this area; despite what many retailers think, it's people not technology who ultimately deliver great service in this area.

This is shopping as an end in itself, and it is very unlikely that much of this type of retail activity will move online until virtual worlds are able to capture the theatre of, for example, French markets or 1,000-year-old Moroccan bazaars. In the meantime, retailers will continue to sell the sizzle as well as the steak by adding services to commodity products. For example, a barbeque will be available with a cooking class or even a barbeque holiday as an optional extra.

Selfridges department store in London is a good example of retail theatre. It describes itself as a theme park where customers are encouraged to buy souvenirs of their visit. Recent foot-fall (business) generators have included a regional food festival, a Brazilian event, and a conceptual art installation in which 600 naked people rode up and down on the escalators. As they say, sex sells. Remember, too, that Selfridges attracts 21 million 'visitors' each year — about the entire population of Australia. If it can persuade even a tiny number of its customers to buy something, this translates into significant revenue.

Of course, this could all be temporary. Generally speaking, department stores are in trouble because they have lost touch with younger shoppers, who generally prefer big-box discounters, category killers, specialist retailers and, of course, the internet. The result is that some department stores have started to add restaurants and hotels, while shopping centres have started to approach discounters to become anchor tenants in new developments, whereas previously department stores would have been the automatic choice.

Moreover, outdoor lifestyle centres, a fast-growing sector in retail, are now regularly built without any department store presence. Is there a solution to what is generally a downward trend? Looking at Selfridges, you'd think so, but pulling off an iconic destination-experience isn't easy.

Department stores will therefore move their brands online, while in the physical world they will continue to become destinations — days out — in their own right, thanks to a mixture of high-energy, crowd-pleasing theatre and hands-on personal pampering, cocooning, and relaxation, although one suspects that much of this might be rearranging deckchairs on the *Titanic*.

Big box versus smallification

To re-state a point, the more life becomes virtual and high-tech, the more people will crave the opposite — low tech, high touch.

This means that there will always be a need for physical shops. Some people will always want physical interaction with human sales assistants and physical products, so don't knock down the old department store just yet.

However, shoppers are getting fed up with giant retailers bulldozing local communities and turning streets into homogenised strips devoid of life after dark. In fact, 75 per cent of people in Britain think that supermarkets like Tesco, which takes £1 for every £8 spent in Britain, have become too powerful, and would support stricter government controls. This has not escaped the attention of the world's largest retailer, which is testing smaller neighborhood stores dubbed 'Small-Marts'.

Maybe the future is stealth retail — shops that don't operate like shops, and malls that don't look like malls. This is not a new idea. Back in the 1960s, Victor Gruen, the architect of the modern mall, called for retailers to incorporate civic and educational facilities. In other words, shopping malls and supermarkets should function more like old-fashioned town centres, with non-retail elements like schools, doctors, libraries, churches, and sport facilities. For example, Swiss retailer Migros has created health and education centres. However, connecting with the local community doesn't just mean parents collecting tokens for school computers. It means placing the school *alongside* the supermarket (Sainsbury's), or using retail space for community purposes by putting a police station *inside* a supermarket (Tesco). Going local also means utilising local labour and selling local produce. Farmers' markets have been so successful in recent years that there's even been talk of allowing them to use supermarket carparks after hours.

Another area where retail is changing is in the creation and development of stores and products themselves. Once upon a time, stores, and the products displayed within them, were fairly static in the sense that store designs changed infrequently, and once a product became a bestseller it wasn't messed with. But two trends have converged to create 'pop-up' stores and limited-edition products, where even an annual model change is considered slow.

The pop-up retail trend, blending business and conceptual art, has been around for a while. Shops like the Meow Mix cat food café in New York (I kid you not) work because they generate a buzz, and people have short attention-spans. People are also increasingly fed up with everything always looking the same. Thus we get 'guerrilla' stores like Comme des Garcons in Berlin or Target's pop-up store in the Rockefeller Centre, which suddenly appear without warning and then disappear in a similar manner, regardless of their success.

The idea of pop-up also recognises that in retail you can only be hot for so long. It is also arguably a reaction to high-concept retail (that is, flagships like the Rem Koolhass-designed Prada store). So where will pop-up go in the future? The answer is pop-up products and brands.

One of the big retail hits of Christmas 2004 in the UK was a website called Asos.com (formerly known as As Seen On Screen). This pure e-tailer is a combined personal stylist and shopping destination that allows people (mainly women aged sixteen to thirty-five) to copy the look of their favourite celebrity, right down to their toenails. So when Gwyneth Paltrow was seen wearing a 'Golden Balls' T-shirt given to her by David Beckham, the website had a batch of identical T-shirts made up within hours and up for sale the following day. Shoppers can search by celebrity (say, Liz Hurley) or by category (say, sunglasses). Like.com is a similar site that allows shoppers to conduct a visual search for a fashion item they have seen on a celebrity.

Zara, the Spanish fashion retailer, is another example of pop-up or fast fashion, where designs are on a catwalk one day and in a physical store the next, although Zara is perhaps even more interesting because of the feedback loops between what customers walk in wearing and what shop managers report back to head office. Zara also works on the basis of producing limited batches, so that popular items automatically become scarce and you never know entirely what will be available when you visit, thus encouraging additional store visits. In an average year, Zara launches 11,000 new products, versus 2,000–3,000 from rivals such as Hennes and Mauritz and Gap, and spends just 0.3 per cent of sales on advertising. It also hires unknown designers and keeps its manufacturing local, thus tightening its distribution networks.

Everything from food products to electricals is playing the same game, with the creation of limited-edition 'specials' or celebrity-endorsed (or designed) products. I predict an increase in the influence of celebrities over everything we consume from bathrobes to butter.

We'll also see limited-edition materials, colours, and packaging, many of which will converge with regional and seasonal variations of nationally available brands. These trends clearly can't last forever, as the strength of pop-up retail and limited-edition products lies in their being an alternative to the mainstream. If they become too common they will lose their value, and will have to be replaced by something else.

Nevertheless, we have at least five to ten years left in the trend, and what we'll probably see next are stores questioning what they are for. Tchibo (with over 1,000 stores worldwide) is a chain of German coffee shops that sells other products along with the coffee. There's nothing new here — just another example of the blurring between retail sectors — but the company seems to have dispensed with the idea that you should focus on one core skill and align new products to the core offer. Instead, Tchibo has adopted a philosophy of 'a new experience every week', so one week they sell bikes and the next ski suits alongside the latte. It's certainly different.

Too much choice is an important global trend that will drive profound change in retail circles over the next few decades. Put simply, there are too many choices available, and customers don't have either the time or the inclination to edit or assess the choices themselves.

In the film *Moscow on the Hudson*, Robin Williams plays a Russian defector living with a family in New York. As a goodwill gesture he volunteers to do the shopping — but passes out alongside the coffee aisle because the choices are just too overwhelming. The average supermarket in the US now sells 30,000 items. Typically, this will include twenty-six types of Colgate toothpaste — there were just two in 1970 — and 724 types of fruit and vegetables, including ninety-three organic items. But why?

To some extent, this proliferation of choice is due to retailers responding to customer demand. However, while some level of choice can be liberating, too much can induce paralysis. For example, in one study, people entering a supermarket were offered six jams to taste; on another occasion, people were offered twenty-four. Both groups were given a $1-off coupon to spend on the jam. Thirty per cent of those tasting six jams bought a jar, compared to only 3 per cent of those tasting twenty-four — apparently the decision-making process was just too complex and time-consuming. Similarly, when people were asked to react to a discounted Sony product in a shop window, most reacted with enthusiasm. But when a second discounted product was put alongside it, their enthusiasm waned.

Consequences? Given that time is a vanishing resource, I'd expect more shoppers to outsource choice to various editors, curators, sifters, and filters. In the US, a chain of wine shops called Vino 100 sells just 100 different wines, all for under $25 per bottle. This I can empathise with. It's currently 4.30 p.m., and within the next thirty minutes I'm going to receive a phone call or email asking what we should eat for dinner. I have no idea. We have about sixty cookbooks at home, but only eat about fifteen different dishes. Whatever we choose to eat we haven't bought yet, and we may well end up eating out, in which case the very last thing I want to see is a sixty-page menu offering every specialty under the sun. No surprise, then, that when a supermarket decreased the number of products it sold by 20 per cent, it saw an 11 per cent increase in sales.

According to Professors Gourville (of Harvard University) and Soman (of the University of Toronto), there are two types of choice: 'alignable choice', a variety of offerings along a single dimension such as size or colour — such as Levi 501 jeans — and 'non-alignable' choice, where companies add features that involve trade-offs across dimensions. For example, toothpaste and cold medicines come with an almost overwhelming number of choices of features and benefits. Of course, cynics will say we've seen this all before, and they'd be right: in 1879, Frank Woolworth opened a store that featured limited choice and fast access.

Another important trend is everyday low pricing, which often carries a high cost for other countries. Moreover, increased consumption doesn't seem to be where people are heading. *Growth Fetish* by Clive Hamilton and *Status Anxiety* by Alain De Botton both make this point. If you put a coat- and bag-checking service into a store, people will be able to carry — and therefore buy — more stuff. But this misses the bigger picture. Some people are beginning to realise that buying more things doesn't make them happier; it just makes them more confused. For example, Wal-Mart is accused of offering prices that are too low due to a business model that's too efficient. Tesco is suffering much the same fate, although the two cases differ slightly in that Wal-Mart is accused of exploiting cheap labour and materials while Tesco is primarily accused of destroying local shops and communities.

However, customers are free to shop anywhere they want, and in most cases there is an alternative — albeit one that may take extra effort. And that, in a nutshell, is the problem. We feel that we should be doing something to save the local high street; but when it comes to an US$8 pair of jeans, our principles go out the window. It's the same with the environment. We see nothing ironic about filling the car with petrol to drive out of our way to Body Shop to refill a plastic bottle so we don't waste packaging that uses oil and damages the environment. We are all becoming conflicted, contrary, and confused.

So what would happen if the world's largest retailer — and arguably one of the most powerful companies on Earth — decided to save the planet? Well, we're about to find out. Wal-Mart (with revenues of US$300+ billion per year) recently laid out a plan to turn itself (and by default its suppliers, staff, and customers) green. Its aims include increasing the fuel and emissions efficiency of its vehicle fleet by 25 per cent by 2009, and doubling this by 2016. The company also plans to lower solid waste (that is, packaging) in its US stores by 25 per cent by 2009. Critics say this is obviously a 'greenwash', but the company says otherwise. It has already become the world's largest buyer of organic milk and organic cotton, and is also starting to buy food locally to reduce food miles and increase freshness.

But there's a dilemma. Wal-Mart set up its stall on the basis of low prices, which helped the little guy. This is fine if the little guy wants to save the planet, but what if she or he does not? What if, for instance, ordinary Americans still want to buy bottled water when most experts agree that the product harms the environment? The answer, in the short-term, is that Wal-Mart will respond to existing customer needs, but there is a bigger game at stake. Wal-Mart, through its sheer size, has the power to affect what people think and want, and therefore to democratise the sustainability issue. Watch this green space.

If Wal-Mart's plans succeed we will start to see fringe products such as organic shoes and organic furniture move into the mainstream. This could gather some serious momentum if localisation also takes hold, and pretty soon we'll see shops selling loose products without packaging — like a century ago — and these will mostly be made or grown locally. This will correspond with the a rise in nationalism and economic protectionism mentioned in chapter 2.

Realistically, though, we will live in a world where both extremes co-exist. There will be big-box retailers selling globally produced products at knock-down prices, while up the road the local mum-and-dad store will be selling local apples and homemade cakes. The future will therefore be a heavily polarised and confusingly paradoxical place. The retail market will be split between austere low-cost and indulgent luxury sectors, and we will become passionate about single issues while simultaneously displaying contradictory shopping attitudes and retail behaviour.

Low-cost goods exist as a historical and political accident. They are dependent on process innovations, which suffer from the law of diminishing returns and are dependent on access to low-cost labour and materials brought about by globalisation. Eventually, labour rates will equalise and materials will start to run out, especially if the global population continues to increase. In the long term, resources and labour problems will be solved through technology; but in the short term, low-cost products could very well become a thing of the past.

This issue doesn't apply to virtual goods and services, and it's possible that accelerated technological innovation would allow the low-cost model to last for longer, but it will end sooner or later. Until then, markets will continue to polarise between the luxury and economy segments, and most retail areas will continue to experience some level of premiumisation or trading up. For example, we'll see the emergence of high-security 'black card' malls and stores where customers will only be allowed in if the storeowner or mall knows who you are (either personally or via electronic identity verification).

Why will this happen? The reason luxury has become so essential is the steady growth in household and individual incomes over the past ten or twenty years. As well, more women are working and earning more, and there are more single-person households, too (often without children), which tends to raise incomes even further.

Add to this ageing populations with high levels of asset wealth and a billion new middle-class consumers in Asia, Africa, and elsewhere, and you can start to see why there's now a market for Gucci toolkits and pet carriers.

Another more mundane example is coffee. In barely more than a decade, real coffee has moved from a US east-coast boutique phenomenon to an everyday necessity across an increasingly large part of the world. If you add up what you now spend on coffee across a year you might be in for a shock — but you can afford it. Will this all last?

I think ultimately not. The luxury bubble will eventually burst, probably due to a global recession caused by the collapse of a major economy such as the US or China.

Perhaps this is no bad thing. Perhaps we will witness a shift away from consumerism and physical consumption to the consumption of experiences. Maybe the current trend towards bigger and bigger global retailers will reverse, and we'll see a resurgence in all things local. There is some evidence of this happening already.

Location, location, location

Ever since Henry Ford invented mass production, companies have pursued a strategy of standardisation. Given globalisation, you'd think that standardisation would be intensifying, but you'd be wrong. The problem is twofold. First, consumer markets are fragmenting. In the 1970s the US population was typically segmented into forty lifestyle groups. Nowadays there are sixty-six.

This diversity comes in many forms: lifestyle, beliefs, values, income, ethnicity, family structures, and so on, all with one thing in common — they dislike homogenisation. The second problem is that standardisation stifles innovation. Making things the same reduces points of difference and leads towards commoditisation. Customisation, on the other hand, encourages experimentation, which drives innovation. Local customisation is also very difficult for competitors to track, let alone copy. As a result, retailers are starting to customise store formats, products, and even service offers according to local tastes.

Equally, manufacturers are formulating specific products for specific regions or groups. For example, Coca-Cola has created four different canned coffee drinks for the Japanese market (each one targeting a particular region), while Wal-Mart varies selections of canned chilli peppers according to store location. Wal-Mart carries about sixty varieties of chillies in total; but only three are stocked nationally, as the company tailors its stores to its local clientele. Too much localisation or personalisation can obviously breed logistical chaos and dilute the brand, so customisation is usually carried out in clusters using local geographic or lifestyle data.

So what, apart from customer fragmentation, is driving this trend? The answer is information. Customer data can pinpoint not only who is buying what, but increasingly when and why. So data from Tesco can identify need states based on the time of day, allowing an inner-city store to stock sandwiches at lunchtime and ready-to-eat meals in the evening. This is hardly rocket science, but retailers like Best Buy in the US have found that localising stores can result in a sales increase that is twice the company average. Websites like Nearbynow come at this localisation trend from another angle by making the inventory of local malls searchable by local shoppers.

In other words, price and choice will no longer be as important to shoppers as they once were. Location will become the most important factor, both in the sense of being most convenient (closest) and the most local (made locally or in tune with local tastes and history). The idea of 'local' will be an important factor in other ways, too, with some enlightened retailers seeing it as their purpose to help build and support local communities. This is perhaps another example of going back to the future.

12 January 2010

Dear Alexandro

You asked me at Christmas how retail had changed since I was a kid, and I've finally had a chance to sit down for more than five minutes to think about it. First of all, there was no internet. Letters and postcards like this were the only way we could order things from far away. Shops were also closed on Sundays (it was actually illegal to sell some things on a Sunday). Some were closed on Wednesday afternoons, too. Shopping was more of a necessity, not a form of leisure activity, and some popular products used to regularly run out. Supermarkets had just been invented, but shopping centres and malls were non-existent where I lived, as were superstores and factory outlets. Most shopping was still done by women, too, in the local high street or town centre. Shops closed at about 5.30 p.m. — no late-night shopping or 24/7 convenience stores. Most of the local names have disappeared now, too, replaced by giant overseas retailers. Perhaps the most amazing thing though was how little choice there was. Products from abroad just didn't exist generally. There were no croissants, no fresh mangoes, no lemongrass, and no pesto unless you knew a small shop run by a foreigner. Believe it or not, we also used cash to pay for things — nobody took credit cards — and most people cooked meals by themselves from scratch.

Hope this helps with your homework project.

Lots of love

Vasiliki

PS. Don't forget to send the RoboAnt back to Torna if it still frightens the cat.

Five trends that will transform retail

Luxury versus low cost   Retail is polarising between luxury and low-cost segments, and this will continue well into the future — or at least until there is a recession, at which point we will all become economy shoppers again. However, shoppers are contradictory and will happily buy standard $15 T-shirts one minute and custom-made $500 jeans the next. However, because customers shop across all segments, customers will expect high-quality service all of the time regardless of what they are paying.

Speed and simplicity   People are busy, and they want whatever they want right now. This is particularly true of Gen Y, which has grown up with high-speed internet connections and therefore suffers from what's been termed digital instant gratification syndrome. However, we are all running out of time, and any retailer that can speed up a simple transaction will be rewarded. For example, queuing will become an even-greater source of stress and aggravation. DIY customer-service kiosks, vending machines, contactless payment, drive-through, home delivery, city-centre convenience stores, and e-tail will therefore all do well in the future. So, too, will retailers that offer edited choice as a response to the avalanche of information and too much choice.

Changes in household composition   The future will contain many more old people, so retailers will slowly respond by designing stores and products that appeal to the fifty-five-and-over crowds who have both time and money to spend. The continued rise of single-person households (lived in by young and old alike) will also have profound implications on everything from store design to product formatting and packaging. Products will thus have to be available in 'ones' as well as twos and fours. Similarly, 'old favourites' and classics will enjoy a resurgence of popularity as older shoppers go all misty eyed about the distant past. Products that are healthy or that promise 'immortality' will also do well.

Sustainability   Last century, shoppers compared prices. This century, they will compare ethical standards. We've already seen sweatshop-free clothing brands and the return of neighborhood retail, but we haven't really seen anything yet. In the future, shoppers will be swayed by various green and ethical issues, some of which will be serious while others will be just plain silly. For example, there will be a crusade against retailers that sell lettuce on the basis that growing lettuces uses too much water, and a campaign to stop drinking bottled water on the basis of its carbon footprint. Thus fair trade products, food miles, minimal and reusable packaging, and products that benefit a local community or the wider world in some way will be in demand in the future.

Story-telling, authenticity, and trust   We are constantly being fed an endless diet of half-truths and manipulated statistics from companies (and governments) wanting us to buy something. The result is cynicism and an interest in authenticity or realness. People want information. They want to know where things (and people) are coming from physically and metaphorically. They also want to know what the story or narrative is so that they can make their own minds up about the 'facts'. There will be a growing interest in information about how things are made and where they are from. This means real people with real stories to tell. This will be good news for brands with history and heritage, but it will also benefit retailers that can tell a story through a hands-on experience.

Chapter 9

Healthcare and Well-being: older and better than well

The future is already here; it's just unevenly distributed.
–William Gibson

D o you want to live forever? How about to 130? Neither of these thoughts is too far-fetched. Already half of those born today into a middle-class family anywhere in the world will almost certainly reach their 100th birthday. A century ago few people lived to see their fifty-sixth birthday. Today most of us make it to eighty. A few decades of medical innovations could easily push this figure to 110 and then onwards until 130. If you really want to explore the boundaries of what's possible, the ultimate sci-fi future is one where humans have figured out a way to download consciousness into a machine, thereby effectively becoming immortal. But back to the more immediate future.

I'm sitting in Foot Heaven trying to have a massage. I'm still suffering from something that I caught in economy class on a plane almost a month ago, so I thought a bit of relaxation might help.

Unfortunately though, the person right next to me is on the phone — and stays on it for an hour. I leave feeling more stressed. Still feeling a bit wobbly a few days later, I stagger into my local doctor's surgery and wait my turn. On the wall is a bank of leaflets, and one in particular catches my eye. The leaflet is entitled 'Your Genetic Sports Advantage: ACTN3 Sports Gene Test'.™ The idea here is that a simple genetic test will identify whether you — or your child — is naturally oriented towards sprint/power sports or endurance events. Again, I'm not making any of this up. This exists right now.

A future pill for every ill

Amongst a host of new medical developments and discoveries in the next few decades, we'll be presented with techniques to grow artificial teeth, artificial bladders, and new breasts. And if you are still feeling queasy about human face transplants, get ready for brain transplants. We'll also see artificial blood, brain food for babies, pills that remove the need for exercise, female Viagra, biodegradable scaffolding (for new organs such as breasts), memory pills, bionic eyes, human limb farms, brain-function tests, anti-suicide pills, artificial hearts, gene silencing, 'cluster bomb' treatments for cancer, and age-retarding pills. There will be vaccinations to help people resist food, alcohol, cigarettes, and drugs such as cocaine, along with jabs to treat asthma, arthritis, and high blood-pressure. Developments in genomic medicine and molecular biology will drive the creation of a host of new compounds, some of which are likely to make it onto pharmacists' shelves in the very near future. For diabetics, daily injections of insulin could soon be a thing of the past, and sufferers will inhale insulin instead. There will be various drugs to manipulate hunger, and a plethora of new treatments to help people get to sleep or stay awake.

Indeed, we aren't that far away from a society where there's a pill for every conceivable ill. As society speeds up and becomes more competitive, many perfectly healthy people will also regularly use pills to enhance their daily lives and performance. Drugs will therefore move from specialist areas into routine domestic and work use. An example is Ritalin (methylphenidate), which is already used by some students to improve test results and by some business people to improve performance in high-pressure situations such as key presentations.

In the US, the military has used Modafinil to help soldiers stay awake and improve concentration and planning skills, and it is looking increasingly likely that various Alzheimer's drugs will eventually be used to improve the memory of otherwise perfectly healthy people.

There will also be a revolution in how medical professionals and patients monitor health and work out whether or not they are ill. There are already some interesting developments in this area. Russian researchers say they have found a way to detect whether someone is about to become ill by looking into their eyes. Apparently the eye is one of the very first parts of the human body to register a temperature increase, often a prelude to infection or a more serious condition. Add a dose of technology to this idea and you can come up with highly sensitive thermal-imaging devices that individuals can use themselves. In theory, such devices could also be used on people without their consent — for example, crowds of people at airports during flu pandemics — which takes us into the area of medical ethics. Maybe one day you will be able use your mobile phone to scan your eyes every morning and wirelessly send the test results to your doctor. Any irregularities would result in an instant appointment sent by SMS.

Sound is another way of telling whether you are ill. Back in 2001 James Gimzewski (a US nanotech expert) had an epiphany — if human cells have tiny moving parts, then surely they must produce tiny vibrations? This in turn would create tiny noises. In theory, the sound produced by cells would also vary according to levels and types of sickness, so it might be possible to literally listen for cancer. And then there's smell. The use of dogs to smell whether someone is sick is seen by some people as crank science. But Professor Michael Philips at New York Medical College has created a machine that can analyse an organ-transplant patient's breath to see whether he or she is suffering from organ rejection. Future breath tests could test for breast cancer, lung cancer, eclampsia, and angina. The theory here is that we all have two types of breath: 'dead space' breath from the upper air passages and alveolar breath from deep within the lungs, and it's the latter that can tell doctors what's going on deep inside your body.

I'd also predict that there will be a boom in regeneration research. The human body has a remarkable ability to regenerate itself (new skin, fingernails, hair, and so on), but animals like the humble newt are on another planet. Newts can self-repair lost legs and even eyes, so the question is whether the human body can be assisted to do the same.

But it won't just be the healthcare industry that will be innovating in the future. There are approximately 1400 pathogens in the world that can kill people. According to researchers at Columbia University, new pathogens have emerged or re-emerged 409 times over the past fifty years, and the trend is accelerating. Moreover, most of the new human pathogens are coming from animals. So what's driving this increase? Nobody knows for sure, but somehow the way the world is changing is giving pathogens new opportunities to infect new species or get into new areas. The list of likely culprits includes rapid urbanisation (more people living closer together), the intensification of agriculture (more animals living closer together and closer to people), and globalisation, which means that everyone is increasingly connected to everyone else.

However, it is probably globalisation that is the most likely suspect. First, it means that animals are moved from one place to another more frequently. Second, people are moving more frequently and faster. SARS (which was of animal origin) was spread by international travel and, as we become more connected through cheap travel, the globalisation of jobs, and mass migration, we are more susceptible to new and old diseases alike.

This brings us on to the issue of global pandemics. The 1918–19 flu pandemic killed somewhere in the region of 20 to 100 million people. Nobody knows for sure how many people died, but the figure is almost certainly greater than the number killed during the First World War. Most (but not all) experts agree that another pandemic is overdue, possibly not on the same scale but devastating to our mental state nevertheless.

Of course, you could argue that we already have a pandemic — HIV/AIDS — but this seemingly doesn't count because it's largely confined to other continents and minority groups. So what else is most likely to kills millions of people in the future? There's still the possibility that H5N1 chicken flu will make it big, but perhaps the most likely future plague is something from our past. Smallpox and polio could make a comeback due to a lack of immunisation, and of course there are the 1957 or 1968 variants of flu. There could even be a bug from outer space. However, none of these, to my mind, are very likely, for reasons I'll explain later.

Closer to home, global warming will also influence sicknesses in the future. Currently, 13 million people in the UK suffer from hayfever, and 2006 saw record pollen-counts across much of Europe. Part of the problem is that the hayfever season is starting earlier and running for longer, but the severity is also increasing. This may be linked to higher temperatures putting plants under greater stress, which in turn causes them to produce more protein on pollen grains. And it is this protein that is the allergen.

CO_2 emissions related to the burning of fossil fuels (to run more air-conditioning units to compensate for the higher temperatures) could also be linked to the increase in asthma cases, according to some sources.

Even old diseases are becoming new again. Cases of gout have doubled in Britain over the past fifty years because people are eating and drinking too much (and arguably eating too fast, too). Ricketts is back, possibly because children are spending too much time playing indoors and are not exposed to enough sunlight, a major source of vitamin D.

Osteoporosis is also enjoying a new moment in the sun. Traditional wisdom says that drinking more milk and eating more dairy products is the way to prevent it; but, according to some experts, this could be contributing to the problem. High-protein diets and foods (such as meat) that are highly acidic may cause a leaching effect that removes calcium from our bones. One study has even suggested that teenage girls are suffering from bone fractures because they are drinking too many soft drinks, which contain phosphoric acid, which again leaches bones of calcium. In fact, the future isn't looking very good for young teens because another study claims their teeth are being damaged because they have stopped drinking tap water, which often contains fluoride, in favour of bottled mineral waters that do not.

Other future 'diseases' include a variety of illnesses and conditions caused by people who are too busy. 'Leisure sickness' is an affliction whereby seemingly healthy people get sick the second they go on holiday. The theory is that as soon as busy people relax, they start to recognise signals from their body that are ordinarily covered up when they are at work and busy. Or perhaps there is some positive relationship between stress and resistance, so when people become less stressed they are more susceptible to infections. There is very little research in this area and, more worryingly, there are almost no drugs in the pipeline to deal with superbugs and antibiotic resistance generally.

It's a similar story with kids. Back in the 1980s, the hygiene hypothesis was put forward to explain the growing epidemic of allergies affecting children. The idea was that the lack of childhood infections (caused by too much vaccination and too many antibiotics) was damaging children's well-being. As a result, their immune systems overreacted when exposed to otherwise harmless allergens. This hypothesis is slowly being replaced by a new theory that, even though a lack of early-childhood infections may have an influence, the real culprit is the lack of exposure to common microbes. In other words, our houses and children are far too clean for our own and their own good.

Given the lower incidence of allergies among people who grow up on farms, perhaps in the future we will see 'dirt holidays' where children are exposed to farmyard animals, mud, and filthy water. Or perhaps, next to the Microban in the supermarket you'll be able to buy aerosols of common bugs to spray on kitchen surfaces, baths, and children.

Talking of supermarkets, retailers have used so-called precision marketing using sophisticated social-segmentation techniques for years to help them decide where to build stores and to achieve maximum impact with their marketing budgets. In the future, health planners and strategists will use similar techniques to target local communities and even individuals most in need of health intervention. The process can even be used to target specific streets, schools, and workplaces. Recently a campaign in Slough (in the UK) targeted individuals in need of screening for type-2 diabetes. Of the 2,000 people identified using social categorisation, 106 were discovered to be undiagnosed type-2 sufferers.

However, while 'precision healthcare' can be highly effective, what are the costs in terms of privacy and even social stigmatisation? What are the implications of health departments (and, in the future, private healthcare providers and insurance companies) targeting people who aren't actually ill yet but who will be in the future? Moreover, should governments then be allowed to restrict the sale of certain products such as alcohol in certain areas if it is found to be a hotbed of future illness? The mind, as they say, boggles.

So here's an idea. In the past, healthcare was about making sick people well. In the future, it will revolve around making well people even healthier for those who can afford it, and we will see a shift from reactive to preventative healthcare. This doesn't just mean curing an illness before it takes hold, either. We will increasingly delve into people's deep hereditary history to solve diseases they would otherwise suffer from — perhaps twenty, thirty, or even sixty years hence.

A future shortage of death

But enough of this idle speculation. Instead, let's turn to a few trends that will impact on healthcare and medicine in the future. The first that is impossible to ignore is ageing. This is a megatrend that will have an enormous influence on healthcare in the future as people not only live longer but expect to remain well for longer, too. Obvious impacts include higher expenditure on pharmaceuticals for the elderly, which is already at record levels in many countries. Overall healthcare spending in the US, for example, was a staggering $1.3 trillion way back in 2003. We'll see anti-ageing drugs on sale at the local Wal-Mart, and anti-ageing surgery will develop into a multi-billion dollar industry with people opting for voice-lifts so that they sound as young as they look. Older people will also receive transplants of young blood or, more likely, artificial blood or pills that mimic the fast-repair qualities of a young person's blood.

We'll also see some convergence between the life expectancy of men and women, although women will still live longer on average than men. As a result, we'll see the emergence of four- and even five-generational families. This shift will make aged care even more complicated and expensive, not least because young couples and individuals will have to devote more time and money to the care of more aged relatives. And because seniors will be around for longer in the future, hospitals will become even more clogged up unless hospitals at home or telemedicine can take up the strain. There has been an increase of over 150 per cent in the number of Americans being treated for heart failure in the US, not because of an increased disease or diagnosis rate but simply because people are living for longer. Also, very old people tend not to suffer from just one disease, but five or six simultaneously. Add to this the cost of treatment, which often goes through the roof in the weeks and months before someone dies, and we have what is in many ways an unsustainable situation — or, as one commentator put it rather unsentimentally, there will be a future shortage of death.

People are supposed to grow old and die so that the next generation — with new thoughts and ideas — can take over. But what if they don't? What if older generations simply refuse to go away? The obvious implications are financial; but socially and attitudinally there are some interesting potential consequences, too. For example, innovation and change are generally driven by the young, so an imbalance of older people could have seriously adverse effects.

People are already starting to question the need to live beyond a certain point (a point defined, one imagines, by some measure of quality of life for yourself or for others), and this debate will intensify in the future. Assisted suicide is an ethically charged issue the world over, but we are starting to see its legalisation, and so-called suicide tourists travelling to places such as Belgium and the Netherlands where euthanasia is legal.

In theory, drugs could be produced by pharmaceutical firms to be administered by doctors, thereby avoiding the rather shady 'exit specialists'. The problem here, of course, is that it's a slippery slope between voluntary killing and involuntary killing, and spurious arguments can easily be made to justify eugenics on the grounds of removing individuals considered dangerous to the rest of society.

In the past, religion gave life and death meaning, and provided a ritualised exit, but now that religion is receding in many western

(Christian) societies there is for many a feeling of hopelessness. The last thing society should do is give these people the proverbial push off the bridge, no matter how bad their suffering.

It's also interesting to me that there has been a kind of reversal since Victorian times, in that sex is now talked about while death has become taboo. There is a feeling in modern societies that medicine can cure everything. Death is something that most people (and the media) now avoid. However, as healthcare budgets become more stretched, dying at home will become more common, and this will make death and dying more visible.

According to Marie Curie (a UK cancer charity) 64 per cent of people would prefer to die at home if they were diagnosed with a terminal illness. Only 25 per cent actually do, but this will change in the future, not least because more seniors will live with their children and grandchildren. Indeed, there is some evidence to suggest that seniors who are surrounded by young people are likely to live a longer and certainly happier life than those who aren't. At the moment, most aged-care facilities are pretty dreadful places, but this will change. Old people's homes will be part of mixed-use developments and will be built alongside and even within schools, so that the different generations can interact and learn from each other.

But enough of this morbid thinking. What are some of the other consequences of an ageing population? Growing numbers of people aged sixty-plus mean that the science of memory recovery and preservation will become a major growth industry in the future because people lose their capacity for recollection when they get older. Conversely, the removal of memories for younger people will receive an increasing amount of attention. For example, 49 per cent of rape victims suffer from some kind of post-traumatic stress disorder (PTSD), as do 17 per cent of people involved in serious car accidents and 14 per cent of people who suddenly face the loss of a member of their immediate family. Add to this an increase in war and terrorism-related PTSD (in both soldiers and civilians), and you could perhaps see why venture capital is flowing into this area. The US government is even researching how combat experience can be downloaded into the heads of raw air-force recruits. So how long before you and I can download other people's experiences into our brain or download our own consciousness?

Don't forget to remember (and vice versa)

In the future, we will be able to buy pills to remove unwanted memories or use memory pills to find memories lost in the sands of time. That's if we remember to take the pills, of course, which brings me to my final point about the ageing population — how to get people to remember not to forget to take their meds. There are already countless innovations aimed at achieving this goal, and we will undoubtedly see more. In Japan, a company called Menicon has developed a contact lens that can slowly release medication. A better idea might be an iPill. An intelligent pill has been developed in Canada that, once swallowed, will dispense the correct amount of drugs according to pre-programmed instructions. The pill is about the size of a five-cent coin, and the brains of the device are no bigger than ten blood cells. Once the pill has done its job it simply disappears, along with your food waste.

Another critical consequence of ageing populations is the shortfall in the number of younger doctors and nurses available to treat the increase in the number of older people needing treatment. To some extent, this will be solved by importing healthcare professionals from other countries (especially Asia), but it will also be partially solved through technology and automation. Nevertheless, there's a skills shortage brewing.

The internet will revolutionise the future of medicine. The Web will aggregate demand for medical services and increasingly help to commoditise the pricing of basic products and services. Patients will use information delivered by search engines to self-diagnose and self-medicate, much to the chagrin of governments and the medical establishment. Already 25 per cent of Americans use the internet at least once a month to access medical information, and you can imagine the doctor's reaction when he walks into a room only to find 'his' patient surfing the Net for a second opinion.

We will see digital plasters that will continually monitor all our body's vital signs. If anything appears abnormal, the plaster will wirelessly send information to your doctor. Power consumption will be almost zero, allowing the device to operate off a printable battery. And if you prefer to wear your heart on your sleeve, you can — we will see clothing embedded with computers that will similarly monitor your heart rate. A few years ago, scientists in Singapore even developed a shirt that calls for help if you fall over.

Our medical records will reside in cyberspace, too. In the short term, e-records will be held by your doctor and will be accessible by any hospital in the world. But, sooner or later, the information will escape and will be accessible by you and me (medical iPods anyone?). In the more distant future, these records will reside in our own bodies, which is the most sensible place for them, when you come to think about it.

Hospitals will be different places, too. First off, information technology will utterly transform care in hospitals. Nurses and doctors will have instant access to life histories, making mess-ups less likely. Currently around 7,000 patients in the US die every year simply due to poor information about drug interaction, while another 7,000 die each year due to doctors' bad handwriting.

Even using PDAs to allow nurses to fill in information at a patient's bedside is said to reduce paperwork errors by as much as 50 per cent. And there will be lots of information in the future. The speed and sheer volume of information will be staggering. First the availability of patient information will increase; but, second, the amount of data available on scientific discoveries and the latest developments will reach a point where no human can possibly keep up-to-date. How to access and digest this information will thus be of critical importance. There will also be robots travelling up and down the corridors dispensing drugs, but hospitals won't really be where the future action is. Hospitals cost money and, ironically, they are breeding grounds for bugs, too, so anything that can be done elsewhere will be. This means that the very idea of a hospital will change from a physical space to a repository of information and expertise accessed through a variety of channels. Developments in remote monitoring and wireless communications will also create a boom in home-based monitoring, diagnosis, and treatment.

Tele-medicine and hospitals at home

The drive to reduce the cost of healthcare services will be a catalyst for a number of DIY medical procedures and services in the future. Areas ripe for self-medication include wound treatment, mental health, and the management of long-term chronic illnesses. Some of these treatments will be provided by the patient, perhaps with the help of remote cameras and the internet, while others will require temporary home visits by healthcare professionals. Telemedicine has been around for a while in some countries, but to date it has largely been confined to hospitals monitoring patients at home in terms of vital signs or drug delivery. Not so in the future.

An emerging area of care is e-therapy, where psychologists and psychiatrists treat patients remotely — either to jump long waiting queues or because the patient lives far away. The technologies used include everything from email and mobile phones to websites and streaming video, and they can treat conditions as varied as PTSD, anxiety, and addiction. In Australia, diabetes patients can send their blood-sugar readings to their doctor via mobile phone (the phone is equipped with a blood glucose meter), while in South Africa patients are sent text messages if they fail to open their medications (the cap of the bottle is connected to the phone, which is in turn connected to the hospital's computer). And in the US My-Food-Phone helps patients with high cholesterol monitor their diet. Patients take photographs of their meals (which is easier than writing a food diary) and send them to a nutritionist for a weekly critique of their food choices.

Even some of the technology once found only in hospitals is now routinely available in ordinary homes. The idea that today's luxuries become tomorrow's mass-market necessities certainly applies in areas such as household goods and electronics, but in the future it will increasingly apply to medical equipment. Take the defibrillator. Once these were only found in city hospitals, but now you can buy one on eBay for US$1,495 or less, second-hand. Mind you, would you buy a second-hand defibrillator? If it worked, you'd imagine the owner would want to keep it; and if it didn't, why would you want to buy it? So what's next? Perhaps your own combined ultrasound, MRI scanner, and 3-D computerised tomography machine from Wal-Mart to treat your own tumours? We'll see.

But again, is all this technology what people really want or need? Sure, such technology saves hospitals time and money, but is our quality of life being improved or reduced? A significant part of medicine is the human element, and physical interaction is surely a vital part of diagnosis and treatment. Research conducted by the Mayo Clinic found that if a doctor sits down during a bedside visit it increases patient satisfaction. For the study, doctors were asked to either stand or sit during their initial evaluation; when questioned later, patients whose doctor stood underestimated the length of the visit by an average of 4 per cent, while those whose doctor sat down overestimated the time by 11 per cent.

In a similar vein, US researchers have found that when people are anxious or in pain, holding hands has a soothing effect on the brain. If more people are going to live alone in the future, a simple service where a person having surgery could hire someone to hold their hand could make a remarkable difference to stress levels and recovery rates. In other words, when it comes to caring for people, technology is only part of the answer; making things too remote or soulless will, while not making people ill, at least make them less well.

This then is yet another example of the dualistic future. On the one hand, we will have nanotech and cellular-based medicine where science will be able to switch genes on and off, build nanomachines to repair severed nerves, or get inside tumour cells and change them. On the other hand, patients are already embracing all manner of alternative and natural treatments. In many ways, 'high-tech' and 'alternative' are opposite and contradictory, but both will happily live side by side in our bathroom cabinet in the future.

If you think I'm kidding about alternative medicine, simply take a trip to the US and visit a pharmacy called either Elephant or Pharmaca. Between 1984 and 1994 the number of independent pharmacies declined by 28 per cent in the US, largely due to the power of Wal-Mart and giant drugstore chains succh as Walgreens (annual revenue $42 billion). So how can small chains like Pharmaca (ten stores) and Elephant (three stores) flourish? The answer is by appealing to a niche that the big guys either haven't noticed or have chosen to ignore. In Pharmaca's case, this means holding seminars on new-age treatments and placing kiosks in-store where customers can read up on alternative medicine. The parallel here is clearly Wholefoods Market, so perhaps Wal-Mart should keep an eye on both of these upstart start-ups.

Another future megatrend will be the personalisation of medicine and the shift of power away from professionals to the end-consumer of healthcare services (that is, patients). Ninety per cent of drugs don't work for 30 per cent of people, so in the future we'll see treatment programs and drugs tailor-made for specific groups and, ultimately, individuals. We'll also see diets customised to specific groups of people and genetically based treatments.

Male and female pain

Personalisation is a megatrend that operates across a number of industries. The trend obviously works at a group and individual level, but it also exists at one of the most fundamental levels — men and women. Until 1990 two-thirds of all research on medical conditions that affect both men and women was done purely on men. Men and women are clearly different when it comes to capacities such as memory, verbal abilities, spatial awareness, and even facial recognition, so why wouldn't they be different when it comes to medicine, too? This has long been recognised on a superficial level with the development of women's clinics and women's medicine, but that's about it. For example, men and women experience heart attacks in different ways. Men tend to have crushing chest pains while women tend to experience upper abdominal pains.

In dentistry, men often have a poor response to a certain group of painkillers. Men and women also process drugs differently, meaning that doses sometimes have to be increased to have the same effect. Similarly, when it comes to severe pain, men and women seem to prefer different painkillers, with men opting for morphine and women choosing nalbuphine. From an evolutionary point of view, this makes perfect sense. Historically, men and women have been subjected to different types of pain, so coping mechanisms may have developed accordingly. This provides a tremendous opportunity to develop male and female versions of all kinds of drugs. Male and female headache pills, anyone?

Personalisation also means that different patients respond differently to different treatment regimes, so gene chips will be developed that allow treatments to be personalised to the genetic make-up of individual patients. This idea is revolutionary in that it will mark a seismic shift away from the blockbuster drug business model that is already at something of a watershed.

In recent times, fewer and fewer drugs have been launched, and more and more have been withdrawn. For example, in 2004 there were 113 submissions for approval in the US compared to 131 in 1996. Second, refocusing R&D towards individuals or, more accurately, sub-groups of individuals, means that pharmaceutical companies will be forced to address sub-populations in regions such as Africa and India. According to a World Bank report published in the *Lancet*, only 16 per cent of drugs registered between 1975 and 1999 were for diseases more common in the developing world than in the west. Moreover, there has been a historical tendency to treat regions such as Africa as cheap testing grounds rather than primary areas for development. If individualised treatments do take off, and I believe they will, genetic diversity will be an integral part of the testing process, and regions such as Africa will be much sought after for both research and treatment.

But back to future ills. Life is speeding up, and more of us are living alone. Stick these two trends together, and you'd expect to see a significant uplift in stress levels in the future.

Various studies, including those conducted by the University of Chicago, have shown that being alone can be bad for you. A Danish study has also found that older people who live alone have a greater risk of a sudden heart episode than those living with others. Moreover, pessimists are more likely to get depression and die from heart disease. What will we get stressed about in the future? The answer will be pretty much the same things that we worry about right now: debt, relationships, work, success, our appearance, terrorism, crime, and so on. The difference is that work hours will be longer and job insecurity will be greater.

We will also be more stressed because of increased levels of change, all of which will make us sick. Maybe. Believe it or not, a study, again by the University of Chicago, found that animals that are frightened by new things are 60 per cent more likely to die than animals that are open to new experiences. Could the same be true of people? Will we adapt to embrace our ever-accelerating societies, or will the speed of change and levels of uncertainty eventually kill us?

Apart from loneliness and depression, one of the biggest problems in future years will be getting enough sleep. Western societies are sleep deprived, and the result is that people are becoming clumsy, stupid, unhappy, and dead according to Dr Stanley Coren. Social observers have coined the term TATT Syndrome to describe people who are Tired All The Time. Whether you buy into the phraseology or not, the condition seems real enough, and sleep is set to become one of the hottest medical and societal issues over the next few decades. The figures certainly speak for themselves. Back in 1900, Americans slept for an average of 9.0 hours per night. The figure is now 6.9 hours, and sleep clinics are popping up to help people fall asleep. In Australia, for example, there were just four sleep clinics in 1985, but now there are over seventy.

In the US, 70 million people now have trouble getting a proper night's sleep, and US$50 billion is lost every year due to sleeplessness. Add to this 100,000 road accidents caused by tiredness, and you can start to see why getting a good night's sleep is keeping a lot of medical researchers wide awake. Conversely, the demands of our twenty-four hour societies mean that people are also looking for ways to stay awake. Sleep science is still a Cinderella area of medical research, but this will change. There is already some evidence to suggest that a lack of sleep is partially behind everything from obesity and irritability to depression and low libido.

So, in the future, expect to see pills that will provide the equivalent of two-, four-, six- or eight-hour doses of 'super sleep'. Eventually, we could even see pills that mean we don't have to sleep at all. But what are the consequences of a society where people sleep less or don't sleep at all?

Globalisation is another key driver of change in the future of medicine. The movement of people caused by globalisation and skills shortages in most western nations have led to an influx of foreign doctors and nurses, with as many as 70 per cent being born outside the country they are currently working in. Meanwhile, many patients are heading in the opposite direction.

Years ago if you were sick, you had no real alternative to the local hospital. Perhaps you would travel a few hundred miles to a centre of excellence, but that was about it. These days, people are jumping on planes and travelling to countries such as India, Costa Rica, Brazil, Thailand, Turkey, and Hungary to have everything from their teeth and hips to their hearts and noses fixed. Medical tourism will enjoy enormous growth in the next few years, and is expected to be worth US$40 billion by 2010. Already 500,000 Americans travel to other countries for medical procedures every year, largely because costs are 30–80 per cent cheaper than in the US. As a result, medical tourism agencies and intermediaries are springing up to advise on everything from hospitals and doctors to hotels and post-operative sightseeing trips.

Equally, since one-fifth of US GDP will be spent on healthcare by 2020, medical outsourcing is set to grow. This is where various services that used to be conducted by your local hospital (or at the very least in your own country) are now exported to low-cost countries such as India, much in the same way that banks are outsourcing their call centres. Hospitals in the US send X-rays to India overnight via the internet for initial screening. What all of this means is that we will slowly see the globalisation and ultimately the commoditisation of all but the most specialist medical services.

Healthcare will therefore essentially become a retail market driven by brands (reputation), price, and convenience, and the patient will be firmly in control of most purchases.

Countries such as China and India will become global centres for certain types of medicine and medical research, including the development of new drugs, at the expense of countries such as the US. However, diseases in countries such as China and India will also start to resemble those in the west and there will be a convergence of diseases, with all countries eventually experiencing the same illnesses and conditions. Obesity will be huge everywhere in the future.

Healthcare in all nations will also be split between health haves and have-nots due to the high cost of treatment. But this may be solved in the long term by technology. Computers will be everywhere, modelling biological systems and processes, and testing drugs.

Computers have consequences for medical training, too, and we'll see the increased use of hyper-realistic patient simulators for training purposes. In fact, in the distant future, people will be amazed that testing and training were ever done on people, let alone animals. Advances in computer modelling and silicon simulations will mean that by 2050 there will be no need to test new drugs on animals or people because software models of human organs and physiological processes will do it instead. Again, this type of activity will be centred in India and China due to the accessibility of inexpensive, highly skilled labour.

Finally, we cannot talk about the future of healthcare and medicine without at least a cursory nod in the direction of ethics, both personal and professional. Technology will continue to revolutionise medicine, but we are on the cusp of an era in which all sorts of choices will have to be made by society about what is and is not acceptable.

The six-million dollar man

There is already a debate about human cloning and, sooner or later, an outlaw scientist will undoubtedly do what many people fear. There is also the debate about what it means to be human and at what point an artificially enhanced person ceases to be one of us. It is interesting to me that steroids are banned in professional sports, but enhancement surgery is perfectly legal. Repairing damage to a ligament has been standard practice for more than a quarter of a century, but new medical and surgical procedures are blurring the line between repair and enhancement. For example, wearing contact lenses is not regarded as cheating, but what if a major league cricket player had eye surgery or a partially robotised arm specifically to improve his or her (it is the future, remember) batting average? Surgical innovations will blur the line between human and machine; and when millions of dollars of sponsorship are involved, the question gets very interesting indeed.

Another area sure to capture the imagination of the media is the use of robots, especially robosurgeons. Put simply, would you allow yourself to be anesthetised and operated on by machines with no human involvement whatsoever? Add in some artificially grown body parts — possibly from a limb farm — and we really do start to enter the realm of science fiction for real. However, the area most likely to cause real consternation is medical privacy; specifically, who owns or controls the information held deep within our bodies? If, as is likely, medical science will be able to tell what a child will suffer from when he or she is twenty or fifty years old, should the child and the parents be told? If the answer is yes, what about their insurance company? Do insurance companies have a right to full disclosure once the hereditary vault is opened?

And what about if links were proven between a parent's current lifestyle and the health of their yet unborn children? What if governments decided to tax the parent on the basis of damage they are doing to the health of the children they haven't decided to have yet? Even better, if unborn children can be tested to determine future intelligence (read earning-power, in some instances), would it be ethical for the parents to interfere to enhance these abilities through the use of drugs or brain surgery? Or what about the ethics of 'cosmetic neurology' — essentially, cosmetic surgery for the mind? Finally, if we are all born with certain impulses such as aggression or selfishness, would it be ethically correct to modify these impulses at birth?

Someday, someone will have to put her mind to all this.

12 December 2033

Dear Annie

What a day! I gave my doctor a sample of my blood a few days ago and today I got a premium email titled 'Re: Nutritional Genomics' from my local supermarket telling me what I could and could not eat to extend my life by a guaranteed twenty years! The diet is not totally unique because I share certain characteristics with other people. But it turns out that I do have a problematic DNA profile, so the supermarket said that a personalised diet would be highly beneficial and recommended the weekly home delivery of certain foods and meals. If I agree to sign up to the program the supermarket-run health insurance scheme will instantly reduce my premiums by 20%. But if I do sign up someone, somewhere, will be watching what I eat and how I live for the rest of my life. All my food purchases, from anywhere in the world, will be automatically entered into their database, and because cash no longer exists, all electronic and digital payments will automatically create a data trail. If I do this, certain foodstuffs will also be impossible to buy unless I can find an underground supply or find a fake ID. My movements will be similarly tracked. If I walk less than 10 km per week my weekly health insurance premiums are adjusted upwards.

What do I do???

Douglas

Five trends that will transform healthcare

Ageing   Ageing is a megatrend that will have enormous influence on healthcare as people not only live longer but expect to be well for longer, too. In China, 134 million people are aged over sixty — 10 per cent of the entire population — and this is predicted to increase to 30 per cent by 2050. Obvious impacts include higher expenditure on pharmaceuticals and care for the elderly, but the type of common diseases we will see will also change. This will impact on everything from memory recovery to the replacement of body parts. Also, expect to see more generations living together under one roof, and more debate about subjects such as euthanasia and sex for the over-seventies.

Telemedicine   Increasing hospitalisation and treatment costs, together with developments in remote monitoring and wireless communications, will create a boom in home-based monitoring, remote diagnosis, and treatment, or 'hospitals at home'. Conversely, there will be a countertrend towards home visits and hands-on physical contact for those who can afford it.

Sleep science   In the future, people will feel increasingly burnt out all of the time, which will cause breakdowns, anxiety, and depression. As a result, there will be a boom in research into the so-called architecture of sleep — the different sleep states, and how they influence health and potentially even learning and intelligence. Indeed, sleep will become so sought after in the future that it's even possible it will replace both money and sex as the new status symbol du jour. Thus we'll see an increase in sleep retail (for

example, MetroNaps) and specialist sleep consulting. Also, expect
a major boom in the sale of high-quality sleep products such as
beds, mattresses, and pillows, some of which will become very
high-tech indeed. There will be pills to provide the equivalent up
to eight-hour doses of quality sleep, freeing us from the need for
genuine sleep, although it is uncertain quite what the longer-term
consequences will be for this or for people who work or play for
twenty-two hours non-stop and sleep for just two.

Medical tourism   Healthcare will become globalised in the
sense that patients (who can afford it) will travel anywhere in
the world to receive high-quality treatment or to save money on
what will become standardised procedures. We will therefore see
the development of menu-pricing for medicine, medical-tourism
agencies, and luxury hospitals that resemble hotels, offering
everything from intelligence implants to memory treatments.

Meanwhile, at the other extreme, there will be drop-in clinics
in supermarkets. Both ends of the market will be owned by just a
handful of global corporations that will outsource mundane tasks
globally to low-cost suppliers.

Memory recovery and removal   To misquote Milan Kundera,
the future will be a struggle of memory against forgetting. Our
individual and collective forgetting will be driven by ageing societies
and by the increasing pace of life, which will contain too much
information. New technologies will also wash away our recent
words and pictures because we can't be bothered to keep proper
records or transfer files from one format to another. Whether it's
a bad date, a corrupt politician, or genocide, we also increasingly
forgive and forget, which is a problem at both an individual and
a societal level because we tend to repeat the mistakes we can't
remember.

Chapter 10

**Travel and Tourism:
'Sorry, this country is full.'**

*We should all be concerned about the future because we will
have to spend the rest of our lives there.*
–Charles Kettering

Why do we go on holiday to places that increasingly look like where we already live? Equally, why do we travel hundreds or thousands of kilometres to visit someone when we could make a phone call instead? These are a couple of the questions we will be asked with increasing frequency in the future as the cost and consequences of physical human movement increases. This may strike some people as an odd thing to say, given that we are currently living in an age of low-cost airlines where distance is effectively dead, but we are on the cusp of a great shift caused by skyrocketing oil prices, increasing population, climate change, and technology.

In the spirit of becoming at one with one's subject, I am writing this lying in bed onboard a Virgin Atlantic Airways flight from London to Sydney via Hong Kong. I have everything I could reasonably expect or need, although the start of the journey in London was far from comfortable. The journey by road to the airport took three-and-a-quarter hours to travel 173 kilometres. The last 32 kilometres took more than an hour. The traffic was bad, but it was a walk in the park compared to what greeted me at the airport. A few months earlier some lunatic had been arrested on suspicion of trying to blow up another plane. As a result, security was paranoid and queues were catastrophic. And that was in the Fast Track queue.

Once past passport and security control, things got much better. I was wafted into a world of peace and serenity, otherwise known as the business-class lounge. This paradox, in a nutshell, is the future of travel. Holidays and travel will become polarised between low cost and luxury, although even the top end will ultimately be reigned in due to the sheer cost, complexity, and environmental damage caused by billions of people moving from one place to another. The result is that we will all start travelling backwards. Foreign travel will once again become the preserve and privilege of the stressed-out, anxious rich, while the less fortunate, stressed-out, and anxious poor will increasingly holiday at home or not at all. So enjoy your next cheap flight, because it may be your last for quite a while.

Sun, sand, and making a difference

According to the World Tourism Organisation, cultural holidays are the fastest-growing sector of the tourism market. Part of this is what I call holidays that help (or reality tourism) — vacations that combine interesting and sometimes exotic locations with helping a local community or local landscape. Examples of travel firms offering such holidays include Earthwatch, which runs trips for volunteers to help scientists track endangered species, and Biosphere Expeditions, a non-profit organisation through which you can study cheetahs in Namibia or Arabian leopards.

This voluntourism has been going on for many years, but it's recently moved from a fringe, student, or gap-year activity into the mainstream tourism market, with families, mid-lifers, and disenchanted business people all swapping sea, sand, and shopping for holidays that make a difference. Why? I think one reason is that it offers a temporary solution to our unease about the future. In other words, it says more about our need to find meaning and to de-stress in a pleasant peasant environment than about our desire to help others. This is borne out by anecdotal evidence from students I've met who have been asked to survey reefs surveyed ten times before. Nevertheless, these forms of experiential travel seem to be what more and more people want. This means that companies expert in cultural activities — museums, for instance — will extend their products and services into travel and tourism. On a related note, a North American company called Vocation Vacations offers its clients the opportunity to try out other jobs on one's holiday. This may be taking the idea of taking your work with you on holiday a little far, but it's certainly another good example of how the pursuit of a work-life balance and happiness are impacting on travel.

Another spin-off from this cultural travel trend is the growth of religious tourism. As societies become more secular, people are becoming more interested in where their ancestors came from, and want to visit places relating to their history or 'tribe' as a result. To put this into perspective, 700 million people travel internationally each year 'for fun', and it's estimated that this figure will reach 1.6 billion by the year 2020 — at which point, tourism expenditure will reach US$2 trillion per year (US$5 billion per day).

According to some experts, tourism is already the single largest industry on Earth, so imagine how big it could get if the industry merges itself into the entertainment business. However, this entertainment element will come under increased ethical scrutiny in the future, with it being talked about in increasingly negative terms by those who would like to regulate travel and tourism on the basis of environmental and cultural damage.

For some people, tourism is neither innocent nor fun, but an out-of-control industry wreaking havoc on the planet. Thus new types of terminology and tourism are being created such as 'green tourism', 'ethical tourism', and 'responsible tourism'. In the UK, Tourism Concern recently lobbied the government and industry to limit developments in some areas due to environmental damage and to pull out of other areas altogether due to human rights abuses.

However, while there is undoubtedly a growing need for holidays that make a difference, one suspects that many of these 'new tourists' are more concerned about escaping the hell that is other people than with saving the planet. Moreover, while tourism has undoubtedly destroyed many places in the eyes of privileged tourists from developed nations, it has also contributed greatly to local economic prosperity and well-being.

As the writer and philosopher Alain de Botton points out, a thousand or so years ago Venice was just a swamp until property developers got their hands on it. Thus this new moral tourism is essentially anti-modernist, and to think of tourists as un-thinking exploiters probably has more to do with the trend for regulating pleasure than any real concern for the well-being of local inhabitants.

A slow boat to China

What else is on the horizon when it comes to travel? According to a report by Deloitte and New York University, the answer — for the year 2010 at least — comes in four parts. First we will see a growth in the market for travel into and out of China, India, and the Gulf States. I would concur with this, especially with parts of the Gulf replacing the Mediterranean as a source of cheap sand, sea, and sun, although some of these new tourism states are quite literally built on foundations of sand. The second prediction from the report entitled 'Holiday 2010' forecasts that the luxury end of the US travel market will continue to grow, along with spending on tourism in general, which is expected to double between 2006 and 2015. This increase is partly a result of growth in disposable incomes, but is also due to a third factor: the increase in the number of older people with both time and money to spend.

The growing number of people aged sixty-five and over will have profound implications on the way people holiday, with more opting for event-based and culturally based activities. The fourth and final factor shaping the future of the travel industry is technology: more people will rely on the internet when researching holidays, and more will go online to book.

The internet has already shaken things up in the travel industry by connecting people to low-cost operators and aggregating demand for various products and services. Crucially, it has also had the effect of removing intermediaries such as travel agents, as customers can use the internet to find out information and access special deals direct. However, this doesn't mean that travel agents will disappear because there is still a need for specialist knowledge; and as people get busier and information becomes more overwhelming, many will continue to delegate their relaxation and entertainment requirements to others.

Nevertheless, the influence of technology on travel and tourism will only accelerate in the future, and eventually many of us will be taking virtual vacations in virtual worlds, aided and abetted by a 5-D interface and experience-enhancing drugs. Fasten your seatbelts.

This is a while off, of course, so in the meantime we'll have to content ourselves with virtual tours of hotels online, checking out which is the best airline seat online (via blogs and user groups), and buying social-network airline tickets and hotel rooms that tell us who else is travelling with similar interests or who knows someone that we know. If you think any of this is pure fantasy, forget it. In Germany you can already use the internet to book hotel sun-beds and towels in advance, and touch-screen kiosks in airports dispense information about the relative safety of countries and the latest security alerts.

Social-network airline tickets may still be a couple of years away, but we already have seat-to-seat texting on board Virgin Atlantic, and most of the airlines are rushing to replicate other communications such as email, internet access, and mobile phone connections. Indeed, it won't be that long before you can download an e-paper airline ticket at home that contains both a flat screen and GPS so that the airline can send information to the ticket about boarding times and delays. It could even flash at you when the gate is closing and help you to find it.

In the US, an airline called DayJet allows business travellers to fly direct to regional airports, thus avoiding time-consuming connections and delays at big airports as well as unwanted overnight stays in small towns and cities. This is quite a good idea, but what's really exciting is how the company does this. The airline operates a small fleet of six-seater micro-jets at a cost of US$1.3 million each, offering airliner-style performance and luxury at a fraction of the cost. But the company has no set routes and no fixed prices. Instead DayJet aggregates demand 'on the fly', linking small groups of people who want to go to roughly the same place at roughly the same time. Routes and pricing therefore fluctuate in real time depending on demand, and passengers are offered a series of prices depending on how flexible they are willing to be. Give a little and save a lot. What's really fascinating about this idea is how the business model of the airline combines a couple of the hottest trends du jour — all of which will affect everyone in some shape another in the future. First there's mass customisation, where customers order a personalised version of an otherwise standard product or service. Second, there's dynamic pricing, where the cost of a product or service changes according to daily or even hourly demand and supply.

While we're on the subject of technology, it's worth a quick detour to mention something called tribal tourism, which is emerging as something of a cross between reality TV and computer gaming. The idea is that holidaymakers can join a virtual tribe on the internet that will eventually exist on a real island in Fiji. For £120, 'Nomads' can join for twelve months and are allowed to visit the real island — once it exists — for seven nights; 'Hunters' join for twenty-four months for £240 and receive fourteen nights' accommodation; and 'Warriors' subscribe for thirty-six months and get twenty-one nights for £350. Once the five thousandth member has joined the virtual community, a real island will be leased and the group will start to make real decisions about what to build on the island.

This is all slightly spooky, and reminds me of those people who go on holiday with the same friends to the same place every single year. Sure it's comfortable and removes any form of risk and uncertainty, but surely the whole point of travel is to see for yourself people and places you wouldn't normally be exposed to.

This brings me to another question: whether it will still be worth travelling in the future if everywhere looks, smells, and tastes the same as everywhere else. One of the upsides of trends such as globalisation and connectivity is that you can get just about anything you want anywhere these days. 'Tastes', ideas, brands, and businesses have all travelled the world, to the point where most airports, shopping centres, and hotels look pretty much alike. So why bother going anywhere? The answer, of course, is that people and places are only similar on the surface; and while mankind is indeed intent on standardisation and homogenisation, history and nature tend to behave otherwise.

Moreover, countries, like companies, are starting to wake up to their unique points of difference or unique selling points (USPs) — and it's these USPs that create 'country brands' to attract tourists. Some countries such as Britain seem to be intent on removing many of these USPs — red double-decker buses and red phone boxes, for instance — but other more future-orientated countries like Dubai are still building them. OK, I know London now has the London

'Eye' but, give me a break, it's hardly the Sydney Opera House, is it?

It occurs to me that what most people really want to see when they go on holiday is great architecture. In some cases, these are man-made — the Eiffel Tower, the pyramids, the Tower of Pisa, Stonehenge, the Great Wall of China, the Taj Mahal, the Empire State Building, and so on. In other cases, it's natural architecture that stirs the soul: Uluru (Ayers Rock), the Grand Canyon, Niagara Falls, Mt Everest, Iguaçu Falls, or a truly great beach. And therein lies both a problem and an opportunity. It's a problem because in the case of natural wonders they aren't really making them any longer, so an expanding global population (that is, at least a billion new tourists in the immediately foreseeable future) will mean that attractions and even whole countries will have to be booked months or years in advance. Want to come and visit Britain in 2010 to see Stonehenge? 'Sorry, the country is full until 2015 — please call again.' Man-made attractions are a slightly better proposition because at least you can re-build them when they get worn out.

Perhaps a more immediate and less iconic architectural opportunity lies in the area of safe, climate-controlled buildings that house things ordinarily found outside. Let me explain. The world is becoming more uncertain and less safe, both in terms of climate and violence. There is already a booming industry in weather hedging and insurance, and it's not too far-fetched to imagine whole countries taking out weather insurance to protect their domestic tourism industries, much in the same way that companies like Coca-Cola or Oktoberfest already hedge against particularly bad weather. A better bet might simply be to build enclosures where the weather — and, up to a point, terrorists — can't dampen an otherwise sunny day. This may seem like a rather frivolous reaction to global climate change and global terror, but it's already happening. In the future, more and more of us will be taking our holidays indoors.

Early examples of the trend towards climate-controlled artificial environments include Phoenix World in Seagaia, Japan, where you can ride 3-metre waves in a giant 300 x 100 metre pool, or lie on a man-made beach and enjoy the warm temperature regardless of what's happening outside. At the other end of the temperature spectrum there's the newly opened 405-metre ski mountain in the middle of the Dubai desert, where the snow and the skiing are always perfect, even if it's 48 degrees Celsius on the outside (no worries about climate change and sustainability there, then). Of course, all we're really talking about here is Disneyland crossed with Centre Parcs (UK), so there's no need to get too excited. Or is there?

All this is happening right now, so imagine what might happen in another twenty or thirty years if you added some technology along with a few trends like the desire for fantasy or escape. What you could very well end up with are worlds like the one portrayed in the film *Westworld*, where guests can visit three different zones of a high-tech amusement park called Delos to indulge in their fantasies or behaviours outlawed in the real world.

Or how about sealed faith-resorts where entry is only available to verified members of a particular religion? To some extent this happens already on a small scale, but what if the idea was pushed even further and incorporated into a sealed environment free from terrorism or the threat caused by non-believers? We're back to a familiar theme here — namely, the impact of anxiety and, to a lesser extent, climate change, although of course the two are somewhat entwined and interrelated.

As I've said before, life is speeding up in the sense that we are sleeping less and doing more. In the case of work, we are expected to do more than we used to and do it faster every year. This means that people are becoming more stressed and in some cases sick, so travel is becoming an antidote to anxiety. If you're got the money, this means ever more luxurious vacations, travelling on planes that resemble hotels and staying in hotels that resemble palaces. Of course, going away makes you even busier when you get back, so people tend to take more work with them, which eventually turns these resorts into the very places they are trying to escape from. Will we see hotels and airlines banning mobile phones and computers in the future? Quite possibly, although they will probably sit on the fence and design tech-free zones rather than applying the principle to entire planes or resorts.

Something we will definitely see is 'Sleep hotels', where guests check in just to check out for a while. We'll also witness a blurring between hotels and hospitals with a return to the spa resorts and convalescence homes of yesteryear. For very busy people there is a growing problem with 'sleep debt' (accumulated tiredness), so in the future we'll see hybrid hospitals. These will not be health farms, but luxury hotels fully equipped with the latest medical technology and expertise.

This need for a respite will also drive a trend for sabbatical vacations, although in most cases what will really take off is the short relaxation-break. Indeed, the idea of the annual family holiday will largely disappear due to time pressures. Instead, family holidays will be replaced by a series of short, selfish mini-breaks, with children taking separate vacations. Couples building 'parent retreats' at home are an early sign of this.

The need for structured environments to help people relax and unwind will also create opportunities for other sealed environments such as cruise ships and trains, where guests relax simply because they cannot get off. This will lead to the further development of long-haul luxury train journeys and cruises, many of which will be fully retro in an attempt to recapture the glamour and innocence of pre-September 11 travel. In some cases, these ships, trains, and resorts will be owned by or operated exclusively for individual companies on the basis that the company will have control over the security of its employees — although, ironically, this may make these places more of a target.

Is the Med dead?

The desire to escape from reality will also drive a few other changes. First, remote real estate will become highly sought after as holiday homeowners flee the crowded and polluted beaches of the Mediterranean, seeking refuge from imaginary threats closer to home. So if you own land somewhere in New Zealand or Tasmania, hang onto it because the isolation that once made it cheap will soon make it very valuable. At the extreme, this means that inaccessible islands will become the ultimate holiday resorts and retreats. Now, you may be thinking that holiday-home ownership is a bit of a niche market, but you'd be wrong. There are 250,000 holiday homes in England and Wales (somewhat ironically, roughly the same number as homeless people), and this figure is growing at a rate of 3 per cent per year and turning some areas of Britain and Europe into ghost towns. For instance, there's a village called Worth Matravers in Dorset (UK) where 60 per cent of the homes are owned by people who don't live there. It's also been estimated that 15 per cent of houses in north-western Europe are now second homes. This is obviously causing great resentment among locals, who can't afford to buy even a first home in these areas, so expect to see 'terrorists' targeting second homeowners in the future, too.

Of course, you don't need to own a second home to get away from the stress and strain of modern living, so hotels will do everything they can think of to make guests feel at home.

At present, this includes video-monitoring systems to enable guests to see who's outside their room (at the Burj Al Arab Hotel in Dubai), motion-detecting lights, biometric safes (at the Langham Palace Hotel in Kowloon), and personalised lighting that can be set to 'business', 'romantic' and 'relaxing' (at the Sofitel Arc de Triomphe in Paris). I've also seen sleep-tight anti-jetlag lighting, iPod mini-bars, mini-bars for kids (no alcohol), personal oxygen bottles and — my personal favourite — the borrow-a-goldfish scheme for lonely travellers at the Monaro Hotel in Chicago.

Other innovations include women-only hotel floors, entire business-class (premium) floors, elevators with wi-fi access (why?), hotel rooms sold by weight (seriously — the more you weigh the more you pay at the Ostfriesland Hotel in Norden, Germany), hotels where you can purchase most of the contents of your room, including the bed, by mail order, and hotels where you can buy your room if you like it.

Over in Los Angeles (where else?) you can check into a hotel with a psychiatrist on call, while in New York, if you're fed up with religious reading, you can book into a room with a copy of the Karma Sutra and a box of condoms where the Gideon's bible used to be. There are also rooms that resemble offices, with printers, faxes, and business centres with personal assistants you can rent by the hour. These will presumably make their way on board aircraft sooner or later, too (the personal assistants, that is — not the bible alternative). That's if you have the money, of course. If you don't, you can check yourself and your bags in by yourself, and even clean your own room, in some budget hotels. At the recently opened Easy hotel in London, the rooms are smaller than the average prison cell and there's no phone, wardrobe, shelving, chair, or toiletries, apart from a rather lonely small bar of soap. There's no TV and no window either — unless you want to pay extra — and the bed linen is fresh when you arrive, but after that it's up to you to keep it clean or pay extra for some more.

On the plus side, the room is dirt cheap — around £20 per night, depending on demand — and you get good security and relative peace and quiet, as long as the bright orange floor doesn't keep you awake. Is this the future? It is certainly another example of polarisation. Hotels will be either very cheap or very expensive.

At the one end, you will check yourself in and out, and will even clean your own bathroom yourself; at the other, everything will be done for you. And people will live for long periods of time, and occasionally indefinitely, in both. Technology will not be applied equally, either. At the budget end, technology will be used to bring costs down; at the other end, guests will demand and receive the human touch, suitably enhanced by technology.

Some of the other things we will definitely see inside hotels in the future include robotic concierges, soundproof rooms (for stress relief), premium-quality air (the more you pay, the cleaner it gets), 'soft' baths that mould to your exact body shape, and rooms that can be personalised through the use of sound and smell.

The same will be broadly true at 8,800 metres. For those who can pay, the whole experience will be personalised, allowing passengers to re-create a series of environments resembling their office, their home, or a favourite hotel. You will even be able to customise the window so that you can look down in real time on the African plains, even if you're flying from New York to Los Angeles. There will be seats with ergonomic memory foam (that can remember your shape from your last flight), live TV, pillow menus (you can get them in hotels, so why not planes?), private fridges, private cabins (with private mist showers), double beds, mini-bars, and private chefs. Some of these ideas exist already if you fly in business or first class, and new ideas will continue to occur here simply because business and first class tend to create high margins which can be reinvested in product and service innovation. However, some of these ideas will slowly trickle down from the pointy end to cattle class because economy is one of the fastest-growing segments of the market.

One point that should be emphasised here is that one of the reasons planes are starting to resemble hotels is that airplanes are one of the last sacred spaces. By this I mean that if you lead a busy and stressful existence, planes offer one of the last places on earth where 'they' can't get you. They are peaceful and private places (in business and first class, at least). You can sleep, watch a movie, or feast like a king. But most of all, planes are one of the few remaining thinking spaces where your mind can drift and dream, and airlines will sooner or later figure this out and design the environment accordingly. Trains and ships will cater to this need, too, but it is aeroplanes where the real opportunity lies.

The death of distance — for a while

So much for how we'll get to where we're going. Where will we actually go? One answer is nowhere. If flying from one city or country to another becomes too expensive, time-consuming, or stressful, many people will simply choose to stay at home. This means that both business and travel will become more localised. People will also stay at home, holidaying in virtual worlds on the internet or transforming their homes and gardens into miniature resorts and entertainment complexes with products and services like swimming pools and room services, all available for purchase or rent. This will create a boom in household outsourcing, although many people will still crave going somewhere different.

In the short term, overcrowding and the unpredictable nature of the weather will mean a move away from the annual mass migration to the southern Mediterranean, and holidaymakers will be spread out more evenly across northern and eastern Europe. Further away from Europe, 'hot' regions will include the Gulf States of the Middle East (especially Oman), and Latin America and Africa. Equally, Australia and New Zealand will both become popular holiday destinations due to cultural familiarity and perceived safety.

However, while all of these destinations will be big in the future, one of the largest trends impacting on the global tourism market is who will be travelling there. Traditionally, the bulk of globetrotters have been relatively wealthy individuals from Europe and the US, with their less-wealthy counterparts booking two weeks of sun slightly closer to home. According to the World Tourism Organisation, there will be 1.5 billion airline trips made by the year 2020. Another September 11-style attack could rapidly move these numbers in the opposite direction, but the emerging middle classes in countries such as China, India, Russia, and Brazil are starting to travel abroad, and their numbers will radically reshape the nature of tourism — or at least they will until the oil price escalates even further, putting long-haul travel out of their grasp once again. Some more figures: whereas it took thirty years for Japan to reach 17 million outbound trips, China reached this figure in just five years. According to the Pacific Asia Travel Association, the Chinese took roughly 800 million internal trips during 2003. That's about the same number taken by the rest of the planet in the same year, so imagine what will happen if even just a third of this number decided to come to Europe one year?

As I've said, sheer numbers will eventually mean that the most popular attractions and countries will have to implement annual quotas, and tourists will have to book months or even years in advance. The vast number of people walking on or past certain attractions will also cause severe environmental damage, and this will also put pressure on owners to limit visitor numbers or even to remove certain famous sights from public view. Similarly, India is another country with a rapidly emerging middle class wanting to spend their money on seeing the rest of the world. In 2003, 4.5 million Indians travelled abroad. This may not sound like much, but it was enough to cause the country to lose millions in foreign currency, due to the imbalance between outbound and inbound tourism.

More extreme destinations will include the Artic and the Antarctic, underwater travel and, of course, space travel. Space has long fascinated Earth dwellers, and the idea of space tourism has caught the collective imagination in recent years. Will it happen? The answer is, it already has; although whether blasting off into Earth orbit will ever feature in a mass-market tour brochure is open to debate. I personally think space flights will appeal to a very niche demographic — namely, rich old men. By the way, if you do still think that space tourism is a flight of fancy, consider this fact. The US

Federal Aviation Authority has already published a set of proposed regulations for space-tourism operators. Regulations include everything from flight-crew qualifications to medical requirements and permits.

While space is certainly a fascinating once-in-a-lifetime experience, many other future destinations will be a little more down to earth. For example, if everyone is rushing about and doing everything at the last minute, why not switch off and start a retro tourism trend of going from point A to point B using the slowest means of transport possible? Or how about using old and quite possibly out-of-date maps to get from one place to another in full anticipation of something awkward or difficult happening along the way?

Getting lost in order to find yourself has always appealed to a certain type of traveller, but doing so will become increasingly difficult in the future. Nevertheless, people will continue to strive for both. As life becomes less private and peaceful, we will desire time and space as never before.

11 February 2038

Dear all

Having a great time here at Holiday World. We're staying in 'America', which is in biosphere two. So far we've seen rattlesnakes, eagles and some buffalo. There's also a whole tribe of native Americans that were brought here in 2011 after the first big North American pandemic. We're not allowed to get up close because of ongoing quarantine restrictions, but it's great to see some of the actual people who were responsible for the new enlightenment movement. However, the best bit so far has been seeing the re-creation of the first Disneyland resort. Granddad says he can remember the real thing before it was blown up by terrorists, but I think that's just the memory pills talking again. By the way, I can't email or call from inside here because it's an enforced-relaxation zone, but if you do somehow get this please don't forget to water the plants and bring the herbs in during the day so they aren't exposed to too much UV.

By the way, we're all off to 'Russia' to hunt virtual terrorists tomorrow. Can't wait.

Love to all

Pam and Reg

Five trends that will transform travel

Growth in numbers   According to the World Tourism Organisation, there will be 1.5 billion airline trips made by the year 2020. Another September 11-style attack could change all that, but in the meantime the emerging middle classes in China, India, Russia and Brazil want to travel and their numbers will reshape the global tourism industry. Sheer numbers will eventually mean that the most popular attractions and countries will have to implement annual quotas, and tourists will have to book months or years in advance. The vast number of people walking on or past certain attractions will also cause severe environmental damage, and this will put pressure on their owners to limit numbers or to remove these famous sights from public view altogether.

Climate change   In fifty years' time the climate will have had a dramatic impact on where people go on holiday. If the climate experts are even half right, some tourist destinations will be underwater while others will be too hot to sustain large numbers of tourists without air conditioning. Conversely, many ski resorts will simply vanish. On the upside, many destinations that were once too cold will be blessed with milder climates, and many tourists will travel back to Northern European resorts that were popular a century or more ago to enjoy a break from the sun. Such shifts could have devastating economic consequences for some regions. One solution might be sealed climate-proof holiday domes and other indoor areas that offer some of the benefits of the great outdoors without being at the mercy of volatile weather.

Resource shortages   You can run cars and coaches on batteries, trains on wood, and ships on wind power; but, apart from alcohol, there are no serious alternatives to jet fuel for aeroplanes. This problem will be solved once the issue reaches crisis proportions, but before that there will be a major switch to other forms of slower transport and a renaissance of local travel. Long-haul aeroplane travel will again become an expensive luxury enjoyed only by the rich who will have to withstand accusations of selfishness and eco-vandalism. Hotels will similarly come under pressure to reduce their carbon footprints and conserve vital resources such as water.

Staying at home   If flying from one city or country to another becomes too expensive, too time-consuming, or too stressful, many people will simply choose to stay at home. This means that both business and leisure travel will become more localised, making people both more insular and parochial. People will also stay at home, holidaying in virtual worlds on the internet or transforming their homes and gardens into miniature resorts and entertainment complexes. Business teleconferencing, especially Web-based virtual meetings and conferences, will become more popular, although the need for face-to-face meetings won't entirely disappear.

Time versus money   The tourism market will become increasingly polarised between the time-rich and the time-poor. In other words, it will be split between those individuals with lots of time but little or no money, and those with lots of money but no time. The former — usually individuals or groups of friends — will take long sabbaticals or holidays using low-cost options such as capsule hotels and pre-erected tents. At the other extreme, wealthy holidaymakers — usually couples — will scour the world to find micro-vacations offering instant luxury and relaxation. Thus we'll see backpacker airlines sitting alongside busines- class only airlines and private jets. We'll also see super-luxurious manifestations of every conceivable type of transport and holiday experience. Also expect to see more luxury brands — especially fashion and 'lifestyle' — entering the holiday market, along with value brands ranging from supermarkets to youth brands.

Chapter 11

Work and Business:
the new right-brain economy

The future is not what it used to be.
–Paul Valery

In the UK, the *Observer* newspaper has claimed that the majority of Britons would rather have a cut in working hours than receive a salary increase. If this is true, what does it say? There are various explanations, and one is that people are doing the wrong kind of work. But what is the 'wrong' kind of work? The answer is highly personal, but in my experience it means working with people you dislike, doing something that's too easy or repetitive. It can also mean having a job that lacks meaning or doesn't make a difference. So perhaps the question we should be asking is whether the nature of work will change in the future and, if so, how and to what?

According to management thinker and philosopher Charles Handy, there are three key forces driving change at work. The first is globalisation. As Thomas Friedman argues in *The World is Flat*, there is a single global market emerging for everything from products to people. In theory, this means you will soon be competing against everyone else on the planet for your job, although in practice there will be a limit to what gets outsourced. Nevertheless, if your current job can be done cheaper somewhere else, it might be worth looking at other employment opportunities. For example, if you are training to be a film editor it might be worth remembering that editing can be done in India, and that Indian editors are cheaper and faster. The same is true of tax returns, X-ray analysis, and dealing with parking-fine disputes, all of which are currently being worked on in cities across Asia. However, there's some good news, too.

The flip side of this global village is that if you're really good at what you do, companies will compete globally for your skills as jobs become more mobile in the future.

The second key driver of change is demographics. Most countries face a demographic double-whammy with an ageing workforce colliding with a declining birth rate. According to the Herman Group, this will mean a shortage of 10 million workers in the US by 2010. There is even a labour shortage in China right now. Employers will therefore have to get smarter about how they attract and retain good people. This will mean companies keeping workers on the payroll for longer, recruiting older people (especially those aged over fifty), and starting a dialogue earlier with potential recruits. Crucially, we will also start to see more flexible working practices and the development of initiatives to attract older workers.

For example, DIY retailer B&Q in the UK offers jobs to retired tradesmen. The results are improved customer service and lower employee turnover. Similarly, BMW in Germany has designed a factory to attract older workers, while Mitsubishi in Japan has already started to rehire its own retirees. Indeed, Ford predicts that the percentage of its employees aged over fifty will increase by 100 per cent in Europe between 2006 and 2008.

Labour shortages will also mean more women in the workforce in the future. In the US, 25 per cent of workers already work for a female-owned company; this percentage is certain to increase, not least because women possess skills that will be highly sought after in the future. First, women make somewhere in the region of 50–90 per cent of all purchasing decisions, so in theory putting more women in charge of corporations would seem to make sense. This is something that management writers such as Tom Peters have been pointing out for years.

Recently, the *Economist* magazine suggested that the appearance of women in the paid labour market has contributed more to the growth of global GDP than either China or new technologies. Moreover, at the risk of generalising, I'd also suggest that women will be preferred over men in the job market of the future because of their empathy and intuition — both of which will be in very high demand. Furthermore, their emotional intelligence translates into a higher level of concern for the well-being of others, whether they're other employees or customers.

Incidentally, one clever idea implemented by P&G is reverse mentoring to help older workers (especially men) understand the problems faced by newly recruited staff (especially women). However, the real solution to the worker shortage will be to offer people a job with real meaning. This will be especially important for members of Generation Y, many of whom are now entering the workforce for the first time. The importance of Gen Y is, in my opinion, overstated, but there are a few things that mark this generation apart when it comes to work. First, the Gen Y cohort has never witnessed a real recession, so they tend to be confident (arguably over-confident) about the future. Second, they have grown up with connectivity and speed of change, which has two important implications for employers: they exchange information and they have very little patience. Add to this their interest in ethics and sustainability, and you have a very explosive cocktail of young people who care passionately about how companies operate and interact with the wider environment.

A while back I overheard a conversation between two Gen X employers. One was complaining to the other that he had offered a very bright female Gen Y graduate a position at his accountancy firm, but before she accepted the job the graduate said she had been offered a similar position at a firm of rival accountants. Therefore she had a few questions. The Gen Xer was obviously expecting a debate about salary or holiday entitlements, but what transpired was a discussion about the ethical principles behind the firm and what the firm was doing in various areas ranging from poverty relief to recycling.

Whether or not companies engage with these issues remains to be seen, although there is anecdotal evidence to suggest that corporate social responsibility (CSR) is moving centre-stage. An international standard for CSR will appear in 2008 (ISO 2600), which will undoubtedly turn the heat up on firms when it comes to transparency and ethical standards. However, if past quality standards are anything to go by, this will be more a case of bureaucratic box-ticking than a paradigm shift in the capitalist economy. First of all, the search by employees for more meaningful work lives and spirituality in their private lives does not necessarily equate with the moral transformation of work. As the late economist Milton Friedman said, the social purpose of a business is to make money for its shareholders.

Having said this, though, ethical investing has become a very hot sector, and people are becoming interested in the ethical dimensions surrounding the products and services they consume. In Australia, The St James's Ethics Centre runs a telephone help-line to help workers whose personal values clash with those of their employers, while Wal-Mart is erecting wind turbines on the roofs of its stores in order to put something back into the environment. The tension here is two-fold.

First there is a mis-match between companies, which are run for profit, and the planet, which is not. If putting windmills on supermarket roofs saves money, companies will do it. Otherwise they won't, unless governments make it mandatory or customers move their business elsewhere. As the German sociologist Max Weber once observed, when people pursue a collective goal there is a 'parcelling-out of the soul' — meaning that the bigger an organisation gets, the less easy it becomes to keep it honest.

Another important element here is trust. If you believe surveys, something between 50–80 per cent of people don't trust their boss, and the feeling seems to be mutual. Some 75 per cent of US companies now regularly monitor employees' email, and around 30 per cent track keystrokes and the amount of time employees spend on their computer. Monitoring employee activity is nothing new — Henry Ford created a sociological department to assess whether his employees gambled or drank at home — but it is becoming more common and more pervasive, thanks to technology that makes it easier to find out where people are and what they are doing.

For example, at most call centres the length of all conversations is monitored, as are lunch and toilet breaks. There is even software like NetIntelligence from firms such as Iomart that, by snooping on internet usage, shows bosses exactly what their staff are up to all day. This makes micro-management relatively easy, but it also makes employees sick. People who are monitored too much or too closely tend to be more prone to conditions such as stress, depression, anxiety, and exhaustion. Moreover, high levels of monitoring tend to reduce trust, which itself is a negative influence on productivity.

In a survey conducted for KPMG a couple of years back, half the workers said they didn't trust their bosses, while an earlier poll by Mercer Human Resources found that 40 per cent didn't trust their line manager. Of course, not all workplace monitoring is bad. Drug-testing in the US is widely endorsed by employees because it makes the workplace safer, and capturing emails for posterity can be useful if you want to defend yourself against a future lawsuit. No wonder paper-use in our supposedly paperless offices has actually gone up.

Bonfire of the certainties

According to psychologists, we get stressed and angry because we have been sold the idea that technology will save us time. So when your computer crashes or develops a mind of its own, it takes your hopes, expectations, and fragile perception of control with it. As a result, we snap.

In the UK, there were 6.5 million workdays lost to stress back in 1995. By 2001 that figure had jumped to 13.4 million, and there is no reason to suppose this trend won't accelerate into the future. However, taking a very long-term view, average hours worked have been declining for a century. So again, what's causing the stress?

One possible explanation is the increased pace of modern life caused by technology, but this doesn't really stack up either. In the 1870s the term 'neurasthenia' was created to describe the nerve-racking effects of modern inventions such as the railway and the telegraph. However, what has changed is people's willingness to admit they are suffering from stress — a badge of honour in many work environments. There is also the argument that as societies become richer there is more time for introspection and people begin to feel a sense of entitlement, which fuels anxiety when expectations are not met. Whatever the reason, the problem is going to get worse in the future. In the US, 40 per cent of workers say they have experienced verbal abuse at work, and murder recently emerged as one of the most common causes of death at work.

One specific consequence of this is an increase in stress-related work compensation claims. In Australia, stress-related claims in New South Wales and Victoria increased by 73 per cent between 1998–99 and 2004–05, and payouts in New South Wales grew from A$5 million in 1991–92 to A$92 million in 2004–05. Email is partly the culprit here but so, too, are open-plan offices, which reduce privacy and increase distractions and disturbances. Meanwhile, in the US, depression is currently costing companies US$31–$44 billion every year.

Something else we'll see more of in the future is drugs. Workers will regularly dose themselves up to improve their performance, in the same way that athletes regularly pop steroids. Back in 1993, Peter Kramer (*Listening to Prozac*) discovered that medicated people were more assertive and better at bargaining — precisely the traits most employers love. People who are already well, with no mood or personality disorders, will therefore take drugs to improve workplace performance and financial reward. We already drink coffee and various caffeine-based drinks and pills, so what if companies actually start prescribing drugs to employees to improve their personality, compliance, or financial results?

Another probable cause of workplace stress is cost-cutting, or de-layering, which increases the workloads of those individuals who still have a job or three. Information overload? It's going to get much worse before it gets better.

The third key driver of change is technology. Thanks to mobile phones, laptops, and the internet, work is becoming less tied to a physical location. Instead we are becoming a tribe of digital nomads working whenever and wherever we choose. This means that future employment contacts will have to change. Companies will realise they are buying people for their ideas, not their time or physical presence, so annual contracts will be related to objectives met, not hours worked. This will mean an increase in sabbaticals, and a further blurring between what's done at home and what happens 'at work'.

But this is just the beginning. In another twenty or thirty years, artificial intelligence and robotics will have displaced yet another layer of workers. So if your job can be reduced to a set of formal rules that an intelligent and emotionally aware machine can learn, it may be worth looking at a career change — because your current profession may disappear.

In other words, we are facing a third industrial revolution. The first revolution swapped fields for factories, while the second — the information revolution — replaced brawn with brains. The third revolution will be the shift from left-brain to right-brain economic production. During the last century, people were paid to accumulate and apply information. The acquisition and analysis of data is logical left-brain activity; but, as Daniel Pink points out, it's an activity that is fast disappearing, thanks to developments in areas such as computing. For instance, speech recognition and GPS systems are replacing people for taxi bookings, while sites like completemycase. com are giving mediocre lawyers a run for their money.

One fascinating statistic I came across recently is that twelve years ago 61 per cent of McKinsey's new US recruits had MBAs. Now it's around 40 per cent. This may be partly because of an oversupply of MBAs in the domestic market or the outsourcing of data analysis to cheaper countries. But it's also probably because arts graduates are in demand. In a globalised world, products and services become homogenised and commoditised. One of the best ways to create differentiation is through innovation, but what some people mean when they say innovation is actually design. Both involve the application of lateral thinking and an appreciation of aesthetics, both of which bring us back to right-brain thinkers.

There are some jobs that cannot be done by a machine or outsourced to India. These include what I'd call high-touch jobs such as nursing and teaching, which involve a high level of emotional intelligence. It also includes jobs that involve the application of creativity and imagination. But, as Richard Florida points out in *The Rise of The Creative Class*, these types of jobs don't work just anywhere. Cities become attractive to right-brained entrepreneurs and cultural innovators when they score highly on the Three Ts — technology, talent, and tolerance. Technology refers to the proximity of world-class research facilities; talent is the clustering of bright, like-minded people from varied backgrounds; and tolerance is an open, progressive culture that embraces 'outsiders' and difference.

Overall then, the workplace will become more decentralised, and there will be a need for workers to become more adaptable in the face of changing technologies such as real-time speech recognition and translation, AI, robotics, and nanotechnology, all of which will accelerate over the next couple of decades. The result will be a demand for a highly educated, highly skilled workforce that is mobile and able to work in multiple locations and on multiple projects simultaneously. In other words, the old factory model of every worker being in the same place at the same time is dead. Instead, individuals will work in small collaborative teams, and once these teams have outlived their usefulness they will be disbanded. People will often work for more than one team, and some will have more than one job.

Indeed, the barriers between companies and individuals will start to blur as separations between working inside and outside an organisation start to fall away. Individuals will also have to look after themselves more, even if they work full-time inside an organisation, because everything from pensions to health and safety will become the responsibility and liability of the individual rather than the corporation. Companies will adopt flexible structures and strategies because the sheer rate of technological change will make products and even entire industries obsolete almost overnight. Companies will also start to look more like academic institutions — especially universities — because this model is based on a fluid, decentralised, and relatively non-hierarchical structure.

Not that this will necessarily help companies survive. Of the Forbes list of the largest companies in the US in 1917, only thirteen exist today in an independent form. The rest have either been swallowed up or have gone out of business. The same is true of many so-called 'world class' companies identified in books such as *In Search of Excellence* and *Built to Last*.

According to McKinsey, only 0.5 per cent of all companies perform well over several decades, so there is every reason to believe that the majority of companies around today won't be in the future.

Why? The primary reason seems to be the need for companies to perform two seemingly contradictory tasks to survive. First, they must execute flawlessly in the present. This requires strict control and tight hierarchies that reward individuals with extensive skills and experience. However, this experience and expertise can create barriers that prevent an organisation from adapting to changed circumstances in the future. In other words, organisations are disabled by their own experience and success, and because senior executives develop mental models about what 'is' and what works based on historical experience. Moreover, successful organisations tend to evolve into large networks that become gridlocked; innovation and change are resisted because they inevitably affect someone, somewhere, negatively. This in-built corporate immune system partly explains why most radical innovations don't come from industry incumbents, and why turnarounds usually involve fresh blood.

Is this the foundation of the next big management idea? According to business writer Jim Collins, one big management idea comes along every twenty years; if true, this means we are overdue for another. In 1900 the corporation was invented, while 1920 saw the development of the idea that management was a science. More recently, we've had continuous improvement in the 1960s, and the idea that entrepreneurship and innovation is a repeatable process in the 1980s. So what's next? Perhaps it's the thought that corporations are no longer the best structures to create value, and that it is finally the individual who will wield the power.

Barriers to market entry are now falling. Scale is less important than it was last century, and physical control is becoming increasingly difficult. Even the idea of short-term value is now under threat from longer-term considerations such as energy and sustainability, so perhaps it really is time for a new model of management thinking to emerge based upon the idea of open innovation and networks.

Currently the vast majority of jobs still reside inside organisations.

In the UK over the last decade, employee jobs have increased by 2 million while self-employed jobs have fallen by 250,000. Reading about 'free agents', home-workers, and tele-commuting, you might think that the trend is the other way around, but it's not. People need somewhere to go, and most people feel happiest working alongside other people. Moreover, over the next decade the UK government predicts that jobs will increase by another 2 million in the UK, but again the number of self-employed jobs will continue to decline. Furthermore, approximately 60 per cent of these new jobs will go to women, while a similar number will be casual or part-time jobs.

To some extent, this is good news. Employees will seek more of a work-life balance and, as a result, there will be a demand for greater flexibility in terms of hours. However, this casualisation is also bad news in terms of emotional security. The average week will get longer, and weekends will be abolished for many people. Work already seeps into our evenings and weekends, and this will continue into the future, particularly as collaboration spreads across countries. As a result, fixed eight-hour days will start to disappear, replaced instead by 14-hour work windows into which people will dip in and out.

One of the most interesting questions, to my mind, is whether companies will continue to exist at all in the future. Corporations, like schools, were largely invented to suit the needs of the day. However, things have changed, and individuals are no longer as dependent on a single employer for life as they once were. These dependencies and resultant obligations could very well change in the future, with individuals being directly responsible for much of the value created in an economy. A good example of this is the trend towards consumer- or user-generated content. This term technically refers to online content produced by users as opposed to professional media companies, but the idea is applicable to other areas. The key point here is that, once, only large corporations could create value on a large scale; but in the internet era, size is becoming increasingly irrelevant.

These days, for example, the cost of creating and distributing digital content is almost zero, so almost anyone can have a go at it. While 99 per cent of the resultant amateur content is rubbish, even the small percentile remaining adds up to a sizeable chunk. In other words, in a knowledge-based economy it is, increasingly, the individual and not the organisation that creates value.

Critically, this structure carries very little in the way of fixed overheads, and can be dismantled and reassembled quickly to respond to changed conditions. Thus, organisationally speaking, networks will replace organisational pyramids.

A global labour shortage will also have a significant impact on how people work. In the US, the workforce grew by around 2.6 per cent in the 1970s; by the 1990s, this growth slowed to 1.1 per cent. Growth rates in the future are unlikely to top 0.5 per cent, and there is even talk of the rate dropping to 0.3 per cent after 2010. As a result, there will be more emphasis placed on recruiting those not currently active or well represented in the workforce. This will include people aged over fifty-five, but it also means that there will be more women and people with disabilities in the workforce. There will also be a push to recruit more immigrants into domestic labour forces, and in some cases we may even see paid immigration — the return of the Ten Pound Poms, in the case of Australia.

Education and training will also become even more important. In the case of adults, this means lifelong learning. The idea here is that education needs to be a continuous process due to the rapid change brought about by science, technology, and globalisation. However, for most people, if they think they need it, it will already be too late.

A study by Harvard Medical School found that after the age of forty around 400 genes become lazy, which impacts on learning, memory, and communication skills. Another study quoted in the *Economist* found that workplace co-ordination and dexterity start to fall after the age of twenty-five, and decline dramatically after thirty-five. This more or less fits with the theory put forward years ago by Thomas Kuhn, in *The Structure of Scientific Revolutions*, that radical breakthroughs tend to come from just three sources: young people, accidents, and the cross-fertilisation of disciplines. In other words, it's younger people who tend to create value. This is obviously problematic from one standpoint — that workplace remuneration tends to be based on age and experience — so maybe in the future we'll see employers putting more time and effort into keeping older minds young and also linking pay to results rather than just age.

Critically, companies will also have to figure out ways to attract and retain the very people they have repelled in the past. Creativity and innovation are vital in economies built on ideas and intellectual property, but vanilla-flavoured corporations tend to shy away from the very people most skilled in these areas and vice versa. The same is true in education, where the very talents needed to become a successful future innovator or entrepreneur are anathema to everyone else. Rebels, not people in suits, start revolutions.

There's another problem with older people, too. As I've said already, developed nations have ageing populations, and older people tend to be conservative and less productive. By contrast, developing nations, particularly those in Asia, have a vast surplus of younger people who, by most historical measures, are the most likely future innovators. One reason it's now fashionable to outsource R&D to Thailand, Brazil, and eastern Europe is because it's cheaper. But it's also to do with the lack of skilled workers in developed nations. In the US in 2005, 220,000 engineers graduated while, in China, 660,000 engineers graduated. According to a Booz Allen/NASSCOM survey, there are now as many as 6 million engineers available for hire in emerging markets such as Asia. But low-cost is only half the story. Young brains drive innovation. They are hungry and, in certain circumstances, adversity drives invention, too. So these regions will become the new powerhouses of innovation and change.

What's going to happen next? First, the pool of low-cost labour will shift to include regions such as Africa, Eastern Europe, Vietnam, and the Philippines. Second, outsourced innovation will move upstream in terms of strategic content, and ultimately there will be a reverse brain-drain with innovators returning to work in their home countries.

This situation could potentially threaten the productivity and innovativeness of nations such as the US, Germany, and Japan unless large numbers of young innovators can be persuaded to migrate to these countries. Therefore, we may see companies adopting the military or sporting model, whereby young people are identified by talent scouts as early as eight, nine, or ten and then offered scholarships right through school and university. Companies and other organisations would also bid on pay and conditions, with the top children being fought over globally in multi-million dollar contract deals. We might also see companies and other organisations bypassing the traditional education system by setting up their own educational establishments to keep a tight reign over their 'investments'.

Another possibility is that the young may affect the old in a very positive way. In the future, we will see three and eventually four generations working alongside each other because people will be working well past the age of sixty-five or seventy. This may have the effect of cross-fertilising experience to produce a melting pot of new ideas. Or it might not work at all. Perhaps we will see generational conflicts rising to the surface, with employers hiring generational consultants to sort out the generational mess. If people stay in the workforce for longer, in theory the final transition from work to retirement will also be more complex and traumatic, which could drive the need for further counselling and consulting.

8 December 2026

Dear Tom

First of all, apologies for using snail mail but I know it will reach Georgie and she'll pass it onto you. Anyway, I just wanted to say thank you for offering me the job at AmazonBay but I've decided to take the job with Tatramobile instead. The reason probably isn't what you expect. Tatra have offered me a starting salary of $296,000, which is the same as AB, but they allow six weeks' annual leave rather than the standard four' and they have also recently adopted a no Sunday work policy. They also have in-house childcare, a works canteen (how retro), and sponsor an insurgency group in Myanmar. However, what really clinched it for me was their ethical standards policy. Maybe it's just an age thing, but at twenty-one I'm really into issues like sustainability and ethical investments, and Tatra's policy of non-investment in China and Russia is way ahead of its time.

Anyway, I really enjoyed hanging out with you guys at the retreat last weekend and please pass my regards onto Bob. I must say that the brain scan was quite revealing. I never knew I had a subconscious bias against women, but I guess that's some kind of inherited trait. The DNA tests were also quite revealing, as it turns out I'm more suited to working on pattern recognition in visually based teams than projects that are purely logic driven. Anyway, I'm having it checked out and I'll beep the money for the retreat next week.

Cheers

Richard

Five trends that will transform work

Workforce shortages, mobility, and promiscuity

Globalisation works both ways. On the one hand, millions of low-skill jobs will be lost to low-cost nations such as China, India, and Africa, while at the same time geography will become irrelevant as highly skilled jobs become more mobile. This means companies will hire globally, and workers will move internationally to follow opportunities. It also means that jobs can exist in one location while the worker is in another. Want to work for an investment bank in New York, but live in London? — no problem in the future. Loyalty to corporations will also dwindle, and it will be very much a case of promiscuous workers moving to wherever the best opportunities lie. The trend of reverse migration will also intensify, with people in countries such as the US moving back to countries such as India because the opportunities are now better 'at home'. However, the biggest future shock will be the lack of workers due to declining fertility-rates in almost every nation. Hence attracting and retaining talented people will become even more critical until robotics and AI solve the problem.

Work-life balance

Twenty or thirty years ago, pundits were predicting the birth of a leisure society. But instead of working less we are working more. We are also commuting for longer periods. Why is this happening? One explanation is technology. Another is globalisation, or it could all be to do with de-layered organisations. Another theory blames low interest-rates, consumerism, and debt. Equally, being busy is also a modern mark of prestige, but this could all be changing. The open-all-hours work culture will be challenged by parents seeking more time with their kids, and there will be law suits and regulation concerning the social costs of long work hours. For example, companies will be forced to pay for ruined marriages, stress-related illnesses, and dysfunctional children caused by a culture of endless work, unrealistic targets, and disappearing evenings and weekends.

Technology and automation   AI and robotics have grabbed the headlines in the past, but we will see more of things like employee tagging and surveillance in the future. Resumés will live online or perhaps inside tamperproof ID chips implanted in our bodies (which could also provide secure office entry and computer login). Online job auctions and online ID checks will also be commonplace. There will be technological solutions to work-related stress, and virtual meetings will increasingly replace the physical variety. People will work from home, on the road, and on the move, but the office will still be vitally important as the central hub, not least because people will still need to physically interact with other people. Having said this, wireless technology and high-speed connectivity will mean that your office will be anywhere, so you will increasingly work on holiday and in remote locations around the world. Previously work-neutral spaces such as planes, trains, and cars will also increasingly resemble offices, and nowhere will you be entirely free from work.

Corporate social responsibility   A large percentage of graduates aged twenty-one to thirty-five in the UK say that work is boring, and almost 50 per cent say their job lacks any form of intellectual challenge.

In the future, companies will have to work harder to attract and retain workers, and issues such as ethical behaviour and corporate social responsibility will be foremost in the minds of potential recruits and customers alike. Indeed, marketing will be turned inwards as organisations fight to create company brands that appeal to potential and existing recruits. Trust and transparency will become more important, and customers will also become more values-driven. As a result, the boundaries between internal and external communications will erode, and organisations will increasingly be forced to tell the truth, the whole truth, and nothing but the truth.

Generation Y   There is a lot of hype surrounding Gen Y, but when it comes to work the next generation will change the rules of the game for themselves and for everyone else. First, if the economy continues to grow and skills shortages are not solved by automation and AI, Gen Y will call the shots simply because there will be more jobs than people. Employers will therefore have to become more flexible about how and where people work and how they are rewarded. Gen Y are also hyper-connected, so virtual networks will grow in importance as a way of getting things done. Decisions will be made using collective wisdom, and innovation will be run using open or distributed innovation principles.

Chapter 12

➡

Conclusions: where to next?

Change is one thing, progress is another. Change is scientific, progress is ethical. Change is indubitable, whereas progress is a matter of controversy.
–Bertrand Russell

Is doom and gloom a new growth industry? The evidence seems to be everywhere. Just scan the shelves of your local bookstore and you'll be assaulted by titles such as *The Long Emergency: surviving the converging catastrophes of the twenty-first century*; *Is It Just Me Or Is Everything Shit?*; and my own particular favourite, *How To Survive a Robot Uprising*.

But is life really getting worse, and will we be anxious and miserable in the future? There are indeed many things to worry about: melting ice caps, flu pandemics, the erosion of privacy, living too long, terrorism, and global economic collapse — even high interest rates that would make second homes unaffordable. According to some great minds, we should add oil, organised crime, loss of biodiversity, space weather, counterfeiting, electromagnetic fields (EMF), earthquakes, hurricanes, TB, malaria, HIV/AIDS, and China.

We're all agreed then, right? Wrong. Some time ago, a lawyer in his late seventies accused me — in the nicest possible way — of living on another planet. Where was the anxiety of which I speak? Where was the evidence of life speeding up, and how could anyone compare a fear of terrorism with the threat of total nuclear annihilation that he had lived with throughout the 1950s and 1960s? Fair point, especially if you don't fly, own a mobile phone, or use email.

The future will not be a singular experience, and neither is it a forgone conclusion. People of the same age, with the same job, living in the same street will experience the future in different ways, and the future will be heavily influenced by local and highly personal events. The future is also something that we alone create. Some of us will embrace technology and globalisation while others will endeavour to escape it. Indeed, to some extent the future will be a battle between those rushing towards it and those wanting to travel backwards in time to a sanitised and personally convenient version of the past.

Crucially, we are already becoming paralysed by future possibilities. It ought to be a place where anything is possible. Unfortunately, this is exactly what's happening. Worst-case scenarios are increasingly being thought of as most-likely scenarios, and we have all but forgotten about present realities, especially the opportunities and threats on our own doorsteps. So let's all worry about influenza pandemics that haven't happened yet and totally ignore the fact that in 2006 2.6 million adults actually died of AIDS; or that, of the 4.9 million new infections the previous year, 700,000 were in children aged under fifteen.

The air we now breathe is, in many instances, far cleaner than it was 100 years ago, but we refuse to recognise this inconvenient truth. Serious acts of crime, especially those aimed at young children, are at the lowest level for years in many places; but, again, we choose not to see it. So what is this new 'miserablism' all about? It seems to me that when it comes to the future, it is safer — and lazier — to be a pessimist. Optimism takes work. It requires commitment, energy, and ideas.

But enough. You probably want to know about the key trends in the future and what you should you be thinking about in terms of new threats and opportunities. Indeed, if you're the busy type, you've probably not even read the rest of the book, but just want a quick summary.

There are three trends and one uncertainty that stand out for me. They are technology, demographics, and sustainability. The key uncertainty is the changing nature of risk, especially the social implications of the new technologies.

First, technology. While it will be possible to sidestep some of the consequences of individual technologies, I for one cannot see anything on the horizon remotely capable of stopping the overall rise of the machines. Whether computers become more intelligent than humans, or whether machines ultimately develop a rudimentary form of consciousness, is uncertain and, in the short term, irrelevant.

Whatever you do will be touched by technology in some way in the future, and in many cases your world will be turned upside down by it. For example, all businesses will to a greater or lesser extent be e-businesses in the future, whether they like it or not. Whether you view this as an opportunity or a risk is entirely personal, and will ultimately fit with whether your view of the future is positive or negative. Whatever you believe, it will probably come true.

Having said this, there will undoubtedly be a reaction against too much technology at some point. Evidence of this will sometimes be obvious — as in people switching things off — but mostly our reactions will be subtle and not recognised for decades.

In the more immediate term, a key question for many organisations will be to what extent people (customers, staff, and suppliers) will accept high tech over high touch. In other words, will we embrace machines for reasons of convenience and speed, or reject further mechanisation in favour of slower, more meaningful relationships with people?

Demographics is the second key trend, in the sense that there is no stopping the ageing of many developed nations. Demographics is still destiny; short of a global pandemic or a nuclear war, it's a very safe bet that there will be a lot more older people in the future. Again, you can view this as either a problem or an opportunity, so the question is to what extent you will thrive or just survive in a world where older people hold the balance of power in terms of voting and spending.

And, of course, it's not simply that there will be more oldies in the future. People will be living longer and feeling younger for longer, too. Personally, I think living longer will, on the whole, be a good thing, although we should be weary of always equating quantity with quality.

If any demographic shift does worry me it's not ageing but the 'singularisation' of society, in the sense that more and more of us will be living alone in the future. This has some very immediate impacts, such as the need for more housing, but it also means that more of us will be spending the future in bubbles protected from the views and needs of other people.

The power of two is important not just in terms of fertility rates but also because of the sex life of ideas. New ideas are inherently social and need conversation, serendipity, and the rubbing together of two or more human brains if they are to grow.

Again, ageing populations and the growth in single-person households are an opportunity, in that both groups will demand products and services tailored to their own particular circumstances and needs, but these shifts could also put a strain on the provision of everything from healthcare and housing to education and employment.

The third key trend is sustainability. I have read various

predictions and forecasts claiming that ethics, corporate social responsibility, corporate governance, and even spirituality will become key business trends in the future. While I accept that these ideas are becoming more important, I cannot see them competing with sustainability in the broadest sense in terms of being a global driver of change across all industries, sectors, and countries. Taking a very long-term view, it is the beginning of the end for non-renewable resources; while climate change grabs the headlines, we should also be thinking in terms of everything from topsoil erosion and ground water to packaging use and transport. Finding alternatives to low-cost inputs, and making better use of natural resources through materials minimalisation, re-use, and re-cycling will be hugely important and tightly regulated issues in the future. Any organisation that thinks otherwise not only has its head buried in the sand but is building on it as well.

Sustainability also means acting in an ethical and socially responsible manner, both for the benefit of the planet and for local communities closer to home. In the future, connectivity will drive transparency, and all companies will be forced to act ethically, either through regulation or by their network of customers. All brands will have an ethical component, and all companies will seek further redemption by taking care of the wider welfare of their employees, customers, and community.

As for key risks and uncertainties, there are many to choose from. The tension between globalisation and localisation is one contender. On the one hand, global connectivity and interdependence may herald the dawning of a new age of cooperation. However, it could play the other way, too. People may grow tired of belonging to a global village, and strive instead to communicate their regional and national differences. This is a world where the individual still reigns supreme, and patriotism and nationalism flourish, along with economic protectionism. In some sense, this is going backwards, but there may be no stopping it. As resources such as oil start to run out, countries will strive to protect what they have, and global trade could easily become local trade as the cost of moving resources, workers, and finished goods no longer adds up.

I have avoided talking in too much detail about economic trends and factors so far because there are people far more qualified than myself to do that. However, money is undoubtedly a critical factor in terms of future risks, and it is perhaps worth exploring this very briefly.

At the moment, money is cheap — ultra cheap by recent historical standards — and this is fuelling economic growth and consumer spending globally. The combination of liquidity and innovation is making it easier than ever to borrow money. This is good because capital is being invested in physical assets (such as new factories), and people are starting new companies. But because money is so cheap, people — individuals and corporations — are making riskier investments. In some cases, this means paying what appears to be too much for something, but it also means lenders are becoming less discriminating about who they lend to and under what circumstances. This in turn allows poorly run corporations — and badly run households — to stay afloat and avoid ruin.

If the cost of money stays low for the next five, ten, or twenty years, this situation is sustainable. But if the cost of money (debt) starts to increase substantially, this could all end in some very big tears affecting emerging markets such as China, India, Russia, and Brazil. At the moment, money is pouring into these countries, but much of this inward investment is going into real estate rather than essential services or infrastructure.

Equally, much of the outbound investment from these regions is doing the same thing. So what happens if real estate bubbles burst or countries such as China start to use their money locally to sort out expensive environmental problems or sustainability issues?

However, the biggest uncertainty or risk factor is technology. As I mentioned earlier, the history of human existence has largely been the history of science and technology, invention and discovery. In other words, our ideas and innovations have shaped who we are, how we act, and what we believe.

Science and technology will continue to influence the future, although it may not be immediately obvious to us that it is happening, and very few of us will stop to think about long-term consequences. What will probably happen is that we will silently wait until there is a disaster — a major nanotech, biotech, or AI accident, for example — and only then will we fully appreciate what is going on, along with the risks and opportunities associated with many of the new technologies, many of which haven't even been invented yet.

On the other hand, technology will offer untold opportunities, and the thought of being six years old and able to see how things pan out over the next fifty or one hundred years fills me with awe. Technology will solve climate change and resource shortages, although in reality we will simply swap these for a set of new fears and anxieties.

Overall then, I'm cynically optimistic. There are ideas, discoveries, and events over the horizon that we can't possibly imagine or comprehend. Yet while the future is unknown and unwritten, we can begin to see and trace its outline, and to start preparing the first drafts. There will obviously be problems — there always have been — but on balance I think the future will be a pretty good place to live in. And if it isn't, we will have only ourselves to blame.

Sources

I know what a few of you are thinking: where are your sources? The
answer is: elsewhere. The immediate sources of almost everything
quoted in this book are my trend reports. Beyond this, sources include
a myriad of newspapers, magazines, reports, and websites. However, to
list every single one of these would double the size of the book, so I've
added a full list of sources, notes, and recommended reading on my
website. If there's something specific that you would like to follow up
on, I suggest that you start there, and if that doesn't work, get in touch
with me directly.

Further reading

If you like what you've read so far, you can find more of the same on my
website at http://www.nowandnext.com. A read-only subscription to
my quarterly trends report is free of charge. Alternatively, if you would
like to know more about some of the general themes highlighted in this
book, I can recommend any of the following titles. Again, you can find
a more extensive reading list on my website.

Scenario planning
Freeman, Oliver, *Building Scenario Worlds*, Richmond Ventures, 2004
National Intelligence Council, *CIA Scenarios — mapping the global
  future*, US Government Printing Office, 2002

Schwartz, Peter, *The Art of the Long View: planning for the future in an uncertain world*, Currency Doubleday, 1991

van der Heijden, Kees, *Scenarios: the art of strategic conversation*, John Wiley & Sons, 1996

van der Heijden, Kees, *The Sixth Sense: accelerating organisational learning with scenarios*, John Wiley & Sons, 2002

Current and future trends

Canton, James, *The Extreme Future*, Penguin, 2006

Knowlson, T Sharper, *Originality*, T Werner Laurie, 1917

Malone, Thomas W, *The Future of Work*, Harvard Business School Publishing, 2004

Taylor, Jim, and Wacker, Watts, *The 500-Year Delta*, Collins, 1997

Toffler, Alvin, *Future Shock*, Pan, 1970

Risk

Bernstein, Peter L, *Against the Gods: the remarkable story of risk*, John Wiley & Sons, 1996

Taleb, Nassim Nicholas, *Black Swan: the impact of the highly improbable*, Allen Lane, 2007

General reading

Brand, Stewart, *The Clock of the Long Now*, Basic Books, 1999

Handy, Charles, *The Empty Raincoat*, Random House, 1995

Handy, Charles, *The Hungry Spirit*, Random House, 1998

Maddox, John, *What Remains to be Discovered*, Touchstone, 1999

Kuhn, Thomas, *The Structure of Scientific Revolutions*, Institute of Religion and Public Life, 1962

Wilson, Daniel, *How to Survive a Robot Uprising: tips on defending yourself against the coming rebellion*, Bloomsbury, 2005

Zeldin, Theodore, *Happiness*, Pan, 1990

Zeldin, Theodore, *An Intimate History of Humanity*, Reed, 1994

Acknowledgements

They say that if you steal an idea from someone it's called plagiarism, but if you steal ideas from several people it's called research. Subconsciously, the thoughts and ideas of many people have influenced my thinking, so I would like to thank as many as my conscious mind remembers. People who have provided wise council and support (whether they know it or not) include Wendy Becker, Sandy Belford, Phil Beresford, Steve Bowbrick, Tom Brigstocke, Wayde Bull, Julian Canny, Napier Collins, Andrew Crosthwaite, Ross Dawson, Matt Doyle, Oliver Freeman, Charles Handy, Elizabeth Handy, Annie Harper, Richard Hytner, Ian Jedlin, Lynne Johnson, Helen Jones, T. Sharper Knowlson, David Maher, Adam Morgan, Charis Palmer, Richard Pearey, Heath Row, Mark Runnals, Jonathan Sands, Douglas Slater, Alan Sekers, Catherine Sheehan, Ellen Sideri, Elizabeth Stephenson, John Trudgian, Margaret Trudgeon, Stephen Tunley, Georgie Vestey, Ron Zeghibe, and Theodore Zeldin. Last but not least, I'd also like to thank Joss Evans for the idea and Russ Radcliffe for the wherewithal.